19.95

JAN 3 1 1991

A Lycanthropy Reader

A Lycanthropy Reader

WEREWOLVES IN WESTERN CULTURE

Medical Cases, Diagnoses, Descriptions;
Trial Records, Historical Accounts, Sightings;
Philosophical and Theological Approaches to Metamorphosis;
Critical Essays on Lycanthropy;
Myths and Legends; Allegory

Edited by
Charlotte F. Otten

DORSET PRESS

Charlotte Otten is Professor of English at Calvin College. She is the author of *Environ'd with Eternity: God, Poems, and Plants in Sixteenth and Seventeenth Century England* and has been published widely in journals such as *Shakespeare Quarterly, Milton Studies,* and *Notes & Queries.* Her poems have appeared in *Southern Humanities Review, Commonweal,* and other journals.

Copyright © 1986 Syracuse University Press
All rights reserved.

This edition published by Dorset Press
a division of Marboro Books Corporation,
by arrangement with Syracuse University Press
1989 Dorset Press

ISBN 0-88029-400-0

Printed in the United States of America
M 9 8 7 6 5 4 3 2 1

Contents

Illustrations

Contributors

Richard Banta, M.D., affiliated with psychiatric residency training programs in Kentucky. He has written on "Elevated Manganese Levels Associated with Dementia and Extrapyramidal Signs."

Sabine Baring-Gould (1834–1924), British cleric, novelist, author of the hymn "Onward Christian Soldiers." A prolific writer with entries in the NUC covering twenty-one pages, his works range from *Lives of the Saints* to travel books to *Freaks of Fanaticism and Other Strange Events*.

Robert Bayfield (b. 1629), British physician. His interest in both medicine and metaphysics is evidenced by his authorship of books on anatomy, disease, pharmacology, and on the theology of the Trinity.

Henri Boguet (d. 1619), demonologist, Chief Justice of Saint-Claude. His commentaries on the Burgundian legal code (1604) set up the procedure necessary to a judge in witchcraft trials; and his *An Examen of Witches*, an erudite commentary from secular and biblical sources, along with personal legal experience, reveals how he attacked disruptive elements in society.

Robert Burton (1577–1640), "Student" of Christ Church, Oxford, and clergyman. Based on his vast reading in the Bodleian Library, his *The Anatomy of Melancholy* (1621, frequently revised and reprinted) is an encyclopedic treatment of mental illness, including religious melancholy and love melancholy.

Giraldus Cambrensis (c. 1146–1223), Welsh cleric, Chaplain to Henry II. He wrote voluminously, filling his histories and travel writing with legends, natural history, and lively anecdotes.

Stuart Clark, Ph.D., Lecturer in History at the University of Wales, Swansea. Author of many essays on witchcraft, he is completing a book for Oxford University Press on *Witchcraft in Early Modern Thought*.

H. R. Ellis Davidson, Ph.D., former Fellow and Vice-President at Lucy Cavendish College, Cambridge, studied English, archaeology, and anthropology at Newnham College, Cambridge. Her works include *Myths of*

Northern Europe, an edition of *Saxo Grammaticus*, and the editorship of *Symbols of Power* and *The Journey to the Other World*.

John Deacon and John Walker, sixteenth-century English preachers. Very little is known about either Deacon or Walker, except that they addressed their anti-exorcism treatise to "the Reverend Fathers, the learned preachers and godlie brethren in this our English Church" and that they wished to avoid schisms and divisions in the Church.

Leland L. Estes, Ph.D., Junior Fellow at the Institute for the Advanced Study of Religion, University of Chicago. Included in his work on witchcraft are articles on "Changing Perspectives on the European Witch Craze" and "Religion and Science in the Opposition to the European Witch Craze."

Eugene Field (1850–1895), American journalist, poet, storyteller. His retellings of legends spring from his avid collecting of books, described in his "The Love Affairs of a Bibliomaniac."

Marie de France (1160?–1215?), Frenchwoman writing at or for the English court. Her best known work, the *Lais*, a collection of Breton tales, reveals her insight into human relationships.

I. (Simon) Goulart (1543–1628), French historian, collector of memoirs and journals. He wrote on medicine and demonology, as well as on *The Most Memorable Accidents and Tragicall Massacres of France* (from Henry II to Henry IV, 1598).

Clemence Housman (1861–1955), Victorian feminist, sister of A. E. and Laurence. She studied art in London, collaborated with Laurence on several projects, and showed her interest in legend and romance not only in *The Were-Wolf* but also in *The Life of Sir Aglovale de Galis* (based on Sir Thomas Malory's *Morte d'Arthur*).

L. Illis, M.D., B.Sc., F.R.C.P., Senior Consultant Neurologist, Wessex Neurological Centre; Clinical Senior Lecturer in Neurology, University of Southampton Medical School. His publications in the field of neurology are extensive.

James VI of Scotland, I of England (1566–1625), successor to Queen Elizabeth I. Recognizing its social and political implications, James argues for the reality of witchcraft in his *Daemonologie*, although he admits melancholy, nightmare, and mental illness as alternative explanations for aberrant conduct.

Heinrich Kramer (1430–1505) and **James Sprenger** (1436–1495), Dominicans, appointed Inquisitors for Germany. Co-authors of the *Malleus Maleficarum* (the *Witches' Hammer*), they provide detailed accounts of every aspect of witchcraft; their book was used as a reference text by European courts, both ecclesiastical and civil, with thirteen editions up to 1520, and another sixteen between 1574 and 1669.

E. William Monter, Ph.D., Professor of History at Northwestern University.

Author of *Ritual, Myth, and Magic in Early Modern Europe* and studies in Genevan government (1536–1605), he has also written on European women's history.

Elliott O'Donnell (1872–1965), British genealogist, historian, professional ghost-hunter, descended from Niall Nóigiallach, the fourth century Irish king associated with magic and the supernatural. O'Donnell's investigations include works on haunted houses, cults, secret societies, accompanied by the disclaimer "to being what is termed a scientific psychical researcher."

Ovid (43 B.C.–A.D. 18), Latin poet whose works inspired poets and painters for centuries, including Chaucer and Shakespeare. Author of *Amores* and *Ars amatoria*, his *Metamorphoses* was made famous in English translations by Caxton, Golding, and Sandys.

Petronius (d. A.D. 66), Master of the Emperor's Pleasures at the Court of Nero, and known for his elegant suicide. His satires on the newly rich, of which only fragments of the fifteenth and sixteenth books remain, were first translated into English in 1694.

Harvey A. Rosenstock, M.D., Clinical Associate Professor of Psychiatry at the University of Texas Medical School (Houston). His studies include "Radical Aspects of Human Sexuality" and "Suicidal Ideation and Suicide Attempts in 900 Adolescents: An Analysis."

Reginald Scot (1538–1599), agriculturalist and lifelong resident of Kent. Scot, who did not believe in the corporeality of demons, attacked "Sprenger's fables" and "Bodin's bables" with evidence from trial records, his interpretation of the Scriptures, and his extensive reading in the demonologies.

Eric Stanislaus Stenbock (Count, 1860–1895), Anglo-Russian whose reputation for eccentricity was documented by the permanent residency of a large toad in his living quarters, by his obsession with a hawthorne tree, by his *Studies in Death*, and by the consigning of his heart after death to a preservative fluid in a glass jar for safe keeping in a cupboard in the church at Kusal. The issue of *The Spirit Lamp* (edited at Oxford) in which his story appeared included contributions by Oscar Wilde, J. A. Symonds, and H. M. Beerbohm.

Frida G. Surawicz, M.D., Department of Psychiatry, University of South Florida, Tampa, Florida. Among other publications, she has authored "Cancer, Emotions, and Mental Illness."

Kenneth R. Vincent, Ed.D., affiliated with the Diagnostic Learning Center of the University of Houston. He is the author of articles on ego development and personality disorders, and on ego development and psychopathology.

Acknowledgments

The editor and publisher gratefully acknowledge permission to reproduce the following copyrighted material:

Josephine L. Burroughs: From "Ficino and Pomponazzi on Man." Reprinted by permission of *Journal of the History of Ideas*.

Stuart Clark: "The Scientific Status of Demonology." Reprinted by permission of Cambridge University Press and Stuart Clark.

H. R. Ellis Davidson: "Shape-changing in the Old Norse Sagas." Reprinted by permission of H. R. Ellis Davidson.

Donald Davie: "Thyestes" from *Collected Poems 1950–1970*. Reprinted by permission of Donald Davie.

Leland L. Estes: "The Medical Origins of the European Witch Craze: A Hypothesis." Reprinted by permission of *Journal of Social History*.

L. Illis: "On Porphyria and the Aetiology of Werewolves." Reprinted by permission of The Royal Society of Medicine and L. Illis.

E. William Monter: reprinted from *Witchcraft in France and Switzerland: The Borderlands during the Reformation*. Copyright © 1976 by Cornell University. Used by permission of the publisher, Cornell University Press.

Ovid: *Metamorphoses*, translated by Mary M. Innes (Penguin Classics, 1955), copyright © Mary M. Innes, 1955. Reprinted by permission of Penguin Books Ltd.

Adrienne Rich: "Meditations for a Savage Child," from *The Fact of a Doorframe: Poems Selected and New, 1950–1984* by Adrienne Rich, are reprinted by permission of the author and W. W. Norton & Company, Inc. Copyright © 1984 by Adrienne Rich. Copyright © 1975, 1978 by W. W. Norton & Company, Inc. Copyright © 1981 by Adrienne Rich.

Harvey A. Rosenstock and Kenneth R. Vincent: "A Case of Lycanthropy." Reprinted by permission of the American Psychiatric Association and Harvey A. Rosenstock.

Frida G. Surawicz and Richard Banta: "Lycanthropy Revisited." Reprinted by permission of Canadian Psychiatric Association.

Preface

$\mathfrak{I}$ first met a lycanthrope in *The Duchess of Malfi*. That strange Duke who robbed graves and went around with the leg of a dead man on his shoulder was suffering from "a very pestilent disease, my lord / They call lycanthropia." I, like Pescara (bluntly), asked, "What's that? / I need a dictionary to't."

From that early ignorance sprang my interest in lycanthropy. I discovered that it was not only the dramatist Webster who was involved in lycanthropy but that physicians, philosophers, preachers, historians, judges, and kings, were also concerned with lycanthropy in the Medieval and Renaissance periods. I began to collect primary materials on the subject. In the course of accumulating materials, this *Reader* took shape. I realized that knowing something about lycanthropy would help to illumine many aspects of life in those periods.

The study of lycanthropy is not a wayward pursuit of the irrational. Today's obsession with the occult and werewolves is frequently an escape mechanism, not a route to sanity and healing. The literature of lycanthropy in the Medieval and Renaissance worlds is not escapist: it is realistic. It helps to clarify the needs, hopes, aspirations, and commitments of a human being and of a society. It addresses the problems, struggles, conflicts, anxieties, triumphs, and joys of humankind. It looks honestly at violence, destructive urges that attack and devour the fabric of human life, at the dark moments in the human soul; but it also looks for sources of healing and restoration.

I am not the first to study lycanthropy. Perhaps the first critical study in English was by Sabine Baring-Gould, whose book on werewolves focuses on the varieties of lycanthropic experience (1865).

Montague Summers's book, *The Werewolf* (1933), although a wide-ranging, erudite study of lycanthropy, is marred by credulity. Within the last fifteen years, historians, anthropologists, and medical historians have been examining the phenomenon; this *Reader* contains five of their essays. This is the first *Reader*, however, to present primary materials from medicine, jurisprudence, history, philosophy, theology, myths and legends, and allegory.

I wish to thank Calvin College for a Faculty Research Grant which enabled me to complete work on the project; the staff of the English Department for typing the manuscript in various stages—Barbara De Vos, Wilma Westra, and Alma Walhout; Conrad Bult, Reference Librarian, for the many courtesies extended to me over the years; Kenneth Baas, Audio-Visual Technician, for his photographic expertise; and Linda DeCelles of Special Collections at the University of Chicago for seeing me through the intricacies of illustration selection. I am grateful to my children for listening to werewolf myths and legends in childhood and for encouraging me to develop a *Reader* on lycanthropy. My debt to my husband is inestimable, for, not only did he engage in discussions about "spiritual substance with corporeal bar," but with him "conversing I forget all time."

Charlotte Otten

Grand Rapids, Michigan
Spring 1986

Introduction

𝕴n our contemporary world the word *werewolf* is associated almost exclusively with the lurid, the sensational, the incredible, the criminal, the irrational. No rational human being today believes that it is physically possible for a human being to be metamorphosed into a wolf, or into any animal, for that matter. (Even sex changes within the species require surgical procedures.) A *werewolf*, one who has literally been transformed from a human being into a wolf, can best be shown on film, where fake brutal attacks, multiple murders, rape, torture, and cannibalism are cinematic tricks to horrify and mesmerize an audience that enjoys vicarious participation in fantasy violence and imaginary savagery. The simulated werewolf is a primitive psychological mechanism to escape the real violence in contemporary society. There are, to be sure, exceptions. When the *Barney Miller* television show picked up a harmless "werewolf" on the streets of New York, the growls (and even agonized cries for a priest and exorcism) evoked laughter from the audience (or from the laugh-machine). It would not have been possible, then, to call this anthology *A Werewolf Reader* and been taken seriously except by devotees of horror fiction and film.

The taste for werewolf fantasy seems to be insatiable. The twentieth century is familiar with werewolf films such as *The Wolf Man* (1941), *Frankenstein Meets the Wolf Man* (1943), *She-Wolf of London* (1946), *The Werewolf* (1956), *I Was a Teenage Werewolf* (1957), *Werewolf in a Girls' Dormitory* (1961), to name only a few of the more than fifty films listed in Walt Lee's *Reference Guide to Fantastic Films* (Chelsea-Lee, 1973). Perhaps the best known werewolf of the screen is Lon Chaney, Jr., whose cinematic transformation from human to wolf took at least six hours of initial preparation in the makeup rooms, and a good many more hours for the gradations in his transformations. Film representations of werewolves can range from the genuinely artistic, even sympathetic, to the deliberately horrifying, to the jocosely bloodthirsty.

Modern werewolf fiction shows a wider range of approaches and perceptions than does film. Although some are horror tales that bristle with terror and sparkle with macabre humor, they do not trivialize the werewolf symbol: stories like Saki's "Gabriel-Ernest" and "The She-Wolf" are forays into the layers of terror underneath the gloss of civilization, showing that the irrational forces in the universe are a constant temptation and a compelling one. Still other modern werewolf stories such as Seabury Quinn's "The Phantom Farmhouse," S. Carleton's "The Lame Priest," Algernon Blackwood's "Running Wolf," and Peter Fleming's "The Kill" deal with basic moral issues: with unavenged murder, expiation for crime, posthumous guilt, love and hate, God and the devil. Often the moral edge is ambiguous.

In addition to film and fantasy fiction, there are journalistic reports of so-called "werewolf crimes." On 17 December 1976, for example, the *London Daily Mail* carried the headline "We Have Werewolf Killer, Say Police," reporting on the capture of the multiple-murderer known as "The Werewolf of Paris." Recognizing its appropriateness for their notorious terrorist organization, the Nazis, during and immediately after the Second World War, carried out unspeakable crimes under the code word "Werewolf." In criminal instances the word *werewolf* functions not metaphysically but as a powerful moral metaphor. It seems to be a linguistic attempt to face the unfathomable: it projects into the word *werewolf* what is sub-moral, sub-rational, sub-human, that is, multiple murders, sexual attacks, cannibalism, torture, sado-masochism, satanism. The irony is that animal wolves (except in case of injury or hunger) do not kill, attack, or mutilate. According to recent research, wolves live in packs and establish congenial, bonding relationships and a society founded on trust. If one of their number develops killer-instincts, that criminal wolf is destroyed for the good of the community.

The "actual" werewolves in our contemporary society are those who appear in hospitals as psychiatric patients, and in Native American ceremonial rites. In delusional states humans (of both sexes) perceive themselves as werewolves; their doctors refer to them as *lycanthropes*. Although the etymological difference between *werewolf* and *lycanthrope* is superficial (werewolf=*vir*, Latin, *manwolf*; lycanthrope=*lykanthropos*, Greek, *wolfman*), the word *lycanthrope* today is a professional term for a pathological condition, and the word *werewolf* is a non-medical term for a fantasy or criminal state. Psychologically, these two words are worlds apart.

In "A Case of Lycanthropy," the first of the three cases which appear in this *Reader*, a female werewolf's symptoms underwent rigorous clinical analysis and treatment. The doctors diagnosed her as suffering from chronic pseudoneurotic schizophrenia and suggested that her *pathological* metamorphosis into a werewolf "provided temporary relief from an otherwise consuming sexual conflict that might have taken the form of a completed suicide."

In the two cases that are discussed in "Lycanthropy Revisited," both patients were males, and both came from the remote mountain regions of the eastern United States. One, a soldier, was a chronic drug-user from early adolescence. Although he was not preoccupied with sex (as was the female in the first case), he had compulsions to devour wild rabbits and was obsessed with satanism. In the other case, a male could no longer function in his occupation as a farmer or even as a human being. He lived outdoors almost exclusively, letting his hair grow into what he considered fur, howling at the moon, and showing signs of diminished mental capacity. He was diagnosed as having chronic brain syndrome. What continued to baffle the investigators, however, was that no organic cause could be found for the patient's increased werewolf activities (prowling and howling) at the time of full moon, in spite of medical treatment. In both cases, hallucination was an important factor in metamorphosis.

In Native American ceremonial rites, the transformation into coyotes is the equivalent of metamorphosis into wolves. In his article on "The Psychodynamics of the Navajo Coyoteway Ceremonial," Daniel Merkur regards lycanthropy as a guilt-expiation mechanism:

> The traditional hunting ritualism of the Navajo Indians, as reconstructed from ethnological literature, uses symbolic lycanthropy to produce catharsis of the horror and guilt of the hunt.

When the psychohygienic function of the ritualism fails, hunting neurosis develops, taking a form described in myth as a transformation into Coyote. Religious lycanthropy inspires the symbolism of repetition-compulsions. The Coyoteway ceremonial addresses the neurosis by reinducing lycanthropy before exorcising the possessing god, Coyote. This enactment of an ecstatic rite of initiation into hunting ritualism provides insights into the origin and artificial nature of the neurosis, channels guilt outward by exteriorizing Coyote (a symbol for guilt), and provides a format for working through these matters. The naive psychotherapy of the Navajo Chanter provides a cure, rather than a remission of symptoms alone.[1]

Buried in these heterogeneous phenomena today are the basic issues faced in the Middle Ages and the Renaissance: the nature of violence, crime, mental health, the involvement of the supernatural in human life, socialization of individuals in the community, jurisprudence, good and evil. (Perhaps the counterpart of film and fantasy fiction is the legends and myths of antiquity.) In passing, it is interesting to observe that when the actual threat to community stability by werewolves was greatest, fictional accounts were replaced by trial records, case histories, and criminal proceedings. Today, when we are confident that humans cannot be metaphysically transformed into wolves, i.e., when there is no threat from werewolves to the tranquillity of communal life, werewolf films and fiction thrive.

Lycanthropy appears to be a depersonalization process. Adrienne Rich's "Meditations for a Savage Child" reflects the ambiguities of the process:

> a red mouth slowly closing
>
> Go back so far there is another language
> go back far enough the language
> is no longer personal
> these scars bear witness
> but whether to repair
> or to destruction
> I no longer know[2]

The paradox in lycanthropy is that by projecting into animals what is unacceptable or unfathomable in human conduct, and by assigning human behavioral patterns to animals, human life's darkest moments are exposed. Whether to destruction or repair is difficult to say.

Although this *Reader* focuses on lycanthropy in the medieval and Renaissance periods, it includes modern psychiatric cases. By looking at lycanthropy in medical, legal, historical, philosophical, theological, and mythological contexts, by recognizing the fact that lycanthropy still exists in our contemporary society, and by reading critical essays on lycanthropy, we can better understand lycanthropes and those who judged them.

II

In English usage the word *werewolf* antedates the word *lycanthrope* by about five centuries. According to Ernest Weekley in *More Words Ancient and Modern*, the word *wer* [*were*] "is found in all the Teutonic languages and is cognate with Lat. *vir*, Gaelic *fear*, Welsh *gwr*, Sanskrit *vira*."[3] The first recorded use of the word *werewolf* appears in the Ecclesiastical Ordinances of King Cnut (1017–1035):

> Thonne moton tha hyrdas beon swydhe wacore and geornlice clypigende, the widh thonne theodsceadhan folce sceolan scyldan, thaet syndon biscopas and maessepreostas, the godcunde heorda bewarian and bewarian sceolan, mid wislican laran, thaet se wodfreca werewulf to swidhe ne slyte ne to fela ne abite of godcundse heorde. [Therefore must the shepherds be very watchful and diligently crying out, who have to shield the people against the spoiler; such are bishops and mass-priests, who are to preserve and defend their spiritual flocks with wise instructions, that the madly audacious were-wolf do not too widely devastate, nor bite too many of the spiritual flock.][4]

Obviously symbolic, this Old English werewolf in ecclesiastical jurisprudence is rooted in the Scriptures. The image of the wolf attacking the flock appears in Christ's Sermon on the Mount: "Beware of false prophets, which come to you in sheep's clothing, but inwardly they are ravening wolves" (Matt. 7:15, AV); and in Paul's address to the Ephesians: "For I know this, that after my departing shall grievous wolves enter in among you, not sparing the flock" (Acts 20:21 AV). The shift in the image of wolf to werewolf may well indicate the perception of a closer alliance with Satan than the word *wolf* (although ravening and and grievous) connotes. The image cluster in the Ecclesiastical Ordinances has roughly the following equivalences:

> sheep/flock = Christian parishioners who are vulnerable to spiritual attack by Satanic forces.
>
> shepherds = bishops and priests who are instructed to protect their "flock" from diabolic attack.
>
> werewolf = Satan and his cohorts who wish to destroy the faith of the "sheep" and to damn them to perdition.

In these Laws of the Church there is no hint that the word *werewolf* could refer to a human being whose mental state of aberration is associated with lycanthropic delusion, a psychological condition recognized for centuries in medicine. Nor is this a reference to St. Augustine's well-known pronouncements on physical metamorphosis:

> It is very generally believed that by certain witches' spells and the power of the Devil men may be changed into wolves . . . but they do not lose their human reason and understanding, nor are their minds made the intelligence of a mere beast. Now this must be understood in this way: namely, that the Devil creates no new nature, but that he is able to make something appear to be which in reality is not. For by no spell nor evil power can the mind, nay, not even the body corporeally, be changed into the material limbs and features of any animal . . . but a man is fantastically and by illusion metamorphosed into an animal, albeit he to himself seems to be a quadruped.[5]

What is remarkable in this Anglo-Saxon legal use of the word *werewolf* is the substitution of *werewolf* for the Scriptural *wolf*. Satan is seen as enlisting humans as allies and servants, adding them to his demonic hosts. This is a covert acknowledgment of Satan's capacity to change humans into werewolves; that is, the instigation to werewolfism is Satan's, but the human will collaborates in the spiritual metamorphosis. Bishops and priests are warned about the subtle, undetectable transformations threatening the spiritual life of the flock.

The spiritual symbolic use continues in Middle English. *Pierce the Ploughmans Crede* (c. 1394) paraphrases Matt. 7:15 and uses *wer-wolves* in place of *wolves*:

> *In vestimentis ouium* but onlie with-inne
> Thei ben wilde wer-wolues that wiln the folk robben. (458–9)[6]

Satan is the specific source of evil: werewolves are his captive agents.

Simultaneous with this use in ecclesiastical and spiritual contexts is the emergence of the werewolf in narrative contexts. Reminiscent of the physical transformation in ancient myth (Homer, Virgil, Ovid, Petronius), these narratives return to physical metamorphosis; the werewolf in the Middle English narratives, however, is not the generalized moral evil of ancient mythology but the helpless victim of domestic crime, usually adultery. The scheming wife (and her lover) are the agents of the transformation. The Celtic tale of *Arthur and Gorlagon* (Latin version, late fourteenth century) is a story of physical transformation through female betrayal. The etymology of *Gorlagon* reveals the werewolf, according to Alfred Nutt: "*Gorlagon* is by metathesis for *Gorgalon*, an expanded form of *Gorgol*=Old Welsh *Guruol* or *Guorguol*, the first syllable of which is cognate to Latin *vir*, Anglo-Saxon *wer*.) (See Section V).

Sir Thomas Malory's *Le Morte Darthur* (1470) has a similar betrayal: a good knight was "bitrayed with his wyf for she made hym seuen yere a werwolf."[7]

In the French *Roman de Guillaume de Palerne*, translated into Middle English about 1350, the werewolf is a Spanish prince who has been transformed by his cruel stepmother. The word *werwolf* occurs frequently throughout the poem, whose subtitle is *William and the Werwolf*:

> For i wol of the werwolf a wile nov speke.
> Whanne this werwolf was come to his wolnk denne. (79–80)[8]

In the narratives of the Middle Ages the werewolf shifted its shapes away from the ancient myths of Greece and Rome, the spiritual uses of the ecclesiastical courts, and the paraphrases of the Scriptures. The ancient myths told of moral changes in humans that converted them into animals; Odysseus's men, for example, were changed by

Circe into beasts. Ovid's *Metamorphoses* records the story of Lycaon, the savage king of Arcadia, who, when visited by the god Jupiter in disguise, served him a dinner of human flesh. Outraged by this display of cannibalism, Jupiter transformed Lycaon into what corresponded to his moral appetites: into an irrational, bestial human-wolf. These myths are a realistic (though symbolic) assessment of the moral dimensions of human life (see Section V). The werewolves of the ecclesiastical courts and the Scriptures were manifestations of the Devil's power in human lives. But the werewolves of medieval narratives were victims of domestic plotting. It is a puzzling change, although the anti-feminist bias of the period may be a factor in the shift. The effect on the reader also undergoes a radical change. While the ancient myths are powerful warnings to humans to abstain from indulging bestial appetites and from obeying irrational promptings, and the ecclesiastical and Scriptural werewolves are to be feared because of the wily stratagems of the Devil who goes about "seeking whom he may devour" (I Peter 5:8 AV), the werewolf in the medieval narratives evokes pity and sympathy for the werewolf, who, banished by fellow humans, was barbarized by his shape and excluded from human fellowship and love.[9]

III

The words *lycanthropia* and *lycanthropus* appeared first in English in Reginald Scot's *The Discoverie of Witchcraft* in 1584 (see Section III). As is obvious from his title, lycanthropy in the sixteenth century was discussed in the context of witchcraft. Not a professional philosopher nor theologian, Scot relied on ancient medical theory as well as the testimony of contemporary physicians to reject the idea of corporeal change in human beings. Doubting the reality of the Devil, and hence the power of the Devil to alter human flesh into animal flesh, Scot regards sufferers from lycanthropic delusions as having the disease *Lupina melancholia* or *Lupina insania*. He discredits the testimony of witchmongers who themselves "rave and rage" about lycanthropes, attacks the Roman Catholic Church's views on demons and magic, and assaults the theories and practices on witchcraft of the great French jurist Bodin. (At this point in English linguistic history the words *werewolf* and *lycanthrope* seem to be interchangeable.)[10]

The question of human metamorphosis was a serious one, with personal, social, religious, and medical implications. Metaphysicians, theologians, kings, judges, historians, physicians, poets, dramatists, and ordinary citizens discussed the question; Scot was a country gentleman. The criminal manifestations of lycanthropy involved the rational processes, community mental health, spiritual well-being, even physical survival. One of the most discussed cases of lycanthropy was brought to trial in France in 1603. Jean Grenier, a young boy, was a self-confessed werewolf. He claimed to have become a werewolf by applying a salve and wearing a wolf-skin which he received from "The Man of the Forest," a secret affiliate of the Devil. When Jean applied the salve to his body and put on the wolf-skin, he developed a voracious appetite for human flesh. At his trial he confessed to having eaten a baby stolen from its cradle, parts of young children, and to having clawed and bitten several young girls. The court, recognizing his mental aberration and limited intelligence, sentenced him to life in a monastery for moral and religious instruction. He died there at age twenty, scarcely human (see Section II).

In other trial transcripts there were admissions to the use of a belt, girdle, or salve received from the Devil or one of his emissaries; to a preoccupation with grave-robbing; to a desire to commit incest and murder; to an appetite for human flesh. The trial of Stubbe Peeter, in 1590, for multiple murders, rape, incest, and cannibalism was known all over Europe; a woodcut illustration shows his execution and death, with his severed head being hoisted on a post and the heads of his victims surrounding him (see Section II).

Other "eye-witness" accounts speak of a poor farmer in Alkmaar, Holland, who skulked in churchyards and around gravestones, his skin pale, his appearance "black, ugly, and fearful." Another frequently repeated description is of packs of werewolves in Livonia who barked and howled all night in cemeteries and in deserts. Their eyes had a hollow look, their legs and thighs were scabbed, their skin was dry and pale. They dug up human bones and gnawed on them.[11] Still another kind of lycanthrope was the medical patient described by the French physician Jacques Ferrand, who, in the throes of erotomania, resembled a wolf.[12]

The question of human metamorphosis, then, was so important that philosophy, theology, jurisprudence, and medicine felt compelled to examine the nature of lycanthropy. It was a baffling metaphysical question. Involved were the nature of matter; the nature of angels, devils, humans, animals; the nature of perception, delusions, mental illness; and, fundamentally, the nature of God the Creator, and of the Devil. Ultimately, the basic moral question of what—or who—is Good or Evil had to be addressed. To regard the Devil as God's antagonist was one thing; to regard him as God's peer (with equal power to create) was to entertain the Manichaean heresy of two co-existing equally powerful forces. From the total skepticism of a Reginald Scot (1584), to the total acceptance of metamorphosis by the philosopher and physician William Drage, who argued as late as 1664 for actual physical transformation on metaphysical grounds, "This world was made of nothing, by Spiritual Power, and may be resolved into nothing again by the same Power; and we can resolve dense Bodies into Air, and coagulate Air into Water; and the Devil . . . a Spirit can do that, that a Spirit can do,"[13] there were many intermediate positions, most of which agreed on diabolical (but illusory) lycanthropy, in which the Devil assumed the body of a wolf or he deluded humans into thinking they were wolves, and pathologic lycanthropy based on humoral theory. Because of the accounts of cannibalism, rape, murder, incest, bestiality, there was a desperate search on the part of society for solutions to these sociocultural and pathological problems. Irving Kirsch's observations on witches are applicable also to lycanthropes:

> Many writers have inaccurately attributed the rise of demonology and witchhunts to the Middle Ages and have associated the decline of these activities with the Renaissance and the period of the scientific revolution (1500–1700). An examination of medieval Church proclamations indicates that during the early part of the Middle Ages, the Church denied the reality of witchcraft and was relatively tolerant toward alleged or self-proclaimed witches. More credulous views were developed during the Renaissance, and the height of the witch mania did not occur until the mid 17th century.[14]

In this environment King James I of England wrote a treatise on demonology which included a brief section on "Men-Woolfes" (see Section III). He concludes that werewolves were neither demon-haunted nor spirit-haunted humans, but were self-deluded "melancholic" humans who counterfeited wolf behavior; that in the absence of Reason, chaotic bestial impulses could run rampant.[15]

Henry Holland, dedicating *A Treatise Against Witchcraft* (1590) to Robert Devorax, Earl of Essex, has a dialogue between Mysodaemon and Theophilus, which combines medical and diabolical lycanthropy:

> **Mysodaemon:** let me heare in a word what can be said of *lycanthropeia*, transfformation of men and women into wolfes and cattes, etc. for these things are cleane contrarie against nature, and must be meere poeticall fables, if the trueth be tryed.
>
> **Theophilus:** these things be not the great ground of witchcraft. Howbeit I denie not, but witches may haue also sundrie such Sathanicall delusions [marginal reference to Fernelkius *de partium morbis*, 5.c.2] in many, which abound in melancholy, but no reall transformations indeede. [Witches] are but Sathans instruments, and can not worke these wonders without him, and as for Sathans power also, it is limited by the Lord.[16]

George Gifford, a preacher at Maulden in Essex, basing his conclusion mainly on English evidence (Scot relied mainly on Continental sources), writes in a similar vein in *A Dialogue Concerning Witches and Witchcraftes* (1593):

> These devils make the witches in some places beleeve that they are turned into the likeness of wolves, that they rend and teare sheepe, that they meet together & banquet, that sometimes they flie or ride in the ayre, which thinges indeed are nothing so, but they strongly delude the fantasies of the witches: Even so the devill can delude a poore woman with the likeness of another woman delivering a mouse or a catte unto her, by appearing in such a likenes. Or he can set a strong fantasie in the mind that is oppressed with melancholie, that such or such a matter was, which indeed was never so. Men must be wise in these causes.[17]

The Devil's power to insinuate himself into the mental processes of melancholics was acknowledged by a number of writers on demonology. Johann Wier (1516–88), the much-quoted tolerant Protestant physician of the Lower Rhine Valley, pleaded in *De Praestigiis Daemonum*

(Basle, 1563) for leniency for witches; and, although he regarded the Devil as wily, and sorcery and magic as dangerous devil-inspired activities, he saw lycanthropes as sufferers from a mental illness exacerbated by the Devil's interference.[18] Jean Bodin's attempts to refute Wier's arguments in *Demonomanie* (1580) became as famous as Wier's.

The position that melancholics were deluded into thinking themselves lycanthropes was carefully examined by William Perkins, who believed that the devil intervened in the visual processes:

> Delusion is then performed, when a man is made to thinke he sees that which indeede he sees not. And this is done by operation of the devill diuersly, but especially three waies. First, by corrupting the humor of the eye, which is the next instrument of sight. Secondly, by altering the ayre, which is the meane by which the object or *species* is carried to the eye. Thirdly, by altering and changing the object, that is, the thing seene, or whereon a man looketh.[19]

Della Porta, attributing transformation to natural magic, describes the phenomenon of altered perceptions as the direct result of using hallucinogenic herbs in potion form:

> For by drinking a certain Potion, the man would seem sometimes to be changed into a Fish; and flinging out his arms, would swim on the Ground: sometimes he would seem to skip up, and then to dive down again. Another would believe himself turned into a Goose: now and then sing, and to endeavour to clap his Wings. And this he did with the aforenamed Plants [Stramonium, Solanum Manicum, Bella Donna]: neither did he exclude Henbane from among his Ingredients: extracting the essences by their Menstruum, and mix'd some of their Brain, Hart, Limbs, and other parts with them. I remember when I was a young man, I tried these things on my Chamber-Fellows: and their madness still fixed upon something they had eaten, and their fancy worked according to the quality of their meat. One, who had fed lustily upon Beef, saw nothing but the formes of Bulls in his imagination, and them running at him with their horns: and such-like things. Another man also by drinking a Potion, flung himself upon the earth, and like one ready to be drowned, struck forth his legs and arms, endeavouring as it were to swim for life: but when the strength of

the Medicament began to decay, like a Shipwreck'd person, who had escaped out of the Sea, he wrung his Hair and his Clothes to strain the Water out of them; and drew his breath, as though he took such pains to escape the danger.[20]

And the physician John Cotta supported "local translation" by attributing to "the Divel, and his associates, Enchaunters, Witches, and Sorcerers" the power to enter into and possess human and animal bodies, and to work magic and mischievous effects "as is evident by the generally knoune power of the Magicke cups."[21]

From earliest times physicians considered lycanthropy as a disease and treated it as such. One of the most influential physicians, Paulos Aigina, who lived in seventh-century Alexandria, described lycanthropy in terms of his clinical experience. His seven-volume encyclopedia of medicine (which was translated into Latin and French in the sixteenth century) analyzes the disease, attributing its causes to brain malfunction, humoral pathology, and hallucinogenic drugs. Paulos describes his lycanthropic patients as suffering from the following symptoms: pallor; feeble vision; absence of tears and saliva, with resultant very dry eyes and tongue; excessive thirst; incurable ulcerated legs (from frequent bruising while travelling on "all-fours"); obsessive compulsions to wander at night in cemeteries, and to howl till dawn. For cures he recommends baths, purging, opening of a vein, control of diet; and, to prevent insomnia and night-wandering, the rubbing of the patient's nostrils with opium to insure uninterrupted sleep.

Francis Adams, nineteenth-century translator of the Seven Books of Paulus Aegineta, comments:

> See Aetius (vi, II); Oribasius (Synops. viii, 10); Actuarius (Mett. Med. i, 16); Anonymus (de Lycanth, ap. Phys. et Med. Min.); Psellus (Carm. de Re Med. ibid.); Avicenna (iii, 1, 5, 22); Haly Abbas (Theor. ix, 7, Pract. v, 24); Alsaharavius (Pract. 1, 2, 28); Rhases (Divis. 10, Cont. 1). All the other authorities give much the same account of this species of melancholy as Paulus . . . Avicenna recommends the application of the actual cautery to the sinciput when the other remedies fail. Haly Abbas describes the disease by the name of *melancholia canina*. He says the patient delights to wander among tombs, imitating the cries of dogs; that his colour is pale; his eyes misty (tenebricosi), dry, and

hollow; his mouth parched; and that he has marks on his limbs of injuries which he has sustained from falls. He recommends the same treatment as our author: indeed he evidently merely translates this section of Paulus. Alsaharavius seems also to allude to this disease by the name of *melancholia canina*. Rhases' account of it is quite similar to our author's.[22]

Over the centuries the symptomatology remained stable, and the disease persisted. Within the ancient classical medical framework Renaissance writers such as Robert Burton wrote his *Anatomy of Melancholy* (1621), taking into account philosophy, psychology, language, literature, and medicine. Burton's view of lycanthropy was that it was a form of insanity (see Section I.). The physician John Webster, in *The Displaying of Supposed Witchcraft* (1677), comments: "many persons, by reason of melancholy in its several kinds, have been mentally and internally (as they thought, being depraved in their imaginations) changed into Wolves."[23]

The long medical history, which extends into the twentieth century, has given birth to many medical theories. Among the theories are two associated with disease: the congenital disease known as porphyria, which discolors the teeth, causes blisters to erupt on the skin when exposed to sunlight, and deforms the shape of the body; and the disease known as hypertrichosis, in which the human body is covered with animal-like hair. Pharmaceutical examination has recognized that in the salves used were hallucinogens that caused delusions. In cannibalism, acute malnutrition can be a contributing factor, or even the major cause. Psychiatrists today attribute lycanthropy to schizophrenia, organic brain syndrome with psychosis, psychotic depressive reaction, hysterical neurosis of the dissociative type, manic-depressive psychosis, or psychomotor epilepsy. A psychologist specializing in mental diseases of childhood, suggests autism as a possibility for feral manifestations in children.[24]

Whatever the causes, diagnoses, prognoses, with so many witnesses to the werewolf phenomenon it is not surprising to discover that a whole body of literature has sprung up around lycanthropy. This *Reader*, in addition to Medical Cases, Diagnoses, Descriptions; Trial Records, Historical Accounts, Sightings; Philosophical and Theological Approaches to Metamorphosis; Myths and Legends, includes

Critical Essays on Lycanthropy, from the viewpoints of anthropology, history, and medicine.

IV

The nineteenth-century allegory in this *Reader* stands in the tradition of *Piers the Plowman* and *Pilgrim's Progress*. There is a main character called Christian and a shimmeringly beautiful temptress who is a werewolf; she kills all whom she kisses. It is Christian in the allegory who saves his twin brother from the fascination and enticement that the werewolf brings. Although the story is by its allegorical nature universal, its human dimension is so personal that specific humans discover that evil is seductive and malevolence is gracious. In the presence of deception and trust, the female werewolf masquerades successfully as lover.

Although no one today believes in actual physical metamorphosis of a human being into a wolf, there is no doubt that a werewolf, a lycanthrope, whether in clinic, forest, courtroom; in legend or myth; in non-fictional or allegorical accounts, evokes terror or pity in the viewer or reader. To admit the werewolf into human consciousness is to admit the need to examine the moral underpinnings of society. The Holocaust is reminder enough of the human propensity for evil. Donald Davie's poem shocks us into an awareness of ever-present dangers:

> The savage poets sang
> Enormities that happen every day.
> No talons raven in a titan's gut
> When dreadful fathers of a fortnight's date
> Are drowning kittens in a water-butt.
> But see, a baby's finger in the plate![25]

Notes

1. Daniel Merkur, "The Psychodynamics of the Navajo Coyoteway Ceremonial," *Journal of Mind and Behavior*, 2 (1981), 243–57.

2. Adrienne Rich, *Diving into the Wreck* (New York: Norton, 1973), 58.

3. Ernest Weekley, *More Words Ancient and Modern* (London, 1927), 181–84.

4. *Ancient Laws and Institutes of England*, edited by B. Thorpe (London, 1840), 160–61.

5. St. Augustine, *De Spiritu et Anima*, cap. 26; *De Civitate Dei*, lib. 18, cap. 17.

6. *Pierce the Ploughmans Crede*, edited by W. W. Skeat, Early English Text Society (London, 1867), 17.

7. Sir Thomas Malory, *Le Morte Darthur*, edited by H. Oskar Sommer, Vol. I (London, 1889), 793.

8. *William of Palerne*, edited by W. W. Skeat, Early English Text Society, (London, 1867), 9.

9. For a curious etymology, see Montague Summers, *The Werewolf* (New York: University Books, 1966), 12, who quotes from *The Booke of huntynge or Master of game* (c. 1400), chap. vii: "Of ye Wolf and of his nature . . . ther ben some that eten chyldren & men and eteth noon other flesh from that tyme that thei be a charmed with mannys flesh, ffor rather thei wolde be deed. And thei be cleped Werewolfes for men shulde be war of him," Bodley MS. 546, 35ᵛ.

10. For an analysis of Scot's *Discoverie*, see Sydney Anglo, "Reginald Scot's *Discoverie of Witchcraft*: Scepticism and Sadduceeism," in *The Damned Art*, edited by Sydney Anglo (London: Routledge & Kegan Paul, 1977), 106–39.

11. See Section I, *Reader*: I. Goulart, *Admirable and Memorable Histories*, and Robert Burton, *The Anatomy of Melancholy.*

12. Jacques Ferrand, *Erotomania*, translated by E. Chilmead (Oxford, 1640), 10, 36, 99.

13. William Drage, *Daimonomageia* (London, 1664), 19.

14. Irving Kirsch, "Demonology and the Rise of Science," *Journal of the History of the Behavioral Sciences*, 14 (April 1978), 149–57.

15. See Stuart Clark, "King James's *Daemonologie*: Witchcraft and Kingship," in Anglo, *The Damned Art*, 156–81.

16. Henry Holland, *A Treatise Against Witchcraft* (London, 1590), G3ʳ.

17. George Gifford, *A Dialogue Concerning Witches and Witchcraftes* (London, 1593), K3ᵛ. For a survey of Gifford's work, see Alan Macfarlane, "A Tudor Anthropologist: George Gifford's *Discourse* and *Dialogue*, in Anglo, *The Damned Art*, 140–55.

18. Johann Wier, *De Praestigiis Daemonum* (Basle, 1563), lib. 4, cap. 23.

19. William Perkins, *A Discourse of Witchcraft* (Cambridge, 1609), 635.

20. Giambattista Della Porta, *Natural Magick*, edited by Derek J. Price (New York, 1957), 219–20. For an illustration of the transformation of men into horses, see Gioseffe Petrucci, *Prodomo Apologetico* (Amsterdam, 1677).

21. John Cotta, *The Triall of Witch-Craft* (London, 1616), 39–43, 91.

22. *The Seven Books of Paulus Aegineta*, edited and translated by Francis Adams (London, 1844–47), III, sec. 16.

23. John Webster, *The Displaying of Supposed Witchcraft* (London, 1677), 95. See also Levinus Lemnius, *The Touchstone of Complexions*, translated by Thomas Newton (London, 1581): "All these sortes of Choler, endued with virulent and poysonous

qualityes, infecte the mynde wyth lewde conditions, and the body wyth loathsome dyseases, whereof many bee of such malignaunt nature, that hardly wil be cured: as eating Cankers, corroding ulcers . . . Herpes . . . and of Courtiers (who commonly more than others are thereto subject) named the Wolfe: for it exulcerateth the skinne, and eateth the flesh to the very Boanes . . . " fol. 134ᵛ. Lemnius is obviously not referring to werewolves, but the dermatological features of those suffering from the "Wolfe" are shared with werewolves.

24. Bruno Bettelheim, "Feral Children and Autistic Children," *American Journal of Sociology,* 64 (1959); reprinted in *Understanding Society* (The Open University Press, 1970). See Christopher Baxter, "Johann Weyer's *De Praestigiis Daemonum:* "Unsystematic Psychopathology," in Anglo, *The Damned Art,* 53–75.

25. Donald Davie, *Collected Poems 1950–1970* (Oxford: Oxford University Press, 1972), 13.

SECTION I

Medical Cases, Diagnoses, Descriptions

Introduction

The first three cases in this section of the *Reader* were recorded in 1975 and in 1977. These patients believed that they had been metamorphosed into werewolves. They were hospitalized, treated with medication, and dismissed on a continuing-medication basis.

Because lycanthropy is admittedly a rare condition in modern industrial societies, the psychiatrists who treated these modern lycanthropes searched older medical literature for descriptions, diagnoses, prognoses, and cures. They discovered that lycanthropes in the ancient world, the Middle Ages, the Renaissance, and into the twentieth century, exhibited many of the following symptoms:

—altered states of consciousness (transformation into the fur, voice, posture of wolves);

—alienation from themselves and from human society (frequenting cemeteries, woods, isolated areas);

—acute physiological stress and anxiety;

—bestial compulsions (wolvish sexual positions, appetite for raw flesh);

—obsession with the demonic (evil eye, invasion of the body by the devil, satanism).

Drug use was involved in many cases, though not in every one. Twentieth-century lycanthropes (at least those described in these three clinical reports and treated in psychiatric clinics) did not engage in sexual violence, cannibalism, or murder, as many of the pre-twentieth century lycanthropes did.

In the first case, the 49-year-old female patient seemed to use metamorphosis to provide relief from conflicts that might have ended in suicide. (She was not a user of toxic substances.) She was diagnosed as suffering from chronic pseudoneurotic schizophrenia. Rosenstock and Vincent drew the following general conclusions about lycanthropy:

> After reviewing ancient and modern literature, it is felt that the differential diagnosis for lycanthropy should include consideration of all of the following possibilities: (1) schizophrenia, (2) organic brain syndrome with psychosis, (3) psychotic depressive reaction, (4) hysterical neurosis of the dissociative type, (5) manic-depressive psychosis, and (6) psychomotor epilepsy. The last item is mentioned because of reports that individuals suffering from lycanthropy have been described as being "prone to epilepsy."

All six of the above distinct categories would have come under the general diagnosis as suffering from *melancholy* in earlier medical writing.

In the second case, the 20-year-old male, a chronic multiple drug user, was put into a lycanthropic state by the use of LSD and strychnine. Under the influence of LSD, he went into the woods, felt himself turning into a werewolf with fur growing on his hands and face, and chased wild rabbits with the desire to devour them raw. His preoccupation with the devil took the form of hallucinations: he was convinced that the devil intervened in his thought processes and that he was demon-possessed. Diagnosed as paranoid schizophrenia, the disease was precipitated and facilitated by drugs. After discharge, he abandoned medication and was again preoccupied with satanism.

In the third case, a 37-year-old male suffered from brain disease. Allowing his facial hair to grow, sleeping in cemeteries, howling at the moon, he was admitted several times to a psychiatric hospital. On the third admission, he claimed that he had been transformed into a werewolf. Although his lycanthropic behavior was controlled with medication, there was evidence of diminished mental activity.

Surawicz and Banta drew the following general conclusions about lycanthropy:

> in both instances an altered state of consciousness existed. Concerning drugs as causative agents, it is interesting to note that opium has been mentioned in a dual capacity, namely as a drug which can cause lycanthropy as well as a drug for its treatment.

Wormwood is described as a cerebral stimulant, which has been used in absinthe and continues to be used in vermouth. The nightshades contain belladonna. Mandrake is described as a narcotic herb which contains hyoscyamine, scopolamine, and atropine. Stramonium is found in Jimson weed which contains hyoscyamine as does henbane. . . . Cohoba . . . produced trances and visual hallucinations . . . peyote . . . [is] a hallucinogenic. All these substances are known to produce altered states of consciousness characterized by perceptual distortion . . . and a loss of ego boundaries, in which the subject experiences transcendental, oceanic, mystical or universal feelings. . . . Some of the substances used then [in antiquity] continue to be in use now, notably Jimson weed, peyote, marijuana and opium.

Ancient physicians, attempting to account for what in modern psychiatry is called "loss of ego boundaries," turned to the theory of humors, a theory that is rooted in the writings of the physicians Hippocrates (460–377 BC) and Galen (AD 129–200). The composition of the human body is viewed in terms of the four elements of the cosmos: earth, air, fire, and water. These four basic elements had their equivalents—their correspondents—in the human body:

Earth = melancholy (black bile)

Air = blood

Fire = choler

Water = phlegm

This classical humoral theory accounted for the human personality (also known as the "complexion") by the domination of one of the humors in the human body. Robert Burton, for example, insists in *The Anatomy of Melancholy*, that he must "make a brief digression of the anatomy of the body and faculties of the soul, for the better understanding of that which is to follow." Burton explains not only how the four humors function in the human body but also how "spirit" rises from the blood and is "the instrument of the soul":

A humour is a liquid or fluent part of the body.

Blood is a hot, sweet, temperate, red humour. . . . And from it spirits are first begotten in the heart, which afterwards by the arteries are communicated to the other parts.

Phlegm is a cold and moist humour, begotten of the colder part of the chylus.

Choler is hot and dry, bitter, begotten of the hotter parts of the chylus.

Melancholy, cold and dry, thick, black, and sour, begotten of the more faeculent part of nourishment, and purged from the spleen. . . .

These four humours have some analogy with the four elements. . . .

Spirit is a most subtle vapour, which is expressed from the blood, and the instrument of the soul, to perform all his actions. (I. 168–170)

John Donne in one of his Holy Sonnets, which attempts to account for sin's invasion of his body and soul, captures the essence of this theory and its implications for human life:

> I am a little world made cunningly
> Of Elements, and an Angelike spright [spirit] (*Divine Poems* V)

Each element had its corresponding temperament. The ideal for human physical and mental health was the balance of all four humors in the human body. An excess of one humor, however, could create an imbalance in the body which would have both physiological and psychological effects. The humoral theory of body composition, then, was both a physiological psychology and a psychological physiology: body health affected mental health, and mental health could alter body health.

In the case of lycanthropy, it was generally agreed that there was an excess of melancholy. This excess of melancholy could cause various kinds of mental derangements, including depression, hallucinations, delusions, and insanity. The word *melancholy* came to represent not only the basic humor but the pathological state of aberration. Repeated often in the Renaissance was a description of "melancholic lycanthropia," adapted from *De Melancholia* by Aëtius (late fifth, early sixth centuries), and quoted here from Garzoni's *Hospitall of Incurable Fooles:*

[Among the] humours of melancholy, the Phisitions place a kinde of madnes by the Greeks called *Lycanthropia*, termed by the Latines *Insania Lupina*, or wolues furie: which bringeth a man to this point . . . that in Februarie he will goe out of the house in the night like a wolfe, hunting about the graues of the dead with great howling, and plucke the dead mens bones out of the sepulchers, carrying them about the streetes, to the great feare and astonishment of all them that meete him . . . melancholike persons of this kinde, haue pale faces, soaked and hollow eies, with a weake sight, neuer shedding one teare to the view of the worlde, a drie toong, extreme thirst, and they want spittle and moisture exceedingly.[1]

Reginald Scot's *Discoverie of Witchcraft*, an attempt to free witches and lycanthropes from the opprobrium and persecution of the community, was based on the humoral theory. An avid reader in the medical literature of aberrant behavior, he returned again and again to the humoral theory to account for pathological states:

This melancholike humor (as the best physicians affirme) is the cause of all their strange, impossible, and incredible confessions . . . these affections, though they appear in the mind of man, yet are they bred in the bodie, and proceed from this humor. (68)

There were, of course, physicians who accepted the humoral theory and used it as the basis for understanding lycanthropy, but who also argued that the devil preys on melancholics and distorts their perceptions. (See Section III for the role of the demonic in lycanthropy.) Shakespeare's Hamlet, for example, a self-admitted melancholic (though obviously not a lycanthrope), was afraid that he might have been delusional when he saw the ghost of his father. Combining humoral theory with the potency of the demonic, Hamlet reflects

> The spirit that I have seen
> May be a devil, and the devil hath power
> T' assume a pleasing shape, yea, and perhaps
> Out of my weakness and my melancholy,
> As he is very potent with such spirits . . . II.ii.610–14

Scot, however, rejected even the suggestion of demonic intervention·

> melancholie abounding in their head, and occupieng their braine, hath deprived or rather depraved their judgements, and all their senses . . . the force which melancholie hath, and the effects that it worketh in the bodie . . . are almost incredible. For as some of these melancholike persons imagine, they are . . . brute beasts. . . . Through melancholie, such were alienated from themselves . . . they may imagine, that they can transforme their owne bodies, which neverthelesse remaineth in the former shape. (64–66)

For those who, like Scot, regarded lycanthropy as strictly a melancholic disease, neither instigated by devils nor exacerbated by them, the humoral theory could provide explanations for hallucinations, delusions, distorted perceptions, states of alienation, simulated brutish conduct, and unacceptable social habits. Basically a "material" psychology and a "spiritual" physiology, the humoral theory accommodated itself to the materialization-spiritualization of personal conflicts. No matter whether the melancholic state was produced by psychological or physical conditions (or a combination of both), the suffering individual seemed to find relief from conflicts by transforming them into a material wolf-like state. Like the first patient in this *Reader*, lycanthropes who found escape from conflicts by materializing them, probably saved themselves from suicide. Although lycanthropes were not necessarily released from pain, anxiety, or stress, conflicts could be played out in a morally depersonalized bestial state.

The causes for the humoral imbalance (and, hence, for lycanthropy) were as baffling then as "chemical imbalances" are today. Burton lists a host of possible causes, among them both external and internal causes: witches and magicians; stars; old age; hereditary disease; bad diet; bad air; immoderate exercise; idleness; passions and perturbations of the mind; solitariness; sleeplessness; poverty; and discontent (I. 230–439).

Throughout the long history of the disease, many lycanthropes confessed to using drugs or an ointment which they smeared on their bodies to initiate feelings of metamorphosis. Drug-induced transformations probably provided welcome release from normal ego boundaries, bringing lycanthropes into states of incredible power—a physical and psychological power out of the range of normal, rational human experience.

Although the deliberate use of drugs in lycanthropy (and witch-craft) is referred to in popular writing as well as in specialized treatises, it should be noted that drugs used for medicinal purposes could inad-vertently cause feelings of metamorphosis, especially since many peo-ple prepared their own herbal remedies. Because the pharmacopeia of mind-altering substances is extensive, only two of the most commonly used drugs in lycanthropy—henbane and nightshade—will be dis-cussed here. (See also the case history of the second patient in this *Reader*.) Before analyzing these drugs, however, it is important to note that the base used in the ointment that was deliberately smeared on the body to achieve transportation (witches) and transformation (ly-canthropes) was made from the boiled, congealed fat of the dead body of an unbaptized infant. Continental Renaissance physicians such as Wier and Cardan, as well as English dramatists of the seventeenth century, refer to the unholy practice of boiling "th' unchristn'd Brat" (Shadwell, *The Lancashire Witches*). This fat apparently created a base that would not only adhere to the skin but would penetrate it. In legitimate medicinal uses, the base consisted of such ingredients as hog's fat, olive oil, turpentine; and today a sedative application of henbane might be made by macerating the leaves in alcohol, mixing the tincture with olive oil, and heating it in a warm bath until the alcohol is dissipated. Whatever the base, Renaissance herbalists regu-larly warned about the dangers of gathering these plants with even the slightest abrasions on the hands, for fear of poisonous penetration through the skin. The skin, both in illegitimate drug use and in legiti-mate, served as a medium in alteration.

Henbane. According to Mrs. M. Grieve in *A Modern Herbal*, henbane (*Hyoscyamus niger.* Linn.) has the following constituents:

> The chief constituent of Henbane leaves is the alkaloid Hyoscyamine, together with smaller quantities of Atropine and Hyoscine, also known as Scopolamine. . . .

> The chief constituent of the seeds is about 0.5 to 0.6 per cent. of alkaloid, consisting of Hyoscyamine, with a small proportion of Hyoscine.[2]

Goya, "Aguarda que te unten" ("Anointing by Witches"). From *The Capriccios*, Etching No. 67, *The Complete Etchings of Goya* (1943). Reprinted by permission of Crown Publishers.

The ancient physicians such as Dioscorides and Celsus (first century AD) and herbalists such as Gerard and Culpeper (seventeenth century) described the uses of henbane: to relieve rheumatic pains; as a sedative for both brain and spine, which causes loss of recollection and insensibility; to induce sleep; as a remedy for toothache (seeds were burned to produce smoke which the patient inhaled; the root boiled with vinegar was held hot in the mouth). A drug similar in action to belladonna and stramonium, though not as potent, henbane could cause indistinctness of vision, giddiness, sleepiness, delirium, convulsions, and sometimes death. Since it was regularly used in many different forms and varying dosages, for such diverse illnesses as rheumatism, disturbances of the central nervous system, insomnia, and toothache, it is not surprising to discover that it could cause, as a side-effect, delusions of metamorphosis into a wolf, or dreams of transportation and transformation.

Nightshade. According to Mrs. M. Grieve, nightshade (*Atropa Belladonna.* Linn.) has the following constituents:

> The total alkaloid present in the root varies between 0.4 and 0.6 percent., but as much as 1 per cent. has been found, consisting of Hyoscyamine and its isomer Atropine, 0.1 to 0.6 percent.

> The amount of alkaloids present in the leaves varies somewhat. . . . The proportion of the total alkaloid present in the dried leaves varies from 0.3 to 0.7 per cent.[3]

Dioscorides prescribed it for "S. Anthonies fire, the shingles, paine of the head . . . and other like accidents proceeding of sharp and biting humours"[4]. Gerard himself, in describing "Dwale, or deadly Nightshade," observed that it "causeth sleep, troubleth the minde, bringeth madnesse if a few of the berries be inwardly taken," and warned about lethal doses. He urged his readers to banish it from their gardens.[5] Since nightshade was a potent drug regularly used medicinally as a narcotic, sedative, antispasmodic, mydriatic (dilation of pupils), it is again not surprising to discover that even small doses could cause paralysis of nerve endings in the involuntary muscles, which consequently affected the central nervous system and caused excitement and delirium[6]; and that the madness referred to by Gerard could have included feelings of metamorphosis through hallucination, delirium, and delusion.

The vivid accounts of lycanthropy given by Goulart are based on his reading in medical history. A French historiographer, not a physician, he was familiar with the works of Aëtius, Aegineta, Donatus, Fincel, Peucer, Bodin, and Wier. His analysis of individual cases of lycanthropy reflects his authors' opinions: some individuals whose brain, or imagination was "corrupted" suffered from melancholy; others, who deluded themselves into thinking they were werewolves, were "impaired and hurt" by Satan. Goulart also records instances of mass lycanthropy. Thousands in Livonia were beaten by chains and compelled to join in sado-masochistic lycanthropic rites, following their torturer into attacking cattle and engaging in sub-human activity. The strange thing, however, is that they were actually in a trance for twelve days, during which time they experienced metamorphosis. Upon recovery they believed that their souls, under the direction of Satan, had left their bodies and entered into wolves; in an involuntary way, then, they had been involved in demonic lycanthropic activity.

Robert Bayfield, a physician, concludes this section of the *Reader* with a personal account of a patient he treated for lycanthropy. Diagnosing this case of lycanthropy as a melancholy disease, Bayfield prescribed a potion and a vomitive after he had drawn from his patient a quantity of blood that was as black as soot. This case ends on a happy note: "he became perfectly well."

Notes

1. Tommaso Garzoni, *Hospitall of Incurable Fooles* (London: 1586, 1600), 19.
2. Mrs. M. Grieve, *A Modern Herbal* (New York: Dover, 1931, 1971), 397–404.
3. Ibid., 582–591.
4. John Gerard, *The Herball* (London: 1597). Enlarged and amended by Thomas Johnson (London: 1633, 1636), 339.
5. Ibid., 337–41.
6. Ibid., 582–91.

A Case of Lycanthropy

HARVEY A. ROSENSTOCK and KENNETH R. VINCENT

Delusions of being a wolf or some other feared animal are universal and, although rare in the industrialized countries, still occur in China, India, Africa, and Central and South America. The animals in the delusional transformation include leopards, lions, elephants, crocodiles, sharks, buffalo, eagles, and serpents.

Case Report

A 49-year-old woman presented on an urgent basis for psychiatric evaluation because of delusions of being a wolf and "feeling like an animal with claws." She suffered from extreme apprehension and felt that she was no longer in control of her own fate: she said, "A voice was coming out of me." Throughout her 20-year marriage she experienced compulsive urges toward bestiality, lesbianism, and adultery.

The patient chronically ruminated and dreamed about wolves. One week before her admission, she acted on these ruminations for the first time. At a family gathering, she disrobed, assumed the female sexual posture of a wolf, and offered herself to her mother. This episode lasted for approximately 20 minutes. The following night, after coitus with her husband, the patient suffered a 2-hour episode, during which time she growled, scratched, and gnawed at the bed. She stated that the devil came into her body and she became an animal. Simultaneously, she experienced auditory hallucinations. There was no drug involvement or alcoholic intoxication.

Hospital Course

The patient was treated in a structured inpatient program. She was seen daily for individual psychotherapy and was placed on neu-

American Journal of Psychiatry 134:10 (October 1977):1147–49.

roleptic medication. During the first 3 weeks, she suffered relapses when she said such things as "I am a wolf of the night: I am a wolf woman of the day. . . . I have claws, teeth, fangs, hair . . . and anguish is my prey at night . . . the gnashing and snarling of teeth . . . powerless is my cause. I am what I am and will always roam the earth long after death . . . I will continue to search for perfection and salvation."

She would peer into a mirror and become frightened because her eyes looked different: "One is frightened and the other is like the wolf—it was dark, deep, and full of evil, and full of revenge of the other eye. This creature of the dark wanted to kill." During these periods, she felt sexually aroused and tormented. She experienced strong homosexual urges, almost irresistible zoophilic drives, and masturbatory compulsions—culminating in the delusion of a wolflike metamorphosis. She would gaze into the mirror and see "the head of a wolf in place of a face on my own body—just a long-nosed wolf with teeth, groaning, snarling, growling . . . with fangs and claws, calling out 'I am the devil.'" Others around her noticed the unintelligible, animal-like noises she made.

By the fourth week she had stabilized considerably, reporting, "I went and looked into a mirror and the wolf eye was gone." There was only one short-lived relapse, which responded to reassurance by experienced personnel. With the termination of that episode, which occurred on the night of a full moon, she wrote what she experienced: "I don't intend to give up my search for [what] I lack . . . in my present marriage . . . my search for such a hairy creature. I will haunt the graveyards . . . for a tall, dark man that I intend to find." She was discharged during the ninth week of hospitalization on neuroleptic medication. . . .

Discussion

We believed that the patient suffered from chronic pseudo-neurotic schizophrenia. What is of particular interest is that the delusional material was organized about a lycanthropic matrix. Her symptom complex included the following classic symptoms:

1. Delusions of werewolf transformation under extreme stress.

2. Preoccupation with religious phenomenology, including feeling victimized by the evil eye.
3. Reference to obsessive need to frequent graveyards and woods.
4. Primitive expression of aggressive and sexual urges in the form of bestiality.
5. Physiological concomitants of acute anxiety.

These symptoms occurred significantly in the absence of exposure to toxic substances. Furthermore, the patient responded to the treatment protocol used for acute schizophrenic psychosis. After reviewing ancient and modern literature, it is felt that the differential diagnosis for lycanthropy should include consideration of all of the following possibilities: (1) schizophrenia, (2) organic brain syndrome with psychosis, (3) psychotic depressive reaction, (4) hysterical neurosis of the dissociative type, (5) manic-depressive psychosis, and (6) psychomotor epilepsy. The last item is mentioned because of reports that individuals suffering from lycanthropy have been described as being "prone to epilepsy."

We believe that the metamorphosis undergone by the patient we have described provided temporary relief from an otherwise consuming sexual conflict that might have taken the form of a completed suicide.

Lycanthropy is a rare phenomenon, but it does exist. It should be regarded as a symptom complex and not a diagnostic entity. Furthermore, although it may generally be an expression of an underlying schizophrenic condition, at least five other differential diagnostic entities must be considered.

2.

Lycanthropy Revisited

FRIDA G. SURAWICZ and RICHARD BANTA

𝔐 ost contemporary textbooks, with the exception of the *American Handbook of Psychiatry* do not mention the term lycanthropy—the delusion of being changed into a wolf. Recently, two patients with symptoms of this disorder were admitted and studied on an inpatient service. Their cases are reported here because of the unusual symptomatology of this allegedly extinct condition.

Case I

Mr. H., a 20-year-old single, unemployed white male from Appalachia, was admitted with a history of long and chronic drug abuse, including marijuana, amphetamines, psilocybin, and LSD. His present sickness was precipitated by LSD and strychnine taken while he was in Europe with the United States Army ten months previously. He was out in the woods while he ingested the LSD, and felt himself slowly turning into a werewolf, seeing fur growing on his hands and feeling it grow on his face. He experienced a sudden uncontrollable urge to chase and devour live rabbits. He also felt that he had obtained horrible insight into the devil's world. After having been in this condition for two days, he rejoined his Army post but remained convinced that he was a werewolf. Looking for clues, he believed that the mess hall sign "feeding time" proved that other people knew he was a wolf. He was sent to a psychiatrist who treated him with chlorpromazine for a few months. Six months thereafter he was returned to the United States on medical evacuation status to a drug program, where he was observed for a few weeks with a diagnosis of "drug abuse— amphetamines." During the next few months, the patient quit all drugs except marijuana, but continued to be preoccupied with the werewolf transformation. He felt worse after he saw the movie "The Exorcist" two weeks prior to admission.

Canadian Psychiatric Association Journal 20:7 (November 1975):537–42.

The background history reveals that the patient's father left home during Mr. H.'s infancy and denied his paternity of the patient, but not that of his two older brothers. The patient felt that the father did this to maintain credibility with his mistress, whom he subsequently married. His first stepfather with whom he was very close, died in his presence, when he was seven. He lost his second stepfather through divorce in his early teens. The patient was very close to his mother. There is a family history suggestive of mental disease, and an older brother and a maternal cousin were denied admission to the Army because they were "weird and nervous."

The patient was sociable as a child. He started experimenting with hallucinogenic drugs in junior high. While in high school, he became interested in the occult and identified with a male priest who claimed to be a satanist. After high school the patient joined the Army where his drug use was intensified. Following his discharge from the Army after fourteen months he returned home and has been restless, hostile, agitated, anhedonic, socially withdrawn, and unable to maintain steady work. His complaints increased after the mother was notified that she would require a nephrectomy.

On admission the patient presented as a tense and suspicious young man who felt that the staff members might be possessed by or be tools of the devil. He had paranoid delusions, feeling that the devil at the end of each performance of "The Exorcist" goes out of the screen and possesses one of the movie goers. He had auditory hallucinations, hearing his thoughts aloud or his name being called, as well as visual hallucinations, during which he saw goats and black mass paraphernalia on the floor. When he looked in a mirror he occasionally saw a devil's claw over his eyes. He also believed that his thoughts were broadcast, and that the devil inserted thoughts into his mind and enabled him to read minds. He had unusual powers and felt that he could stare down dogs with his demoniacal gaze. He felt that the doctors put drugs in the patients' food to make them crazy. He showed marked ambivalence, seeking out doctors for long conversations, while at the same time expressing his fear of them. His affect was inappropriate and he would appear angry for no obvious reason, or giggle while discussing his stepfather's sudden death. There were somatizations of his delusion, and he attributed a shooting pain from the neck through the arms as a sign of possession. The patient gave a history of heavy and multiple drug use including LSD, amphetamines, mescaline, psilocybin, heroin, and marijuana until his bad trip ten months ago, when he stopped taking LSD but continued to take amphetamines and marijuana. Since his discharge from the Army he continues to smoke marijuana regularly but has not taken any other drugs.

The MMPI was interpreted as "compatible with an acute schizophrenic or toxic psychosis characterized by anxiety, obsessional thinking, agitation, religious delusions as well as bizarre sexual preoccupations and fears regarding homosexuality. Delusions of grandeur, ideas of reference, and hallucinations may be present. A delusional system involving omnipotence, genius and special abilities may be present that could also be compatible with the profile of a male hysteric who has decompensated into a psychotic reaction."

The patient was treated with trifluo perazine and showed gradual improvement. At the time of his discharge thirty-two days after admission, he had dropped the belief that he was a werewolf or that he was possessed, and displayed no other overt psychotic determinants.

The patient was referred to an outpatient clinic near his hometown, two hundred miles from this hospital. He was seen for an interview at that clinic two weeks after his discharge and appeared polite but guarded, was preoccupied with satanism and had stopped his medications because they made him feel uneasy. No further contact was established with this patient, and it was thought by the staff that he perhaps felt threatened by the clinic. Attempts to call him for further visits failed.

Case II

Mr. W. is a 37-year-old single male farmer from Appalachia. At the time of his service in the United States Navy he had a normal and average IQ. Since his discharge after four years of service he has progressively and insidiously failed to function both as a farmer and in his daily activities. He has episodically behaved in a bizarre fashion, allowing his facial hair to grow, pretending that it was fur, sleeping in cemeteries and occasionally lying down on the highway in front of oncoming vehicles. There is also a history of patient howling at the moon. Following two of these occasions, he was admitted to a psychiatric hospital. On the first admission he was given a diagnosis of "psychosis and mental deficiency," and marked deterioration of higher cortical functions was noted. During his second hospitalization, he was diagnosed as suffering from chronic undifferentiated schizophrenia, based on his bizarre behaviour since delusions or hallucinations could not be elicited while he was in hospital. During his third hospitalization, one year after his second hospitalization, the patient explained his bizarre behaviour by saying that he was transformed into a werewolf. The mental status examination showed a patient who was tidy yet dirty and sat in a slumped position. His facial expression was blank and he showed paucity of motor activity. He did not display any concern about his hospitalization and his affect was flat. His speech was slow, but in general logical and coherent, with impoverished thought processes. Although little rapport could be established, the patient was in general cooperative and compliant. On cognitive function testing he showed markedly impaired attention and concentration. His ability to calculate was severely impaired, recent memory was moderately impaired, and remote memory was spotty. The ability to make objective judgments and to abstract was adequate. On physical examination, soft neurological signs were found, including bilateral hyporeflexia of the triceps, a slow second phase of both knee jerks and a thick speech with retarded flow. The remainder of the neurological examination was negative and the family history was noncontributory and negative for neuropsychiatric problems. The patient's symptoms began after he was discharged from the Navy.

The patient had a positive brain scan, static, in the region of the right frontal cortex. Skull X-rays showed a lucid area in the right frontal region. The cerebral arteriogram did not show a mass lesion in the brain. The pneumoencephalogram showed no evidence of dilatation, but the third ventricle was somewhat atypical in appearance. No pathological changes could be identified.

Psychological testing showed ". . . a mental age on the Peabody Picture Vocabulary Test of eight years one month and ten years five months respectively, corresponding to an IQ score of 57 and 68. On the Shipley Hartford Scale his vocabulary mental age was eleven years, nine months, his abstract mental age was eight years, four months and his conceptual quotient was 70. There was a variation in the testing and his verbal functioning level was at best in a mild retardation range with an IQ between 52 and 67. Considering his figure drawings and the Shipley Hartford Conceptual Quotient his level of impairment was even greater, probably in the moderate mental retardation range with an IQ between 36 and 51 or lower. There seemed to be indication of brain damage. On a concrete level, his ability to comprehend was surprisingly almost adequate. He was not capable of any abstract reasoning and psychomotor retardation was pronounced. If care was taken to communicate with him, he could communicate on a simple concrete level."

Because of his bizarre behaviour and his increasing dementia at an early age, a brain biopsy was performed. It was noted that the sub-arachnoid space was quite enlarged. The neurosurgeon noted at the time of the operation that the gyri of the brain were quite small, whereas the sulci were large, suggesting a "walnut" brain. On microscopic examination, the cortical tissue revealed an unusual degree of astrocytosis with areas of cortical degeneration. There was no evidence of senile plaques or neurofibrillary traglex. These findings were not compatible with Alzheimer's disease.

The patient was discharged with a diagnosis of chronic brain syndrome of undetermined etiology. His psychotic behaviour has been successfully controlled with thioridazine hydrochloride 50 mgm b.i.d., and no further episodes of lycanthropy have been reported since his discharge one year ago, but he continues to be inactive, seldom reads, and on his last visit to the Outpatient Clinic it was noted that he offers little spontaneous conversation. He appears quiet and childlike, answering most questions with "yes," or "no," or "I don't know," but he did not show any evidence of abnormal behavior or psychosis.

Comments

Lycanthropy, by its very definition, would appear to point to a severe type of depersonalization. Many medical treatises from the past have indeed suggested that it is a form of hysteria. The endemic occurrence of the disorder and its mystical superstitious content have been used as supporting arguments. Many contemporary psychiatrists, when faced with the description of the recorded cases of the sixteenth and seventeenth centuries, would undoubtedly focus on the severe withdrawal, bizarre behaviour and delusions, impaired impulse control, and habit deterioration to support a diagnosis of schizophrenia.

The two presented cases shared lycanthropy but had a different diagnosis. The first was complicated by the history of drug use but was diagnosed as paranoid schizophrenia, perhaps precipitated and facilitated by drugs. The second case represented a chronic brain syndrome with periodic psychotic flare-ups. The common denominator would appear to be an onset precipitated by changes in brain disease in the second. Depersonalization has of course been frequently described by contemporary hallucinogenic drug users. The occurrence of depersonalization in convulsive disorders has also been noted. Therefore, the authors propose that in both instances an altered state of consciousness existed. In the first case, this was brought on by LSD and strychnine and continued casual marijuana use. In the second it must be assumed that a chronic altered state of consciousness was caused by irreversible brain disease, although the periodicity of his psychosis, occurring during the full moon, remains unexplained on an organic level.

Concerning drugs as causative agents, it is interesting to note that opium has been mentioned in a dual capacity, namely as a drug which can cause lycanthropy as well as a drug for its treatment. Wormwood is described as a cerebral stimulant, which has been used in absinthe and continues to be used in vermouth. The nightshades contain belladonna. Mandrake is described as a narcotic herb which contains hyoscyamine, scopolamine, and atropine. Stramonium is found in Jimson weed which contains hyoscyamine as does henbane, which is a narcotic, and is poisonous to fowl—hence its name. Columbus, while in the Caribbean, discovered cohoba, a snuff which produced trances and visual hallucinations among the Indians. Peyote was discovered by the Spanish explorers in West America as a hallucinogenic. All these substances are known to produce altered states of consciousness characterized by perceptual distortion such as hallucinations and illusions and a loss of ego boundaries, in which the subject experiences transcendental, oceanic, mystical, or universal feelings. During this stage, the subject is highly vulnerable to suggestions and manipulations. One may assume that excessive bloodletting with fainting or excessive purgation or vomiting, with subsequent changes in the electrolyte bal-

3.

Admirable Histories

I. GOULART

To the former Histories, we will joynesome, touching the Licanthropes and mad-men, the which wee will consider of two
sorts. For there be Licanthropes in whom the melancholike humor
doth so rule, as they imagine themselves to be transformed into
Wolves. This disease as Aetius doth witnesse lib. 6. Chap. 11. and Paulus
lib. 3. Chap. 16 with other late writers, is a kinde of melancholie, but
very black and vehement: for such as are toucht there-with, goe out of
their houses in Februarie, counterfet Wolves in a manner in all things,
and all night doe nothing but runne into Church-yardes, and about
graves, so as you shall presently discover in them a wonderfull alteration of the braine, especially in the imagination and thought, which is
miserably corrupted, in such sort, as the memorie hath some force: as I
have observed in one of these melancholike Licanthropes, whom we
call Wolves: for he that knew mee well, being one day troubled with
his disease, and meeting me, I retired my selfe a part, fearing that he
should hurt me. Having eyed me a little, hee passed on, being followed by a troupe of people. Hee carried then upon his shoulders the
whole thigh and the legge of a dead man. Beeing carefully looked
unto, hee was cured of this disease. Meeting mee another time, hee
asked mee if I had not beene afeard, when as hee incountred mee in
such a place, which makes mee to thinke that his memorie was not hurt
nor impayred, in the vehemencie of his disease, although his imagination were much. Donat de Hautemer, Chap. 9. of his *Treatise of the cure of*
Diseases.

William of Brabant writes in his Historie, that a man of a setled
judgement, was some-times so tormented with an evill spirit, that at a
certaine season of the yeare, hee imagined himselfe to bee a ravening
Wolfe, running up and downe the Woods, Caves and Deserts, especially after young Children. More-over hee saith, that this man was
often found running in the Desarts, like man out of his wittes, and that

Admirable and Memorable Histories. Translated from the French by Ed. Grimeston (London: 1607), 386–92.

in the end by the grace of GOD, hee came to himselfe againe, and was cured.

There was also as Job Fincel reports, in his 2.*Booke of Miracles*, a Countri-man unto Pavia, in the yeare 1541. who thought himselfe to bee a Wolfe, setting upon divers men in the fields, and slew some. In the end being with great difficultie taken, hee did constantly affirme that hee was a Wolfe, and that there was no other difference, but that Wolves were commonlie hayrie without, and hee was betwixt the skinne and the flesh. Some (too barbarous and cruell Wolves in effect) desiring to trie the truth thereof, gave him manie wounds upon the armes and legges: but knowing their owne error, and the innocencie of the poore melancholie man, they committed him to the Surgions to cure, in whose hands hee dyed within fewe dayes after. Such as are afflicted with that disease, are pale, their eyes are hollow, and they see ill, their tongue is drye, they are much altered, and are without much spittle in the mouth. Plinie and others write, that the braine of a Beare provokes brutish imaginations. And he saith, that in our time some made a Spanish Gentleman eate thereof, whose phantasie was so troubled, as he imagined that he was transformed into a Beare, flying into the Mountaines and deserts. J. Wier, lib. 4. Chap. 13. *Of Divelish devices.*

As for those Licanthropes, which have the imagination so impayred and hurt, that besides by some particular power of Sathan, they seeme Wolves and not Men, to them that see them runne, doing great spoile. Bodin disputes very amply in his *Demonomana.*lib. 2. Chap. 3. where he maintaines, that the Divell may change the figure of one body into another, considering the great power which GOD hath given him in this elementarie world. Hee maintaines that there be Licanthropes transformed really from Men into Wolves, alledging divers examples and Histories to that purpose. In the end, after many arguments, hee maintaines the one and the other sort of *Licanthropia.* And as for this represented in the end of this Chapter, the conclusion of his discourse was, that men are some-times changed into Beasts, the humaine reason remaining: whether it bee done by the power of GOD immediatly, or that this power is given to Sathan, the executioner of his will, or rather of his fearefull judgements, And if we confesse (saith he) the truth of the holy writte in Daniel, touching the transformation of Nabuchodonoser, and of the Historie of Lots wife, changed into an immovable Piller, it is certaine, that the change of a Man into an Oxe, or into a Stone is possible, and by consequence possible into all other creatures. But for that Bodin cites Peucer touching the transformation of the Pilappiens, and doth note relate plainly that which he doth observe worthy of consideration upon that subject, I will transcribe it as it is conteined in his learned worke, intituled. *A Commentarie of the principall sorts of divinations.*lib. 4. Cap. 9. according to the French edition. In the ranke and number of Ecstatiques, are put those which they call Licaons and Licanthropes, which imagine themselves to bee changed into Wolves, and in their forme runne up and downe the fields, falling upon troopes of great and small Cattell, teare in peeces what they incounter, and goe roring up and downe Church-yardes and Sepulchers. In the forth booke of Herodotus, there is a passage touching the Neuriens, a people of Scythia, who transformed them-selves into Wolves, the which hee saith, hee could not beleeve, not withstanding any report that was made unto him. For my part, I have held it fabulous and rediculous, that which hath beene often reported of this transformation of men into Wolves. But I have learned by certaine and tryed signes, and by witnesses worthy of credit, that they be not things altogether invented, and incredible, which are spoken of such transformations, which happen every yeare twelve dayes after Christmas in Livonia and the Countries thereabout: as they learned by their confessions which have beene imprisoned and tormented for such crimes. Behold how they report it to be done. Presently after that Christmas day is past, a lame Boye goes through the Countrie, and calles the Divels slaves together, being in great numbers, and injoynes them to follow him. If they staye any thing, then presently comes a great man, holding a whippe made of little chaines of Iron, where-with he makes them to advance, and some-times he handles these wretches so roughly, as the markes of his whippe sticke long by them, and puts them that have beene beaten to great paine. Being upon the way, behold they are all (as it seemes to them) changed and transformed into Wolves. They are thousands of them together, having for their conductor and guide this Whippe-carrier, after whom they marche, imagining that they are become Wolves. Beeing in the open champian Countryes, they fall uppon such troupes of Cattell as they finde, teare them in peeces, and carrye away what they can, committing many other spoiles: but they are not suffered to touche nor to hurt any reasonable creature. When they approche neere unto any River, their guide, (say they) devides the water with his whippe, so as they seeme to open, and to leave a drye path betwixt both to passe through. At the end of twelve dayes, all the troupe is dispersed, and every one returnes unto his house, having layde away his Wolves forme, and taken that of Man againe. This transformation (say they) is done after this manner. Those which are transformed fall sodenly to the ground, like unto them that have the Falling-sicknesse, and remaine like dead men, voyde of all feeling. They stirre not from thence, neither goe into any other place, neither are they transformed into Wolves, but are like unto dead carcasses: for although you shake them and rowle them up and downe, yet they make no shewe of life. From thence is sprung an opinion, that the soules taken out the bodyes, enter into these fantosmes or visions, running with the shapes of Wolves: then when the worke enterprized by the Divell is finished, they returne into their bodyes which then recover life. The Licanthropes them-selves confirme this opinion, confessing that the bodyes doe not leave their humaine forme, neyther yet receive that of a Wolfe: but onelie that the soules are thrust out of their prisons, and flye into Wolves bodyes, by whom they are carried for a time. Others have maintained, that lying in Irons in a Dungeon, they have taken the forme of a Wolfe, and have gone to finde out their companions many dayes journey off. Beeing examined how they could gette out off a strong and close prison? Why they have returned, and how they could passe over Rivers that were large and deepe? They answered, that no Irons, walles, nor doores, could hinder their getting out: that they returned by constraint, and that they did flye over Rivers, and runne by land.

Hetherto I have set downe the wordes of Doctor Peucer, the which shew, that this transformation of Licanthropes, nor that of Sorcerers mentioned by Bodin, have no affinitie with the transmutation of the King of Babilon, nor with that of Lots wife: and that in this Licanthropia, there are manifest illusions of Sathan, the which ought not to bee confounded with apparent testimonies of GODS visitation upon some persons: as the Divines which have expounded these Histories, doe shewe more at large. Moreover, John Wier is of a contrary opinion unto Bodin touching the Licanthropes whereof wee speake, and disputes at large thereof, in the sixt Booke of *Divelish Devises*, Chapter thirteenth and fourteenth: where hee manifestlie denyes Bodins reall transformation, and doth maintayne that it is onely in the fantasie troubled by the indisposition of the person, and by the illusion of Sathan. But we will leave their controversie to such as will looke into it.

4.

Diseases of the Mind

ROBERT BURTON

Madness, phrenzy, and melancholy, are confounded by Celsus and many Writers; others leave out phrenzy, and make madness and melancholy but one disease, which Jason Pratensis especially labours, and that they differ only *secundum majus* or *minus*, in quantity alone, the one being a degree to the other, and both proceeding from one cause. They differ *intenso & remisso gradu*, saith Gordonius, as the humour is intended or remitted. Of the same mind is Areteaus, Alexander Tertullianus, Guianerius, Savanarola, Heurnius; and Galen himself writes promiscuously of them both by reason of their affinity: but most of our neotericks do handle them apart, whom I will follow in this treatise. Madness is therefore defined to be a vehement dotage, or raving without a fever, far more violent than melancholy, full of anger and clamour, horrible looks, actions, gestures, troubling the patients with far greater vehemency both of body and mind, without all fear and sorrow, with such impetuous force & boldness, that sometimes three or four men cannot hold them. Differing only in this from phrenzy, that it is without a fever, and their memory is most part better. It hath the same causes as the other, as choler adust, and blood incensed, brains inflamed, &c. Fracastorius adds, a due time, and full age, to this definition, to distinguish it from children, & will have it confirmed impotency, to separate it from such as accidentally come and go again, as by taking henbane, nightshade, wine, &c. Of this fury there be divers kinds; ecstasy, which is familiar with some persons, as Cardan saith of himself, he could be in one when he list; in which the Indian priests deliver their oracles, and the witches in Lapland, as Olaus Magnus writeth, 1.3. cap. 18, *ecstasi omnia praedicere*, answer all questions in an ecstasy you will ask; what your friends do, where they are, how they fare, &c. The other species of this fury are enthusiasms, revelations, and visions, so often mentioned by Gregory and Bede in their works; obsession or possession of devils, Sibylline Prophets, and poetical Furies; such as come by eating noxious herbs, tarantula's stinging, &c.

Anatomy of Melancholy, edited by A. R. Shilletto (London: Bell, 1912) (Part 1, Sect. 1. Mem. 1. Subs. IV.), Vol. I, 160–64.

which some reduce to this. The most known are these, *Lycanthropia, Hydrophobia, Chorus Sancti Viti.*

  Lycanthropia, which Avicenna calls *Cucubuth* others *Lupinam insaniam* or Wolf-madness, when men run howling about graves and fields in the night, and will not be persuaded but that they are wolves, or some such beasts. Aetius and Paulus call it a kind of Melancholy; but I should rather refer it to Madness, as most do. Some make a doubt of it whether there be any such disease. Donat. ab Altomari saith, that he saw two of them in his time: Wierus tells a story of such a one at Padua, 1541, that would not believe to the contrary, but that he was a wolf. He hath another instance of a Spaniard, who thought himself a bear: Forestus confirms as much by many examples; one amongst the rest of which he was an eye-witness, at Alkmaar in Holland, a poor husbandman that still hunted about graves, & kept in churchyards, of a pale, black, ugly, & fearful look. Such belike, or little better, were King Proetus' daughters, that thought themselves kine. And Nebuchadnezzar in *Daniel,* as some interpreters hold, was only troubled with this kind of madness. This disease perhaps gave occasion to that bold assertion of Pliny, some men were turned into wolves in his time, and from wolves to men again: and to that fable of Pausanias, of a man that was ten years a wolf, and afterwards turned to his former shape: to Ovid's tale of Lycaon, &c. . . .* This malady, saith Avicenna, troubleth men most in February, and is now-a-days frequent in Bohemia and Hungary, according to Heurnius. Schernitzius will have it common in Livonia. They lie hid most part all day, and go abroad in the night, barking, howling, at graves and deserts; they have usually hollow eyes, scabbed legs and thighs, very dry and pale, saith Altomarus, he gives a reason there of all the symptoms, and sets down a brief cure of them.

*Burton here refers to additional sources including St. Augustine, Mizaldus, Schenkius, Hildesheim, Forestus, Olaus Magnus, Vincentius Bellavicensis, Pierius, Bodin, Zwinger, Zeilger, Peucer, Wier, Spranger.

A Treatise

ROBERT BAYFIELD

Wolf-madness, is a disease, in which men run barking and howling about graves and fields in the night, lying hid for the most part all day, and will not be persuaded but that they are Wolves, or some such beasts.

. . . they have usually hollow eyes, scabbed legs and thighs, very dry and pale. . . .

A certain young man, in this City, tall, slender, and black, of a wild and strange look, was taken with this kind of malady, for he run barking and howling about the room where he was. . . . I remember I opened a vein, and drew forth a very large quantity of blood, black like Soot; after which, I gave him this Potion. . . . And lastly I gave him this vomit. . . . This wrought upward and downward; after which, he became perfectly well.

A treatise De Morborum Capitis Essentiis & Prognosticis (London, 1663), 49–51.

SECTION II

Trial Records, Historical Accounts, Sightings

Introduction

The trial records of cases of lycanthropy contain detailed accounts of rape, incest, murder, savage attacks, and cannibalism. Among the most famous of the cases of lycanthropy in France was that of Jean Grenier (1603). This case is noteworthy for its judgment and sentence. Basing the sentence not only on the review of precedents but on a realistic assessment of demonic theory, the court determined that Jean Grenier was mentally incompetent, and, hence, not morally culpable; he was sentenced to life imprisonment in a monastery, where he was to receive spiritual care and moral instruction.

The details of the case presented at the trial revealed a young man-wolf who had been apprehended in a clumsy murder. Corroborating evidence recorded the disappearance of children from the community, the discovery of partially eaten children, the sighting of a man-wolf attacking children. Confessing to an uncontrollable appetite for the flesh of young girls, Jean Grenier told the court that he had been transformed into a wolf through the salve and wolfskin given him by the Man of the Forest.

The court determined that Jean Grenier was of deficient intelligence, was deluded into thinking himself a werewolf, was incapable of socialization, and could not be executed for the crimes that he had committed. Although Jean Grenier did not plead insanity, the judge determined that he was incapable of rational thought. The startling statement made by the president of the assize was that "the change of shape existed only in the disorganized brain of the insane, consequently it was not a crime which could be punished."

Henri Boguet, a prominent and respected judge of his day, tried werewolves in his court. Appointed judge of the lands of the Abbey of St. Claude in 1596, he remained a judge for twenty years, during which time he recorded (and defended) his judgments in his *Discours des Sorciers*. Its printing history shows that it had both popular and professional appeal: it was printed and enlarged almost every year until 1610. (Boguet tried his last witchcraft case in 1609). His *Discours* is a history of precedents and a theoretic discussion of witchcraft, including lycanthropy.

In the cases of lycanthropy, his theory (somewhat simplified) runs like this: Satan deludes humans into thinking they are wolves by confusing the humors of the body and by giving them an ointment to deaden their senses. Humans who suffer from hallucinations and delusions of metamorphosis are instruments of Satan. Witnesses to transformation of humans into werewolves are also deceived by Satan: Satan confuses their vision so that what they see and report is an illusion. The battle, then, in the courts was against demonic and disruptive elements in the life of the community. Witches and werewolves had to be punished (and eliminated).

Boguet stressed, however, that the Devil has no power to alter the human nature which God created in His own image; only God can create new forms. On the other hand, the power of the Devil in the lives of ordinary human beings should not be underestimated, since Satan is the father of lies and the instigator of all evil.

Boguet's theory of the demonic is similar to that of judges like Jean Bodin and Nicolas Remy. Remy, for example, in his *Demonolatry* (1595) reported cases of lycanthropy that came to him from reliable sources. His views of metamorphosis are summed up in the headnote to Book II, Chapter V:

> That the much-talked—of Examples of Metamorphosis, both in Ancient and Recent Times, were true in Appearance only, but not in Fact; for the Eyes are deceived by the Glamorous Art of the Demons which cause such Appearances. And although these False Appearances are accompanied by Actions which are found to be perfectly Genuine, this does not prove the Truth of such Metamorphoses; for it is agreed that such Actions are performed by the Demons which control the whole Matter; they being by Nature able very quickly to bring their Designs to Effect. [1]

The theological and legal ambiguities that arise from both Boguet's and Remy's theories of metamorphosis reveal the tension between demonic theory and individual moral responsibility. The justification for criminal prosecution of lycanthropes comes from the distinction Boguet and Remy make between *metaphysical* and *moral:*

> It is not only the external physical shape that appears to be changed; the witch is also endowed with all the natural qualities and powers of the animal into which she is seemingly changed. For she acquires fleetness of foot; bodily strength; ravenous ferocity; the lust of howling . . . and other such animal characteristics, which are far beyond human strength or ability. For it is a matter of daily experience that Satan does actually empower them. Thus they easily kill even the biggest cattle in the fields, and even devour their raw flesh. [2]

Remy concludes his treatise: that those (including lycanthropes) whose lives are "so notoriously befouled and polluted by so many blasphemies, sorceries, prodigious lusts and flagrant crimes . . . I have no hesitation in saying that they are justly to be subjected to every torture and put to death in the flames."[3] (For a statistical study of witchcraft cases tried by Boguet, see Monter, Section IV; for a philosophical study of Boguet's demonology, see Clark, Section IV. See also Bodin, *Démonomanie.*)

One of the most notorious criminal werewolves was Stubbe Peeter. A pamphlet describing his trial and his crimes was circulated all over Europe and in England soon after he was tortured and executed. Described as a man who from his youth had been evil, Stubbe Peeter was the cause of many violent crimes in Germany over a twenty-five–year period. He confessed to committing incest with his daughter and sister, to murdering his son, to attacking animals and humans and eating their raw flesh, to committing adultery with many women. He admitted that he had made a pact with the Devil and that the Devil had given him a girdle to transform him into a wolf. Since the scabrous details of the crimes strain credibility, the testimony of many witnesses appears in the pamphlet. Added to the testimony of witnesses is the statement of one Master Tice Artine, a German brewer living at Puddlewharf in London, who testified to having received letters substantiating firsthand the werewolf attack on the child of a relative.

The account of Stubbe Peeter's trial can be seen in the Lambeth Palace Library, and, except for the modernization of the spelling and the elimination of a few repetitious phrases, reads as it did in the sixteenth century. This document, with its vivid illustrations of Stubbe Peeter's torture and punishment, was meant as a warning to anyone who might be contemplating an alliance with the Devil.

The twentieth-century sightings of a werewolf in this section of the *Reader* come from a man who devoted the greater part of his life to research of psychic phenomena. It was in the course of his studies and research on ghosts that O'Donnell met people who claimed that they had seen a werewolf. After inquiry into the circumstances and credentials of his informants, he decided that these werewolf encounters bore the marks of authenticity. His informants, who did not want to believe in the existence of werewolves, reported that their sightings had indeed upset their mental equilibrium.

O'Donnell discovered that most of the werewolf sightings occurred when the bones and skull of an alleged werewolf had been moved. Simply by disturbing those restless bones (their abnormal anatomical proportions had fascinated their finders), unwary humans had inadvertently brought a werewolf back to a troubled phantom life. He reasoned that if ghosts were the displaced souls of those condemned to walk the earth as punishment for their corrupt lives on earth, why should werewolves be exempt from the same torment, especially since their lives had been less than exemplary?

The sightings in this section of the *Reader* raise the fundamental question about the relationship of unholy living to post-death appearances. O'Donnell's probings into the areas where the sharp distinctions between metamorphosed human forms and posthumous moral responsibility are blurred, continue the basic discussions about the nature of the human form.

The account of werewolf sightings in the chronicles of Giraldus Cambrensis differs sharply from those in the trial records of the Renaissance. Giraldus, an ecclesiastic who was elected to be Bishop of St. David's in 1198 (but not confirmed by Rome), tells the story of a werewolf pair who requested last rites for the dying female werewolf. Giraldus was concerned with the ecclesiastical issues raised by this request: (1) Since the divine nature took on human nature (Christ became man), it is possible that God will exercise his power in trans-

Wolf symbolizing the demonic destruction of the Christian sheep. From Joachim Camerarius, *Symbolorum et emblematum ex animalibus* . . . , Noribergae, 1595. Courtesy of University of Chicago Library, Department of Special Collections.

forming a human being into a wolf; (2) what is the nature of a werewolf?, is it human or animal? (3) the Devil cannot change the human form, although he can alter perceptions of it; (4) the transubstantiation of the bread and wine into the body and blood of Christ in the Communion rite is an alteration not of appearance but of substance; this change of substance is "far beyond the powers of the human intellect."

The sympathetic account of the two aging werewolves in this history shows how important it was to exercise compassion in the presence of human metamorphosis, but also how vital it was to distinguish between the works of the Devil and of the Creator. Giraldus reveals something of the unease and anxiety he experienced in trying to make the distinction.

Notes

1. Nicolas Remy, *Daemonolatria* (Lyon, 1595), translated by E.A. Ashwin (London, 1930), 108.

2. Ibid., 112.

3. Ibid., 188.

Topographia Hibernica

GIRALDUS CAMBRENSIS (1187)

Of the Prodigies of our Times,
and First of a Wolf Which Conversed With a Priest

I now proceed to relate some wonderful occurrences which have happened within our time. About three years before the arrival of Earl John in Ireland, it chanced that a priest, who was journeying from Ulster towards Meath, was benighted in a certain wood on the borders of Meath. While, in company with only a young lad, he was watching by a fire which he had kindled under the branches of a spreading tree, lo! a wolf came up to them, and immediately addressed them to this effect: "Rest secure, and be not afraid, for there is no reason you should fear, where no fear is!" The travellers being struck with astonishment and alarm, the wolf added some orthodox words referring to God. The priest then implored him, and adjured him by Almighty God and faith in the Trinity, not to hurt them, but to inform them what creature it was that in the shape of a beast uttered human words. The wolf, after giving catholic replies to all questions, added at last: "There are two of us, a man and a woman, natives of Ossory, who, through the curse of one Natalis, saint and abbot, are compelled every seven years to put off the human form, and depart from the dwellings of men. Quitting entirely the human form, we assume that of wolves. At the end of the seven years, if they chance to survive, two others being substituted in their places, they return to their country and their former shape. And now, she who is my partner in this visitation lies dangerously sick not far from hence, and, as she is at the point of death, I beseech you, inspired by divine charity, to give her the consolations of your priestly office."

At this word the priest followed the wolf trembling, as he led the way to a tree at no great distance, in the hollow of which he beheld a she-wolf, who under that shape was pouring forth human sighs and

Completed in 1187. Translated by Thomas Forester in *The Historical Works of Giraldus Cambrensis*, edited by Thomas Wright (London: Bell, 1913), 79–84.

groans. On seeing the priest, having saluted him with human courtesy, she gave thanks to God, who in this extremity had vouchsafed to visit her with such consolation. She then received from the priest all the rites of the church duly performed, as far as the last communion. This also she importunately demanded, earnestly supplicating him to complete his good offices by giving her the viaticum. The priest stoutly asserting that he was not provided with it, the he-wolf, who had withdrawn to a short distance, came back and pointed out a small missal-book, containing some consecrated wafers, which the priest carried on his journey, suspended from his neck, under his garment, after the fashion of the country. He then intreated him not to deny them the gift of God, and the aid destined for them by Divine Providence; and, to remove all doubt, using his claw for a hand, he tore off the skin of the she-wolf, from the head down to the navel, folding it back. Thus she immediately presented the form of an old woman. The priest, seeing this, and compelled by his fear more than his reason, gave the communion; the recipient having earnestly implored it, and devoutly partaking of it. Immediately afterwards, the he-wolf rolled back the skin, and fitted it to its original form.

These rites having been duly, rather than rightly, performed, the he-wolf gave them his company during the whole night at their little fire, behaving more like a man than a beast. When morning came, he led them out of the wood, and, leaving the priest to pursue his journey, pointed out to him the direct road for a long distance. At his departure, he also gave him many thanks for the benefit he had conferred, promising him still greater returns of gratitude, if the Lord should call him back from his present exile, two parts of which he had already completed. At the close of their conversation, the priest inquired of the wolf whether the hostile race which had now landed in the island would continue there for the time to come, and be long established in it. To which the wolf replied:—"For the sins of our nation, and their enormous vices, the anger of the Lord, falling on an evil generation, hath given them into the hands of their enemies. Therefore, as long as this foreign race shall keep the commandments of the Lord, and walk in his ways, it will be secure and invincible; but if, as the downward path to illicit pleasures is easy, and nature is prone to follow vicious examples, this people shall chance, from living among us, to adopt our depraved habits, doubtless they will provoke the divine vengeance on themselves also."

The like judgment is recorded in Leviticus: — "All these abominations have the inhabitants of the land done, which were before you, the land is defiled. Beware, therefore, that the land spue not you out also, when ye defile it, as it spued out the nation which was before you." All this was afterwards brought to pass, first by the Chaldeans, and then by the Romans. Likewise it is written in Ecclesiasticus: — "The kingdom is made over from one nation to another, by reason of their unjust and injurious deeds, their proud words, and divers deceits."

It chanced, about two years afterwards, that I was passing through Meath, at the time when the bishop of that land had convoked a synod, having also invited the assistance of the neighbouring bishops and abbots, in order to have their joint counsels on what was to be done in the affair which had come to his knowledge by the priest's confession. The bishop, hearing that I was passing through those parts, sent me a message by two of his clerks, requesting me, if possible, to be personally present when a matter of so much importance was under consideration; but if I could not attend, he begged me at least to signify my opinion in writing. The clerks detailed to me all the circumstances, which indeed I had heard before from other persons; and, as I was prevented by urgent business from being present at the synod, I made up for my absence by giving them the benefit of my advice in a letter. The bishop and synod, yielding to it, ordered the priest to appear before the pope with letters from them, setting forth what had occurred, with the priest's confession, to which instrument the bishops and abbots who were present at the synod affixed their seals.

It cannot be disputed, but must be believed with the most assured faith, that the divine nature assumed human nature for the salvation of the world; while in the present case, by no less a miracle, we find that at God's bidding, to exhibit his power and righteous judgment, human nature assumed that of a wolf. But is such an animal to be called a brute or a man? A rational animal appears to be far above the level of a brute; but who will venture to assign a quadruped, which inclines to the earth, and is not a laughing animal, to the species of man? Again, if any one should slay this animal, would he be called a homicide? We reply, that divine miracles are not to be made the subjects of disputation by human reason, but to be admired. However, Augustine, in the 16th book of his Civit. Dei, chapter 8, in speaking of some monsters of the human race, born in the East, some of which had the heads of dogs, others had no heads at all, their eyes being placed in their breasts, and others had various deformities, raises the question whether these were really men, descended from the first parents of mankind. At last, he concludes, "We must think the same of them as we do of those monstrous births in the human species of which we often hear; and true reason declares that whatever answers to the definition of man, as a rational and mortal animal, whatever be its form, is to be considered a man." The same author, in the 18th book of the Civit. Dei, chapter 18, refers to the Arcadians, who, chosen by lot, swam across a lake and were there changed into wolves, living with wild beasts of the same species in the deserts of that country. If, however, they did not devour human flesh, after nine years they swam back across the lake, and reassumed the human form. Having thus further treated of various transformations of man into the shape of wolves, he at length adds, "I myself, at the time I was in Italy, heard it said of some district in those parts, that there the stable-women, who had learnt magical arts, were wont to give something to travellers in their cheese which transformed them into beasts of burthen, so that they carried all sorts of burdens, and after they had performed their tasks resumed their own forms. Meanwhile, their minds did not become bestial, but remained human and rational." So in the Book which Apuleius wrote, with the title of the Golden Ass, he tells us that it happened to himself, on taking some potion, to be changed into an ass, retaining his human mind.

In our time, also, we have seen persons who, by magical arts, turned any substance about them into fat pigs, as they appeared (but they were always red), and sold them in the markets. However, they disappeared as soon as they crossed any water, returning to their real nature; and with whatever care they were kept, their assumed form did not last beyond three days. It has also been a frequent complaint, from old times as well as in the present, that certain hags in Wales, as well as in Ireland and Scotland, changed themselves into the shape of hares, that, sucking teats under this counterfeit form, they might stealthily rob other people's milk. We agree, then, with Augustine, that neither demons nor wicked men can either create or really change their natures; but those whom God has created can, to outward appearance, by his permission, become transformed, so that they appear to be what they are not; the senses of men being deceived and laid asleep by a strange illusion, so that things are not seen as they actually exist, but are strangely drawn by the power of some phantom or magical incantation to rest their eyes on unreal and fictitious forms.

It is, however, believed as an undoubted truth, that the Almighty God, who is the Creator of natures, can, when he pleases, change one into another, either for vindicating his judgments, or exhibiting his divine power; as in the case of Lot's wife, who, looking back contrary to her lord's command, was turned into a pillar of salt; and as the water was changed into wine; or that, the nature within remaining the same, he can transform the exterior only, as is plain from the examples before given.

Of that apparent change of the bread into the body of Christ (which I ought not to call apparent only, but with more truth transubstantial, because, while the outward appearance remains the same, the substance only is changed), I have thought it safest not to treat; its comprehension being far beyond the powers of the human intellect.

7

Jean Grenier, a French Werewolf

Retold by SABINE BARING-GOULD

One fine afternoon in the spring, some village girls were tending their sheep on the sand-dunes which intervene between the vast forests of pine covering the greater portion of the present department of *Landes* in the south of France, and the sea.

The brightness of the sky, the freshness of the air puffing up off the blue twinkling Bay of Biscay, the hum or song of the wind as it made rich music among the pines which stood like a green uplifted wave on the East, the beauty of the sand-hills speckled with golden cistus, or patched with gentian-blue, the charm of the forest-skirts, tinted variously with the foliage of cork-trees, pines, and acacia—all conspired to fill the peasant maidens with joy, and to make their voices rise in song and laughter, which rung merrily over the hills, and through the dark avenues of evergreen trees.

Now a gorgeous butterfly attracted their attention, then a flight of quails skimming the surface.

"Ah!" exclaimed Jacquiline Auzun, "ah, if I had my stilts and bats, I would strike the little birds down, and we should have a fine supper."

"Now, if they would fly ready cooked into one's mouth, as they do in foreign parts!" said another girl.

"Have you got any new clothes for the S. Jean?" asked a third; "my mother has laid by to purchase me a smart cap with gold lace."

"You will turn the head of Etienne altogether, Annette!" said Jeanne Gaboriant. "But what is the matter with the sheep?"

She asked because the sheep which had been quietly browsing before her, on reaching a small depression in the dune, had started away as though frightened at something. At the same time one of the dogs began to growl and show his fangs.

The girls ran to the spot, and saw a little fall in the ground, in which, seated on a log of fir, was a boy of thirteen. The appearance of the lad was peculiar. His hair was of a tawny red and thickly matted, falling over his shoulders and completely covering his narrow brow.

Book of Were-Wolves (London: Smith, Elder and Co., 1865), 85–98.

His small pale-grey eyes twinkled with an expression of horrible ferocity and cunning, from deep sunken hollows. The complexion was of a
dark olive colour; the teeth were strong and white, and the canine
teeth protruded over the lower lip when the mouth was closed. The
boy's hands were large and powerful, the nails black and pointed like
bird's talons. He was ill clothed, and seemed to be in the most abject
poverty. The few garments that he had on him were in tatters, and
through the rents the emaciation of his limbs was plainly visible.

The girls stood round him, half frightened and much surprised,
but the boy showed no symptoms of astonishment. His face relaxed
into a ghastly leer, which showed the whole range of his glittering
white fangs.

"Well, my maidens," said he in a harsh voice, "which of you is the
prettiest, I should like to know; can you decide among you?"

"What do you want to know for?" asked Jeanne Gaboriant, the
eldest of the girls, aged eighteen, who took upon herself to be
spokesman for the rest.

"Because I shall marry the prettiest," was the answer.

"Ah!" said Jeanne jokingly; "that is if she will have you, which is
not very likely, as we none of us know you, or anything about you."

"I am the son of a priest," replied the boy curtly.

"Is that why you look so dingy and black?"

"No, I am dark-coloured, because I wear a wolf-skin sometimes."

"A wolf-skin!" echoed the girl; "and pray who gave it to you?"

"One called Pierre Labourant."

"There is no man of that name hereabouts. Where does he live?"

A scream of laughter mingled with howls, and breaking into
strange gulping bursts of fiendlike merriment from the strange boy.

The girls recoiled, and the youngest took refuge behind Jeanne.

"Do you want to know Pierre Labourant, lass? Hey, he is a man
with an iron chain about his neck, which he is ever engaged in gnaw-
ing. Do you want to know where he lives, lass? Ha, in a place of gloom
and fire, where there are many companions, some seated on iron
chairs, burning, burning; others stretched on glowing beds, burning
too. Some cast men upon blazing coals, others roast men before fierce
flames, others again plunge them into caldrons of liquid fire."

The girls trembled and looked at each other with scared faces,
and then again at the hideous being which crouched before them.

"You want to know about the wolf-skin cape?" continued he. "Pierre Labourant gave me that; he wraps it round me, and every Monday, Friday, and Sunday, and for about an hour at dusk every other day, I am a wolf, a were-wolf. I have killed dogs and drunk their blood; but little girls taste better, their flesh is tender and sweet, their blood rich and warm. I have eaten many a maiden, as I have been on my raids together with my nine companions. I am a were-wolf! Ah, ha! if the sun were to set I would soon fall on one of you and make a meal of you!" Again he burst into one of his frightful paroxysms of laughter, and the girls unable to endure it any longer, fled with precipitation.

Near the village of S. Antoine de Pizon, a little girl of the name of Marguerite Poirier, thirteen years old, was in the habit of tending her sheep, in company with a lad of the same age, whose name was Jean Grenier. The same lad whom Jeanne Gaboriant had questioned.

The little girl often complained to her parents of the conduct of the boy: she said that he frightened her with his horrible stories; but her father and mother thought little of her complaints, till one day she returned home before her usual time so thoroughly alarmed that she had deserted her flock. Her parents now took the matter up and investigated it. Her story was as follows: —

Jean had often told her that he had sold himself to the devil, and that he had acquired the power of ranging the country after dusk, and sometimes in broad day, in the form of a wolf. He had assured her that he had killed and devoured many dogs, but that he found their flesh less palatable than the flesh of little girls, which he regarded as a supreme delicacy. He had told her that this had been tasted by him not unfrequently, but he had specified only two instances: in one he had eaten as much as he could, and thrown the rest to a wolf, which had come up during the repast. In the other instance he had bitten to death another little girl, had lapped her blood, and, being in a famished condition at the time, had devoured every portion of her, with the exception of the arms and shoulders.

The child told her parents, on the occasion of her return home in a fit of terror, that she had been guiding her sheep as usual, but Grenier had not been present. Hearing a rustle in the bushes she had looked round, and a wild beast had leaped upon her, and torn her clothes on her left side with its sharp fangs. She added that she had defended herself lustily with her shepherd's staff, and had beaten the creature off.

It had then retreated a few paces, had seated itself on its hind legs like a dog when it is begging, and had regarded her with such a look of rage, that she had fled in terror. She described the animal as resembling a wolf, but as being shorter and stouter; its hair was red, its tail stumpy, and the head smaller than that of a genuine wolf.

The statement of the child produced general consternation in the parish. It was well known that several little girls had vanished in a most mysterious way of late, and the parents of these little ones were thrown into an agony of terror lest their children had become the prey of the wretched boy accused by Marguerite Poirier. The case was now taken up by the authorities and brought before the parliament of Bordeaux.

The investigation which followed was as complete as could be desired.

Jean Grenier was the son of a poor labourer in the village of S. Antoine de Pizon, and not the son of a priest, as he had asserted. Three months before his seizure he had left home, and had been with several masters doing odd work, or wandering about the country begging. He had been engaged several times to take charge of the flocks belonging to farmers, and had as often been discharged for neglect of his duties. The lad exhibited no reluctance to communicate all he knew about himself, and his statements were tested one by one, and were often proved to be correct.

The story he related of himself before the court was as follows: —

"When I was ten or eleven years old, my neighbour, Duthillaire, introduced me, in the depths of the forest, to a M. de la Forest, a black man, who signed me with his nail, and then gave to me and Duthillaire a salve and a wolf-skin. From that time have I run about the country as a wolf.

"The charge of Marguerite Poirier is correct. My intention was to have killed and devoured her, but she kept me off with a stick. I have only killed one dog, a white one, and I did not drink its blood."

When questioned touching the children, whom he said he had killed and eaten as a wolf, he allowed that he had once entered an empty house on the way between S. Coutras and S. Anlaye, in a small village, the name of which he did not remember, and had found a child asleep in its cradle; and as no one was within to hinder him, he dragged the baby out of its cradle, carried it into the garden, leaped the hedge, and devoured as much of it as satisfied his hunger. What remained he had given to a wolf. In the parish of S. Antoine de Pizon he had attacked a little girl, as she was keeping sheep. She was dressed in a black frock; he did not know her name. He tore her with his nails and teeth, and ate her. Six weeks before his capture he had fallen upon another child, near the stone-bridge, in the same parish. In Eparon he had assaulted the hound of a certain M. Millon, and would have killed the beast, had not the owner come out with his rapier in his hand.

Jean said that he had the wolf-skin in his possession, and that he went out hunting for children, at the command of his master, the Lord of the Forest. Before transformation he smeared himself with the salve, which he preserved in a small pot, and hid his clothes in the thicket.

He usually ran his courses from one to two hours in the day, when the moon was at the wane, but very often he made his expeditions at night. On one occasion he had accompanied Duthillaire, but they had killed no one.

He accused his father of having assisted him, and of possessing a wolf-skin; he charged him also with having accompanied him on one occasion, when he attacked and ate a girl in the village of Grilland, whom he had found tending a flock of geese. He said that his step-mother was separated from his father. He believed the reason to be, because she had seen him once vomit the paws of a dog and the fingers of a child. He added that the Lord of the Forest had strictly forbidden him to bite the thumb-nail of his left hand, and had warned him never to lose sight of it, as long as he was in his were-wolf disguise.

Duthillaire was apprehended, and the father of Jean Grenier himself claimed to be heard by examination.

The account given by the father and stepmother of Jean coincided in many particulars with the statements made by their son.

The localities where Grenier declared he had fallen on children were identified, the times when he said the deeds had been done accorded with the dates given by the parents of the missing little ones, when their losses had occurred.

The wounds which Jean affirmed that he had made, and the manner in which he had dealt them, coincided with the descriptions given by the children he had assaulted.

He was confronted with Marguerite Poirier, and he singled her out from among five other girls, pointed to the still open gashes in her body, and stated that he had made them with his teeth, when he attacked her in wolf-form, and she had beaten him off with a stick. He described an attack he had made on a little boy whom he would have slain, had not a man come to the rescue, and exclaimed, "I'll have you presently."

The man who saved the child was found, and proved to be the uncle of the rescued lad, and he corroborated the statement of Grenier, that he had used the words mentioned above.

Jean was then confronted with his father. He now began to falter in his story, and to change his statements. The examination had lasted long, and it was seen that the feeble intellect of the boy was wearied out, so the case was adjourned. When next confronted with the elder Grenier, Jean told his story as at first, without changing it in any important particular.

The fact of Jean Grenier having killed and eaten several children, and of his having attacked and wounded others, with intent to take their life, were fully established; but there was no proof whatever of the father having had the least hand in any of the murders, so that he was dismissed from the court without a shadow of guilt upon him.

The only witness who corroborated the assertion of Jean that he changed his shape into that of a wolf was Marguerite Poirier.

Before the court gave judgment, the first president of assize, in an eloquent speech, put on one side all questions of witchcraft and diabolical compact, and bestial transformation, and boldly stated that the court had only to consider the age and the imbecility of the child, who was so dull and idiotic that children of seven or eight years old have usually a larger amount of reason than he. The president went on to say that Lycanthropy and Kuanthropy were mere hallucinations, and that the change of shape existed only in the disorganized brain of the insane, consequently it was not a crime which could be punished. The tender age of the boy must be taken into consideration, and the utter neglect of his education and moral development. The court sentenced Grenier to perpetual imprisonment within the walls of a monastery at Bordeaux, where he might be instructed in his Christian and moral obligations; but any attempt to escape would be punished with death.

No sooner was he admitted into the precincts of the religious house, than he ran frantically about the cloister and gardens upon all fours, and finding a heap of bloody and raw offal, fell upon it and devoured it in an incredibly short space of time.

After seven years in the monastery, he was found to be diminutive in stature, very shy, and unwilling to look any one in the face. His eyes were deep set and restless; his teeth long and protruding; his nails black, and in place worn away; his mind was completely barren; he seemed unable to comprehend the smallest things.

He died at the age of twenty.

8

A True Discourse Declaring the Damnable Life and Death of One
Stubbe Peeter,
A Most Wicked Sorcerer, Who in the Likeness of a Wolf
Committed Many Murders, Continuing This Devilish Practise 25 Years,
Killing and Devouring Men, Women, and Children.
Who for the Same Fact Was Taken and Executed
the 31st of October Last Past
in the Town of Bedbur Near the City of Collin in Germany.

Truly translated out of the high Dutch, according to the copy printed in Collin,
brought over into England by George Bores ordinary post, the 11th day
of this present month of June 1590, who did both see and hear the same.

In the towns of Cperadt and Bedbur near Collin in high Germany,
there was continually brought up and nourished one Stubbe Peeter,
who from his youth was greatly inclined to evil and the practising of
wicked arts, surfeiting in the damnable desire of magic, necromancy,
and sorcery, acquainting himself with many infernal spirits and fiends.
The Devil, who hath a ready ear to listen to the lewd motions of cursed
men, promised to give him whatsoever his heart desired during his
mortal life: whereupon this vile wretch, having a tyrannous heart and a
most cruel bloody mind, requested that at his pleasure he might work
his malice on men, women, and children, in the shape of some beast,
whereby he might live without dread or danger of life, and unknown to
be the executor of any bloody enterprise which he meant to commit.
The Devil gave him a girdle which, being put around him, he was
transformed into the likeness of a greedy, devouring wolf, strong and
mighty, with eyes great and large, which in the night sparkled like
brands of fire; a mouth great and wide, with most sharp and cruel
teeth; a huge body and mighty paws. And no sooner should he put off
the same girdle, but presently he should appear in his former shape,
according to the proportion of a man, as if he had never been changed.
Stubbe Peeter herewith was exceedingly well pleased, and the
shape fitted his fancy and agreed best with his nature, being inclined to
blood and cruelty. Therefore, satisfied with this strange and devilish

Original trial transcript. STC 23375, f. E. Venge. Entered 22 June 1590.

gift (for it was not troublesome but might be hidden in a small room), he proceeded to the execution of heinous and vile murders; for if any person displeased him, he would thirst for revenge, and no sooner should they or any of theirs walk in the fields or the city, but in the shape of a wolf he would presently encounter them, and never rest till he had plucked out their throats and torn their joints asunder. And after he had gotten a taste hereof, he took such pleasure and delight in shedding of blood, that he would night and day walk the fields and work extreme cruelties. And sundry times he would go through the streets of Collin, Bedbur, and Cperadt, in comely habit, and very civilly, as one well known to all the inhabitants thereabout, and often-times was he saluted of those whose friends and children he had butchered, though nothing suspected for the same. In these places, I say, he would walk up and down, and if he could spy either maid, wife, or child that his eyes liked or his heart lusted after, he would wait their issuing out of the city or town. If he could by any means get them alone, he would in the fields ravish them, and after in his wolvish likeness cruelly murder them. Often it came to pass that as he walked abroad in the fields, if he chanced to spy a company of maidens playing together or else milking their kine, in his wolvish shape he would run among them, and while the rest escaped by flight, he would be sure to lay hold of one, and after his filthy lust fulfilled, he would murder her presently. Besides, if he had liked or known any of them, her he would pursue; such was his swiftness of foot while he continued a wolf that he would outrun the swiftest greyhound in that country; and so much he had practised this wickedness that the whole province was frightened by the cruelty of this bloody and devouring wolf. Thus continuing his devilish and damnable deeds, within the compass of a few years, he had murdered thirteen young children, and two goodly young women bit with child, tearing the children out of their wombs, in most bloody and savage sort, and after ate their hearts panting hot and raw, which he accounted dainty morsels and best agreeing to his appetite.

Moreover, he used many times to kill lambs and kids and such like beasts, feeding on the same most usually raw and bloody, as if he had been a natural wolf indeed.

He had at that time living a fair young daughter, after whom he also lusted most unnaturally, and cruelly committed most wicked incest with her, a most gross and vile sin, far surmounting adultery or fornication, though the least of the three doth drive the soul into hell fire, except hearty repentance, and the great mercy of God. This daughter of his he begot when he was not altogether so wickedly given, who was called by the name of Stubbe Beell, whose beauty and good grace was such as deserved commendations of all those that knew her. And such was his inordinate lust and filthy desire toward her, that he begat a child by her, daily using her as his concubine; but as an insatiate and filthy beast, given over to work evil, with greediness he also lay by his own sister, frequenting her company long time. Moreover, being on a time sent for to a Gossip of his there to make merry and good cheer, ere he thence departed he so won the woman by his fair and flattering speech, and so much prevailed, that ere he departed the house, he lay by her, and ever after had her company at his command; this woman had to name Katherine Trompin, a woman of tall and comely stature of exceeding good favour and one that was well esteemed among her neighbours. But his lewd and inordinate lust being not satisfied with the company of many concubines, nor his wicked fancy contented with the beauty of any woman, at length the Devil sent unto him a wicked spirit in the similitude and likeness of a woman, so fair of face and comely of personage, that she resembled rather some heavenly angel than any mortal creature, so far her beauty exceeded the choicest sort of women; and with her, as with his heart's delight, he kept company the space of seven years, though in the end she proved and was found indeed no other than a she-Devil. Notwithstanding, this lewd sin of lechery did not any thing assuage his cruel and bloody mind, but continuing an insatiable bloodsucker, so great was the joy he took therein, that he accounted no day spent in pleasure wherein he had not shed some blood, not respecting so much who he did murder, as how to murder and destroy them, as the matter ensuing doth manifest, which may stand for a special note of a cruel and hard heart. For, having a proper youth to his son, begotten in the flower and strength of his age, the first fruit of his body, in whom he took such joy that he did commonly call him his heart's ease, yet so far his delight in murder exceeded the joy he took in his son, that thirsting after his blood, on a time he enticed him into the fields, and from thence into a forest hard by, where, making excuse to stay about the necessaries of nature, while the young man went forward, in the shape and likeness of a wolf he encountered his own son and there most cruelly slew him, which done, he presently ate the brains out of his head as a most savory and dainty delicious means to staunch his greedy appetite: the most monstrous act that ever man heard of, for never was known a wretch from nature so far degenerate.

Long time he continued his vile and villainous life, sometime in the likeness of a wolf, sometime in the habit of a man, sometime in the towns and cities, and sometimes in the woods and thickets to them adjoining, whereas the Dutch copy maketh mention; he on a time met with two men and one woman, whom he greatly desired to murder. In subtle sort he conveyed himself far before them in their way and craftily couched out of their sight; but as soon as they approached near the place where he lay, he called one of them by his name. The party, hearing himself called once or twice by his name, supposing it was some familiar friend that in jesting sort stood out of his sight, went from his company toward the place from whence the voice proceeded, of purpose to see who it was; but he was no sooner entered within the danger of this transformed man, but he was murdered in that place; the rest of his company staying for him, expecting still his return, but finding his stay over long, the other man left the woman and went to look for him, by which means the second man was also murdered. The woman then seeing neither of both return again, in heart suspected that some evil had fallen upon them, and therefore, with all the power she had, she sought to save herself by flight, though it nothing prevailed, for, good soul, she was also soon overtaken by this light-footed wolf, whom, when he had first deflowered, he after most cruelly murdered. The men were after found mangled in the wood, but the woman's body was never after seen, for she he had most ravenously devoured, whose flesh he esteemed both sweet and dainty in taste.

Thus this damnable Stubbe Peeter lived the term of five and twenty years, unsuspected to be author of so many cruel and unnatural murders, in which time he had destroyed and spoiled an unknown number of men, women, and children, sheep, lambs, and goats, and other cattle; for, when he could not through the wariness of people draw men, women, or children in his danger, then, like a cruel and tyrannous beast, he would work his cruelty on brute beasts in most savage sort, and did act more mischief and cruelty than would be credible, although high Germany hath been forced to taste the truth thereof.

By which means the inhabitants of Collin, Bedbur, and Cperadt, seeing themselves so grievously endangered, plagued, and molested by this greedy and cruel wolf, insomuch that few or none durst travel to or from those places without good provision of defence, and all for fear of this devouring and fierce wolf, for oftentimes the inhabitants found the arms and legs of dead men, women, and children scattered up and down the fields, to their great grief and vexation of heart, knowing the same to be done by that strange and cruel wolf, whom by no means they could take or overcome, so that if any man or woman missed their child, they were out of hope ever to see it again alive.

And here is to be noted a most strange thing which setteth forth the great power and merciful providence of God to the comfort of each Christian heart. There were not long ago certain small children playing in a meadow together hard by the town, where also some store of kine were feeding, many of them having young calves sucking upon them. And suddenly among these children comes this vile wolf running and caught a pretty fine girl by the collar, with intent to pull out her throat; but such was the will of God, that the wolf could not pierce the collar of the child's coat, being high and very well stiffened and close clasped about her neck; and therewithal the sudden great cry of the rest of the children which escaped so amazed the cattle feeding by, that being fearful to be robbed of their young, they altogether came running against the wolf with such force that he was presently compelled to let go his hold and to run away to escape the danger of their horns; by which means the child was preserved from death, and, God be thanked, remains living at this day.

And that this thing is true, Master Tice Artine, a brewer dwelling at Puddlewharfe in London, being a man of that country born, and one of good reputation and account, is able to justify, who is near kinsman to this child, and hath from thence twice received letters concerning the same; and for that the first letter did rather drive him into wondering at the act then yielding credit thereunto, he had shortly after, at request of his writing, another letter sent to him, whereby he was more fully satisfied; and divers other persons of great credit in London hath in like sort received letters from their friends to the like effect.

Likewise in the towns of Germany aforesaid continual prayer was used unto God that it would please Him to deliver them from the danger of this greedy wolf.

And, although they had practised all the means that men could devise to take this ravenous beast, yet until the Lord had determined his fall, they could not in any wise prevail: notwithstanding they daily sought to entrap him and for that intent continually maintained great mastiffs and dogs of much strength to hunt and chase the beast. In the end, it pleased God, as they were in readiness and provided to meet with him, that they should espy him in his wolvish likeness at what time they beset him round about, and most circumspectly set their dogs upon him, in such sort that there was no means of escape, at which advantage they never could get him before; but as the Lord delivered Goliath into the hands of David, so was this wolf brought in danger of these men; who, seeing as I said before, no way to escape the imminent danger, being hardly pursued at the heels, presently slipped his girdle from about him, whereby the shape of a wolf clean avoided, and he appeared presently in his true shape and likeness, having in his hand a staff as one walking toward the city; but the hunters, whose eyes were steadfastly bent upon the beast, and seeing him in the same place metamorphosed contrary to their expectation, it wrought a wonderful amazement to their minds; and, had it not been that they knew the man so soon as they saw him, they had surely taken the same to have been some Devil in a man's likeness; but forasmuch as they knew him to be an ancient dweller in the town, they came unto him, and talking with him, they brought him home to his own house, and finding him to be the man indeed, and no delusion or phantastical motion, they had him before the magistrates to be examined.

Thus being apprehended, he was shortly after put to the rack in the town of Bedbur, but fearing the torture, he voluntarily confessed his whole life, and made known the villainies which he had committed for the space of twenty-five years; also he confessed how by sorcery he procured of the Devil a girdle, which being put on, he forthwith became a wolf, which girdle at his apprehension he confessed he cast it off in a certain valley and there left it, which, when the magistrates heard, they sent to the valley for it, but at their coming found nothing at all, for it may be supposed that it was gone to the Devil from whence it came, so that it was not to be found. For the Devil having brought the wretch to all the shame he could, left him to endure the torments which his deeds deserved.

After he had some space been imprisoned, the magistrates found out through due examination of the matter, that his daughter Stubbe

The Damnable Life and Death of One Stubbe Peeter, London, 1590. Courtesy of His Grace the Archbishop of Canterbury and the Trustees of Lambeth Palace Library, London.

Beell and his Gossip Katherine Trompin, were both accessory to divers murders committed, were arraigned, and with Stubbe Peeter condemned, and their several judgements pronounced the 28 of October 1589, in this manner, that is to say: Stubbe Peeter as principal malefactor, was judged first to have his body laid on a wheel, and with red hot burning pincers in ten places to have the flesh pulled off from the bones, after that, his legs and arms to be broken with a wooden axe or hatchet, afterward to have his head struck from his body, then to have his carcase burned to ashes.

Also his daughter and his Gossip were judged to be burned quick to ashes, the same time and day with the carcase of the aforesaid Stubbe Peeter. And on the 31st of the same month, they suffered death accordingly in the town of Bedbur in the presence of many peers and princes of Germany.

Thus, Gentle Reader, have I set down the true discourse of this wicked man Stubbe Peeter, which I desire to be a warning to all sorcerers and witches, which unlawfully follow their own devilish imagination to the utter ruin and destruction of their souls eternally, from which wicked and damnable practice, I beseech God keep all good men, and from the cruelty of their wicked hearts. Amen.

After the execution, there was by the advice of the magistrates of the town of Bedbur a high pole set up and strongly framed, which first went through the wheel whereon he was broken, whereunto also it was fastened; after that a little above the wheel the likeness of a wolf was framed in wood, to show unto all men the shape wherein he executed those cruelties. Over that on the top of the stake the sorcerer's head itself was set up, and round about the wheel there hung as it were sixteen pieces of wood about a yard in length which represented the sixteen persons that were perfectly known to be murdered by him. And the same ordained to stand there for a continual monument to all ensuing ages, what murders by Stubbe Peeter were committed, with the order of his judgement, as this picture doth more plainly express.

Witnesses that this is true: Tyse Artyne, William Brewar, Adolf Staedt, George Bores. With divers others that have seen the same.

9

Of the Metamorphosis of Men into Beasts

HENRI BOGUET

Of the Metamorphosis of Men into Beasts, and Especially of Lycanthropes or Loups-garoux.

Τ he same method of procedure which was used in the case of Francoise Secretain was followed in those of Jacques Bocquet, Clauda Jamprost, Clauda Jamguillaume, Thievenne Paget and Clauda Gaillard. Jacques Bocquet, otherwise known as Groz-Jacques, came from Savoy, and was apprehended on the accusation of Francoise Secretain. Clauda Jamprost was from Orcieres, and was accused by Groz-Jacques. Clauda Jamguillaume and Thievenne Paget were also from Orcieres, and were accused by Groz-Jacques and Clauda Jamprost. Clauda Gaillard was from Ebouchoux, and was imprisoned as the result of information arising from the preceding trials.

The first four of these confessed that they had turned themselves into wolves and that, in this shape, they had killed several children, namely, a child of Anathoile Cochet of Longchamois, one of Thievent Bondieu known as the rebel of Orcieres, four or five years old; another of big Claude Godard, and another of Claude the son of Antoine Gindre. Finally, they confessed that in the year 1597 they met in the neighbourhood of Longchamois two children of Claude Bault, a boy and a girl, who were gathering strawberries; that they killed the girl, and the boy saved himself by running away. They confessed also that they had eaten part of the children which we have mentioned, but that they never touched the right side. These murders were verified both by the evidence of the parents, and by that of several others in the villages of Longchamois and Orcieres, who deposed that all these children had been caught and eaten by wolves at such a time and such a place.

Clauda Jamguillaume added that she had nearly killed two other children, and that with the intent to do so she had hidden behind a hut in the mountains for about an hour, but had been prevented by a dog,

Discours des Sorciers, 1590, 1602, 1603, 1605, 1606, 1607, 1608, 1610, 1611. Translated by E. Allen Ashwin as *An Examen of Witches* (London: John Rodker, 1929), 136–55.

which she killed in spite; but that nevertheless she contrived to wound one of the children in the thigh.

Jeanne Perrin also gave evidence that Clauda Gaillard had turned herself into a wolf, and had attacked her in that shape in a wood called Froidecombe. It was therefore very convenient that all these witches should have been tried together, since they had all turned themselves into wolves. Pierre Gandillon and his son George Gandillon would also have been tried with them, but that they were hurried too quickly to their execution; for these last two also confessed that they had turned themselves into wolves. Yet the son averred that he had never meddled with any children, but that, in company with his aunt Perrenette Gandillon, he had only killed certain goats, among them one belonging to his father, which as he said, they had done by mistake.

All these witches confessed besides that they had many times been to the Sabbat, that there they had copulated, danced, eaten, and made their ointment; and also that they had caused the death of countless persons and beasts. But since we have dealt in detail with these last matters in their proper place, I shall here confine myself to the consideration of the first of them, namely, lycanthropy and the metamorphosis of men into beasts.

There is much disputing as to whether it is possible for men to be changed into beasts, some affirming the possibility, whilst others deny it; and there are ample grounds for both views. For we have many examples of the fact. The family of Antaeus in Arcadia used to become wolves at a certain season of the year. After Demenetus Parrasius had tasted the entrails of a child, he was changed into a wolf. Baianus, the son of a certain Simeon who was a chieftain of the Bulgarians, used to change himself into a wolf when he wished, as did Moeris, of whom Vergil speaks:

> Moeris I often saw changed to a wolf
> And prowling in the woods.

Ovid reports that Lycaon did the same:

> He was amazed, and howled in loneliness,
> Nor could he speak as he was wont to do.

Job Fincel relates that he saw a Lycanthrope at Padua. Herodotus tells that the inhabitants of a district in Scythia used to turn into wolves; and this is also common among the peoples of the North. When the Romans were trying to prevent Hannibal from crossing the Alps, a wolf came amongst their army, rent those whom it met, and finally escaped without being hurt. In the year 1042 the people of Constantinople were much embarrassed by the appearance of more than 15 wolves at the same time. And in 1148 in the land of Geneva there was seen a wolf of unusual size, which killed thirty persons of both sexes and various ages. Who, then, can doubt but that these wolves were Lycanthropes?

Again, there are the three wolves which were seen on the 18th of July, 1603, in the district of Douvres and Jeurre about half an hour after a hailstorm had very strangely ruined all the fruit of that country. These wolves had no tails; and, moreover, as they ran through herds of cows and goats they touched none of them except one little kid, which one of them carried a little distance away without doing it any harm at all. It is apparent from this that these were not natural wolves, but were rather witches who had helped to cause the hailstorm, and had come to witness the damage which they had caused.

Also there was one which was larger than the others, and always went in front; and Groz-Jacques Bocquet, Thievenne Paget, la Michollette and several others said that, when they ran about in the shape of wolves, Satan used also to assume the form of a wolf and led and guided them.

The people of this country ought to know as much as any others about were-wolves; for they have always been known here. In the year 1521 three witches were executed: —Michael Udon of Plane, which is a little village near Poligny; Philibert Montot; and one called Gros Pierre. These men confessed that they had changed themselves into wolves and in that form had killed and eaten several people. While he was in the shape of a wolf, Michael Udon was wounded by a gentleman, who followed and found him in his hut where his wife was bathing his wound; but he had then resumed the form of a man. There have for a long time been pictures of these three witches in the Church of the Jacobins at Poligny. And in 1573 Gilles Garnier also confessed that he had made himself into a wolf, and in that form had killed and eaten several children, and was burned alive at Dôle by order of the Court. Here it will be relevant to recount what happened in the year 1588 in a village about two leagues from Apchon in the highlands of Auvergne. One evening a gentleman, standing at the window of his chateau, saw a huntsman whom he knew passing by, and asked him to bring him some of his bag on his return. As the huntsman went his way along a valley, he was attacked by a large wolf and discharged his arquebus at it without hurting it. He was therefore compelled to grapple with the wolf, and caught it by the ears; but at length, growing weary, he let go of the wolf, drew back and took his big hunting knife, and with it cut off one of the wolf's paws, which he put in his pouch after the wolf had run away. He then returned to the gentleman's chateau, in sight of which he had fought the wolf. The gentleman asked him to give him part of his bag; and the huntsman, wishing to do so and intending to take the paw from his pouch, drew from it a hand wearing a gold ring on one of the fingers, which the gentleman recognised as belonging to his wife. This caused him to entertain an evil suspicion of her; and going into the kitchen, he found his wife nursing her arm in her apron, which he took away, and found that her hand had been cut off. Thereupon the gentleman seized hold of her; but immediately, and as soon as she had been confronted with her hand, she confessed that it was no other than she who, in the form of a wolf, had attacked the hunter; and she was afterwards burned at Ryon. This was told me by one who may be believed, who went that way fifteen days after this thing had happened. So much for men being changed into the shape of wolves.

But they are sometimes also changed into the shapes of other animals. For we read that Circe changed the companions of Ulysses into swine:

> Circe did with her chants accursed and strange
> The wretched comrades of Ulysses change.

And Lucian and Apuleius confessed that they were formerly changed into asses. It is probable that this is what happened to certain pilgrims who were crossing the Alps, according to the evidence of St. Augustine: as also to an Englishman who, says Guillaume Archbishop of Tyre, was thus metamorphosed by a witch of Cyprus while kneeling in a church; and to another mentioned by Vincent of Beauvais in his "Mirror," and by Baptista Fulgosus, who after he had been dipped in water returned to his former shape. Others also have held that the ass which Belon in his "Observations" says that he saw in Cairo in Egypt was none other than a transformed man.

Others have been changed into cats. In our own time one named Charcot of the bailiwick of Gez was attacked by night in a wood by a number of cats; but when he made the sign of the Cross they all vanished. And more recently a horseman was passing by the Chateau de Joux and saw several cats up a tree: he approached and discharged a carbine which he was carrying, thereby causing a ring with several keys attached to it to fall from the tree. These he took to the village, and when he asked for dinner at the inn, neither the hostess nor the keys of the cellar could be found. He showed the bunch of keys which he was carrying, and the host recognized them as his wife's, who meanwhile came up, wounded in the right hip. Her husband seized her, and she confessed that she had just come from the Sabbat, where she had lost her keys after having been wounded in the hip by a shot from a carbine.

The Inquisitors also tell that in their time there were seen three large cats near the town of Strasbourg, which afterwards resumed the shape of women.

At other times men have been seen in the shape of a horse. Praestantius took the form of a horse; and an Egyptian's wife cured by St. Macharius that of a mare.

Again, there have been those who have been accused of changing themselves into hares, as was Pierre Gandillon, who was burned alive in this place.

But even if we had no other proof than the history of Nabuchodonosor, that would suffice for us to believe that the metamorphosis of a man into a beast is possible. For it is said that this Prince was changed into an ox, and lived for seven years like a beast, eating straw.

The fact of transformation can again be proved from the example of Lot's wife, who was turned into a pillar of salt which was still to be seen in the time of Josephus, as he himself testifies in his "Antiquities." It is again instanced in the transmutation of all sorts of herbs and plants into various kinds of worms and serpents, which are all endowed with

Nebuchadnezzar. Paris, Bibliothèque Nationale. Cod. gr. 923, fol. 259ʳ. Courtesy of the Bibliothèque Nationale.

their appropriate forms and qualities, as we read in Cardan. Also we observe that if a woman's hair be hidden in dung, it is changed to a serpent, as also is a rotten rod or wand. And in the town of Darien, a Province of the New World, drops of water are in summer turned to little green frogs.

Nevertheless it has always been my opinion that Lycanthropy is an illusion, and that the metamorphosis of a man into a beast is impossible. For it would necessitate one of two things: —either the man who is changed into a beast must keep his soul and power of reasons, or he must lose this at the moment of metamorphosis. Now the first point cannot be admitted, since it is impossible for the body of a brute beast to contain a reasoning soul. We know by experience that the wisdom or folly of a man is governed by the temperature of his brain, and that those with small heads are not usually very wise: then how can we believe that a soul gifted with reason can make its lodging in the head of a wolf or an ass or a cat or a horse or a hare? Besides, it is said in Genesis that man was created in the image and likeness of God, and this principally refers to the soul; and would it not be unspeakably absurd to maintain that so beautiful and holy a likeness should inhabit the body of a beast? Therefore I think that Homer was in error when, speaking of the companions of Ulysses who were changed into swine by Circe, he says that they had the hair, head and body of swine, but that their reason remained intact.

But if, on the other hand, man loses his reasoning soul when he is metamorphosed, how is it possible for him to recover it, and for it to return into him when he resumes the shape of a man? If this were possible we should have to admit that the Devil can perform miracles, if we grant the truth of the maxim of the Philosophers, that "That which is lost can never be recovered." But then I ask, Where does Satan put the soul when it is separated from its body? Does he cause it to wander in the air, or does he shut it up somewhere until the Lycanthrope has resumed his human shape? Certainly I cannot think that God permits him who has sworn our utter ruin to play such tricks with us. Aristotle was far nearer the truth when he said that the soul no more leaves its body than a pilot leaves his ship. In conclusion I believe that the transmutation of a man into a beast in the manner we speak of is so much the less possible in that the truth is that He alone to whom creation belongs can change the forms of things. And it would be a shameful thing for man, to whom all the beasts of the earth are subject, to be clothed in the form of a beast. For the Law has so much respect for the human face, since it was formed in the likeness of celestial beauty, that it has not permitted it to be disfigured even by branding or otherwise as a punishment for any crime. A Council has even pronounced those to be infidels who believe in Lycanthropy and the metamorphosis of a man into a beast.

As for Nabuchodonosor, he was never changed into an ox; but he thought he was so changed, and therefore went with the brute beasts and lived as they did. This is very clearly shown by the words of the Holy Scripture, which are repeated three times in the same chapter: "Thou shalt east grass as oxen." But even if we were to admit that this Prince was truly changed into an ox, it would not follow from that that witches have the power, with the help of Satan, to change themselves into wolves. For as to the former case, we must say with the magicians of Pharaoh: "This is the finger of God." In the same light I would regard what I said of Lot's wife.

As for the herbs, and drops of water, and woman's hair which are changed into worms and serpents and frogs, this comes about through corruption and putrefaction, by which imperfect animals are engendered; but this does not apply in the case of Lycanthropes.

There have been those who have flatly contradicted the changing of a man into a beast, holding that the Lycanthrope did its work in the spirit only, whilst its body lay lifeless behind some bush. But there is no more truth in this than in the former opinion; for if it be true that, when the soul is separated from the body, death must necessarily ensue, how is it possible for Satan to bring the witch back to life, seeing that to do so is possible with God only, as we have fully shown elsewhere?

My own opinion is that Satan sometimes leaves the witch asleep behind a bush, and himself goes and performs that which the witch has in mind to do, giving himself the appearance of a wolf; but that he so confuses the witch's imagination that he believes he has really been a wolf and has run about and killed men and beasts. He acts in just the same way as when he causes witches to believe firmly that they have been to the Sabbat, although they have really been lying in their beds; and it is likely that the ointment with which they rub themselves only serves to deaden their senses so that they do not awake for a long time.

And when it happens that they find themselves wounded, it is Satan who immediately transfers to them the blow which he has received in his assumed body.

Notwithstanding, I maintain that for the most part it is the witch himself who runs about slaying: not that he is metamorphosed into a wolf, but that it appears to him that he is so. And this comes from the Devil confusing the four Humours of which he is composed, so that he represents whatever he will to his fantasy and imagination. This will be easier to believe when it is considered that there are natural maladies of such a nature that they cause the sick to believe that they are cocks, or pigs, or oxen. And here I shall set down what Cardan relates of Andre Osiander of Nuremberg, a man well versed in theology. This man was in his youth afflicted with a quartan fever; and when it attacked him, he thought that he was in a forest and that many serpents and other savage beasts attacked him; and there was no means of persuading him that he was only imagining this, and that he was all the time in his father's house. And whenever his father came to him, he always came back to his senses and recognised the house, the room and his friends; but when his father went away again, he again fell into his former sickness and imaginings, which continued for as long as the fever lasted. It is the same way that those who are feverish, having their palates out of order, cannot correctly discriminate between different dishes. And when people see the witch in this shape, and think that it is really a wolf, the fact is that the Devil befogs and deceives their sight so that they think they see what is not; for such fascination is commonly used by the Devil and his demons, as we know from several examples. Simon Magus told the Emperor Nero that he might cut off his head, and he would come to life again on the third day; but he substituted a sheep, which they beheaded thinking that it was he. He also so troubled the eyes of St. Clement and several other holy persons that they mistook Simon for Faustinian. Again, there was once brought to St. Macharius a young woman whom everybody took to be a mare. About twelve years ago at Uzelle, which is a village in the department of Baume in our country, a certain man's house appeared to be all on fire, so that all the inhabitants ran to extinguish it as they usually do in such cases; but after about an hour they saw the house standing whole and quite undamaged; and this happened on three separate occasions, and was contrived by a certain chambermaid, as I was told by Monsieur

Jean Cretenet, the Lord of Thalenay, a Canon of the Metropolitan Church of Besancon, who was himself present on one of these occasions. I also know of this from the report of the trial sent to me by the Lord Ayme Morel of Besancon. Consider also our card manipulators. I have seen an Italian Count named l'Escot, who practised this marvellously: he would put a ten of spades in your hand, and you would always end by finding that it was the king of hearts, or some other different card. Those in whose presence he did these tricks were men of wit who were very careful to make sure whether it was only a matter of sleight of hand. There is no doubt but that he cast some glamour over their eyes; for he also turned his back to them and muttered I know not what between his teeth when he did these sleight-of-hand tricks.

But why should we find anything very strange in this fascination by which Satan makes a man appear like a wolf to us? For, among other naturalists, Albert, Cardan and Giovanni Battista Porta of Naples have taught us how to cause men's heads to seem like those of horses and asses and other animals, and their snouts like a dog's. They even have means to make men appear like angels. And therefore I am the less surprised at the formulas which they also give for causing a house to appear silvery, luminous, green, full of serpents, and to assume other terrible forms. This is consonant with what we have just said of the house at Uzelle.

The following examples also are pertinent to our subject with regard to the last point which we have just touched upon.

About three years ago Benoist Bidel of Naizan, a lad of fifteen or sixteen, climbed a tree to pick some fruit, leaving his younger sister at the foot of the tree. The girl was then attacked by a wolf without a tail; whereupon the brother quickly climbed down from the tree. The wolf then left the girl and turned to the boy, and took from him a knife which he was carrying, and wounded him in the neck with it. People ran to the boy's assistance, and led him into his father's house, where he died of his wounds in a few days. But before he died he declared that the wolf which had wounded him had its two forefeet like a man's hands covered on the top with hair. They knew then that it was Perrenette Gandillon who had killed him; for she tried to make her escape after striking the blow, and was killed by the peasants.

Similarly Jeanne Perrin deposed that while she was going through a wood with Clauda Gaillard, Clauda said to her that she had received more alms than she; and then she went behind a bush, and Jeanne saw come from it a wolf without a tail, which pranced round her and so frightened her that she let fall her alms and ran away, after having protected herself with the sign of the Cross; and she added that this wolf was no other than Clauda Gaillard; for she afterwards told Jeanne that the wolf which attacked her would not have done her any harm. And as for the hands and the toes which were recognized by Benoist Bidel and Jeanne Perrin, are they not evidence that Perrenette Gandillon and Clauda Gaillard were not really transformed into wolves? We may say the same of the wife of the gentleman of Auvergne, of whom we wrote above, whose hand was found in the hunter's pouch instead of a paw. This agrees also with what Job Fincel says of his Lycanthrope of Padua, namely, that, when its paws were cut off, the man was found with his hands and feet cut off.

The confessions of Jacques Bocquet, Francoise Secretain, Clauda Jamguillaume, Clauda Jamprost, Thievenne Paget, Pierre Gandillon and George Gandillon are very relevant to our argument; for they said that, in order to turn themselves into wolves, they first rubbed themselves with an ointment, and then Satan clothed them in a wolf's skin which completely covered them, and that they then went on all-fours and ran about the country chasing now a person now an animal according to the guidance of their appetite. They confessed also that they tired themselves with running. I remember once asking Clauda Jamprost how she was so well able to follow the others, even when they had to climb up rocks, seeing that she was both old and lame; and she answered me that she was borne along by Satan. But this in no way renders them immune from fatigue. For they who are carried by the Devil to the Sabbat say that when they arrive there, or when they return to their houses, they are quite weary and fatigued.

In company with the Lord Claude Meynier, our Recorder, I have seen those I have named go on all-fours in a room just as they did when they were in the fields; but they said that it was impossible for them to turn themselves into wolves, since they had no more ointment, and they had lost the power of doing so by being imprisoned. I have further noted that they were all scratched on the face and hands and legs; and that Pierre Gandillon was so much disfigured in this way that he bore hardly any resemblance to a man, and struck with horror those who looked at him. Finally, the clothes of the children which they have killed and eaten have been found in the fields quite whole and without a single tear; so that there was every appearance of the children having been undressed by human hands.

Who now can doubt but that these witches themselves ran about and committed the acts and murders of which we have spoken? For what was the cause of the fatigue which they experienced? If they had been sleeping behind some bush, how did they become fatigued? What caused the scratches on their persons, if it was not the thorns and bushes through which they ran in their pursuit of man and animals? Again, is it not the work of human hands to unclothe a child in the manner we have described? I say nothing of their confessions, which are all in agreement with one another.

I am well aware that there are those who cannot believe that witches eat human flesh. But such people ought to consider that from all time there have been tribes which use this practice, even if they were not were-wolves, and that they have therefore been called Anthropophagi; and that it is even said that there are still a great number of them in Brazil and the lands of the New World, whose chief boast is to have eaten many of their enemies. Witches go even further; for they take down the corpses from gibbets in order to eat their flesh. Lucan says:

> She gnaws the rope through with her witch's teeth,
> She drags the gibbet down, unhangs the corpse,
> And then in cruel banqueting tears out
> The stomach's entrails and the marrow bones.

Horace also gives us sufficient evidence that witches are hungry for human flesh:

> From the bloated body of an aged witch
> They cut a child which was not yet quite dead.

And Apuleius in the "Golden Ass" says that there were witches in Thessaly who used to search everywhere for dead bodies, so that if a corpse was not carefully guarded it would be found all gnawed about the nose and cheeks and mouth and several other parts. Not long ago at Nancy in Lorraine the corpse of one who had been tortured was left in the road outside the town; and it was found that during the night a thigh and a leg had been cut off from the body. There were many various opinions concerning this event; but for my part I maintain that only a witch did this deed; for on the same night there was seen a spectre hovering about the body, which so frightened a passer-by that, although he put his hand to his sword, he was compelled to run away into the town.

Fulgosus also mentions a villager who was burned alive because she had killed several children and salted them to keep as food for herself.

I am only puzzled by the fact that our witches said that they could not eat the head or the right side of those whom they killed. Groz-Jacques stated that he could not touch the head, by reason of the Holy Chrism with which it is anointed; and Clauda Jamguillaume said that they did not touch the right side because the sign of the Cross is made with the right hand. But I do not know that these are sufficient reasons, although they are largely substantiated by the strength and power which lies in the Cross and the Holy Chrism, of which we shall hereafter speak more fully.

And if anyone ask with what instrument witches, when appearing to be wolves, effect the death of those whom they kill, I shall answer that they have only too many contrivances for this purpose. For sometimes they use knives and swords, as did Perrenette Gandillon, who killed Benoist Bidel with his own knife; and therefore he who painted the three were-wolves of Poligny represented them as each carrying a knife in its right paw. At other times they drag their victims through rocks and stones, and so kill them. Clauda Jamprost, Clauda Jamguillaume and Thievenne Paget confessed that they did this. I make no doubt also that, for the most part, they strangle them.

For the rest, Jacques Bocquet and Pierre Gandillon said that, when they wished to turn into wolves, they rubbed themselves with an ointment given them by the Devil. Michel Udon, Gros Pierre and others confessed the same.

They said also that, when they wished to resume their former shape, they rolled in the dew or washed themselves with water. This agrees with Sprenger's statement that a man who has been changed into a beast loses that shape when he is bathed in running water.

Again, the man mentioned by Vincent of Beauvais, who was changed into an ass, resumed his human shape when he was dipped in the water. Apuleius gives another method for restoring a man from the shape of an ass, which is to eat fresh roses or else anise and laurel leaves together with spring water. Pierre Burgot similarly said that, to lose his wolf's shape, he rubbed himself with certain herbs. But since, as we have shown, the metamorphosis of a man into a beast is for countless reasons a very controversial subject, we must not pay much attention to these remedies. Moreover, I believe that most often witches who think that they are wolves neither wash nor anoint themselves in order to resume their natural shape. I had nearly omitted to say that werewolves couple with natural wolves according to the confessions of Michel Udon and Gros Pierre, who said that they had as much pleasure in the act as if they had been embracing their wives.

So much have I thought good to set down concerning Lycanthropes or were-wolves. Yet I should be sorry to leave this subject without reprimanding those who would excuse them and cast the blame for all that they do upon Satan, as if they were entirely innocent. For it is apparent from what I have said that it is the witches themselves who run about and kill people; so that we may here apply the Proverb which says: "Man is a wolf to man." And even if they were guilty in nothing but their damnable intention, they should still be thought worthy of death, seeing that the law takes cognizance of the intention even in matters which are not very serious, although nothing has actually resulted from such intention. I may add that such people never have this intention, except those who have first renounced God and Heaven.

10

British Werewolves

ELLIOTT O'DONNELL

𝕴n my investigations of haunted houses and my psychical research work generally, I have met people who have informed me they have seen phantasms, in shape half human and half beast, that might well be the earth-bound spirits of werwolves.

A Miss St. Denis told me she was once staying on a farm, in Merlonethshire, where she witnessed a phenomenon of this class. The farm, though some distance from the village, was not far off the railway station, a very diminutive affair, with only one platform and a mere box that served as a waiting-room and bookingoffice combined. It was, moreover, one of those stations where the separate duties of station-master, porter, booking-clerk, and ticket-collector are performed by one and the same person, and where the signal always appears to be down. As the platform commanded the only paintable view in the neighbourhood, Miss St. Denis often used to resort there with her sketch-book. On one occasion she had stayed rather later than usual, and on rising hurriedly from her campstool saw, to her surprise, a figure which she took to be that of a man, sitting on a truck a few yards distant, peering at her. I say to her surprise, because, excepting on the rare occasion of a train arriving, she had never seen anyone at the station beside the station-master, and in the evening the platform was invariably deserted. The loneliness of the place was for the first time brought forcibly home to her. The station-master's tiny house was at least some hundred yards away, and beyond that there was not another habitation nearer than the farm. On all sides of her, too, were black, frowning precipices, full of seams and fissures and inequalities, showing vague and shadowy in the fading rays of the sun. Here and there were the huge, gaping mouths of gloomy slate quarries that had long been disused, and were now half full of foul water. Around them the earth was heaped with loose fragments of rock which had evidently been detached from the principal mass and shivered to pieces in the fall. A few trees, among which were the black walnut, the slippery elm,

Werwolves (London: Methuen & Co., Ltd, 1912), 93–107.

and here and there an oak, grew among the rocks, and attested by this dwarfish stature the ungrateful soil in which they had taken root. It was not an exhilarating scene, but it was one that had a peculiar fascination for Miss St. Denis—a fascination she could not explain, and which she now began to regret. The darkness had come on very rapidly, and was especially concentrated, so it seemed to her, round the spot where she sat, and she could make nothing out of the silent figure on the truck, save that it had unpleasantly bright eyes and there was something queer about it. She coughed to see if that would have any effect, and as it had none she coughed again. Then she spoke and said, "Can you tell me the time, please?" But there was no reply, and the figure still sat there staring at her. Then she grew uneasy and, packing up her things, walked out of the station, trying her best to look as if nothing had occurred. She glanced over her shoulder; the figure was following her. Quickening her pace, she assumed a jaunty air and whistled, and turning round again, saw the strange figure still coming after her. The road would soon be at its worst stage of loneliness, and, owing to the cliffs on either side of it, almost pitch dark. Indeed, the spot positively invited murder, and she might shriek herself hoarse without the remotest chance of making herself heard. To go on with this outre figure so unmistakably and persistently stalking her, was out of the question. Screwing up courage, she swung round, and raising herself to her full height, cried: "What do you want? How dare you?"—She got no further, for a sudden spurt of dying sunlight, playing over the figure, showed her it was nothing human, nothing she had ever conceived possible. It was a nude grey thing, not unlike a man in body, but with a wolf's head. As it sprang forward, its light eyes ablaze with ferocity, she instinctively felt in her pocket, whipped out a pocket flash-light, and pressed the button. The effect was magical; the creature shrank back, and putting two paw-like hands in front of its face to protect its eyes, faded into nothingness.

She subsequently made inquiries, but could learn nothing beyond the fact that in one of the quarries close to the place where the phantasm had vanished, some curious bones, partly human and partly animal, had been unearthed, and that the locality was always shunned after dusk. Miss St. Denis thought as I did, that what she had seen might very well have been the earth-bound spirit of a werwolf.

The case of another haunting of this nature was related to me last year. A young married couple of the name of Anderson, having acquired, through the death of a relative, a snug fortune, resolved to retire from business and spend the rest of their lives in indolence and ease. Being fond of the country, they bought some land in Cumberland, at the foot of some hills, far away from any town, and built on it a large two-storied villa.

They soon, however, began to experience trouble with their servants, who left them on the pretext that the place was lonely, and that they could not put up with the noises that they heard at night. The Andersons ridiculed their servants, but when their children remarked on the same thing they viewed the matter more seriously. "What are the noises like?" they inquired. "Wild animals," Willie, the eldest child, replied. "They come howling round the window at night and we hear their feet patter along the passage and stop at our door." Much mystified, Mr. and Mrs. Anderson decided to sit up with the children and listen. They did so, and between two and three in the morning were much startled by a noise that sounded like the growling of a wolf—Mr. Anderson had heard wolves in Canada—immediately beneath the window. Throwing open the window, he peered out; the moon was fully up and every stick and stone was plainly discernible; but there was now no sound and no sign of any animal. When he had closed the window the growling at once recommenced, yet when he looked again nothing was to be seen. After a while the growling ceased, and they heard the front door, which they had locked before coming upstairs, open, and the footsteps of some big, soft-footed animal ascend the stairs. Mr. Anderson waited till the steps were just outside the room and then flung open the door, but the light from his acetylene lamp revealed a passage full of moonbeams—nothing else.

He and his wife were now thoroughly mystified. In the morning they explored the grounds, but could find no trace of footmarks, nothing to indicate the nature of their visitant. It was now close on Christmas, and as the noises had not been heard for some time, it was hoped that the disturbances would not occur again. The Andersons, like all modern parents, made idols of their children. They never did wrong, nothing was too good for them, and everything they wanted they had. At Christmas, perhaps, their authority was more particularly in evidence; at any rate, it was then that the greatest care was taken that the menu should be in strict accordance with their instructions.

"What shall Santa Claus bring you this time, my darlings?" Mr. Anderson asked, a week or so before the great day arrived; and Willie, aged six, at once cried out: "What a fool you are daddy! It is all tosh about old Claus, there's no such person!"

"Wait and see!" Mr. Anderson meekly replied. "You mark my words, he will come into your room on Christmas Eve laden with presents."

"I don't believe it!" Willie retorted. "You told us that silly tale last year and I never saw any Claus!"

"He came when you were asleep, dearie," Mrs. Anderson ventured to remark.

"Well! I'll keep awake this time!" Willie shouted.

"And we'll take the presents first and pinch old Claus afterwards," Violet Evelyn, the second child, joined in.

"And I'll prick his towsers wif pins!" Horace, aged three and a half, echoed. "I don't care nothink for old Santa Claus!" and he pulled a long nose in the manner his doting father had taught him.

Christmas Eve came at last—a typical old-fashioned Christmas with heaps of snow on the ground and frost on the window-panes and trees. The Andersons' house was warm and comfortable—for once in a way the windows were shut—and enormous fires blazed merrily away in the grates. Whilst the children spent most of the day viewing the good things in the larder and speculating how much they could eat of each, and which would taste the nicest, Mr. Anderson rehearsed in full costume the role of Santa Claus. He had an enormous sack full of presents—everything the children had demanded—and he meant to enter their room with it on his shoulder at about twelve o'clock.

Tea-time came, and during the interval between that meal and supper all hands—even Horace's—were at work, decorating the hall and staircases with holly and mistletoe. After supper "Good King Wencelas," "Noel," and one or two other carols were sung, and the children then decided to go to bed.

It was then ten o'clock; and exactly two hours later their father, elaborately clad as Santa Claus, and staggering, in the orthodox fashion, beneath a load of presents, shuffled softly down the passage leading to their room. The snow had ceased falling, the moon was out, and the passage flooded with a soft, phosphorescent glow that threw into strong relief every minute object. Mr. Anderson had got half-way along it when on his ears there suddenly fell a faint sound of yelping! His whole frame thrilled and his mind reverted to the scenes of his youth—to the prairies in the far-off West, where, over and over again, he had heard these sounds, and his faithful Winchester repeater had stood him in good service. Again the yelping—this time nearer. Yes! it was undoubtedly a wolf; and yet there was an intonation in that yelping not altogether wolfish—something Mr. Anderson had never heard before, and which he was consequently at a loss to define. Again it rang out—much nearer this time, much more trying to the nerves, and the cold sweat of fear burst out all over him. Again—close under the wall of the house—a moaning, snarling, drawn-out cry that ended in a whine so piercing that Mr. Anderson's knees shook. One of the children, Violet Evelyn he thought, stirred in her bed and muttered: "Santa Claus! Santa Claus!" and Mr. Anderson, with a desperate effort, staggered on under his load and opened their door. The clock in the hall beneath began to strike twelve. Santa Claus, striving hard to appear jolly and genial, entered the room, and a huge grey, shadowy figure entered with him. A slipper thrown by Willie whizzed through the air, and, narrowly missing Santa Claus, fell to the ground with a clatter. There was then a deathly silence, and Violet and Horace, raising their heads, saw two strange figures standing in the centre of the room staring at one another—the one figure they at once identified by the costume. He was Santa Claus—but not the genial, rosy-cheeked Santa Claus their father had depicted. On the contrary, it was a Santa Claus with a very white face and frightened eyes—a Santa Claus that shook as if the snow and ice had given him the ague. But the other figure—what was it? Something very tall, far taller than their father, nude and grey, something like a man with the head of a wolf—a wolf with white pointed teeth and horrid, light eyes. Then they understood why it was that Santa Claus trembled; and Willie stood by the side of his bed, white and silent. It is impossible to say how long this state of things would have lasted, or what would eventually have happened, had not Mrs. Anderson, anxious to see how Santa Claus was faring, and rather wondering why he was gone so long, resolved herself to visit the children's room. As the light from her candle appeared on the threshold of the room the thing with the wolf's head vanished.

"Why, whatever were you all doing?" she began. Then Santa

Claus and the children all spoke at once—whilst the sack of presents tumbled unheeded on the floor. Every available candle was soon lighted, and mother and father and Willie, Violet and Horace all spent the remainder of that night in close company. On the following day it was proposed, and carried unanimously, that the house should be put up for sale. This was done at the earliest opportunity, and fortunately for the Andersons suitable tenants were soon found. Before leaving, however, Mr. Anderson made another and more exhaustive search of the grounds, and discovered, in a cave in the hills immediately behind the house, a number of bones. Amongst them was the skull of a wolf, and lying close beside it a human skeleton, with only the skull missing. Mr. Anderson burnt the bones, hoping that by so doing he would rid the house of its unwelcome visitor; and, as his tenants so far have not complained, he believes that the hauntings have actually ceased.

A lady whom I met at Tavistock some years ago told me that she had seen a phantasm, which she believed to be that of a werwolf, in the Valley of the Doones, Exmoor. She was walking home alone, late one evening, when she saw on the path directly in front of her the tall grey figure of a man with a wolf's head. Advancing stealthily forward, this creature was preparing to spring on a large rabbit that was crouching on the ground, apparently too terror-stricken to move, when the abrupt appearance of a stag bursting through the bushes in a wild state of stampede caused it to vanish. Prior to this occurrence, my informant had never seen a ghost, nor had she, indeed, believed in them; but now, she assures me, she is quite convinced as to their existence, and is of the opinion that the sub-human phenomenon she had witnessed was the spirit of one of those werwolves referred to by Gervase of Tilbury and Richard Verstegan—werwolves who were still earthbound owing to their incorrigible ferocity.

This opinion I can readily endorse, adding only that, considering the number of werwolves there must once have been in England, it is a matter of some surprise to me that phantasms are not more frequently seen.

Here is another account of this type of haunting narrated to me some summers ago by a Mr. Warren, who at the time he saw the phenomenon was staying in the Hebrides, which part of the British Isles is probably richer than any other in spooks of all sorts.

"I was about fifteen years of age at the time," Mr. Warren said, "and had for several years been residing with my grandfather, who was an elder in the Kirk of Scotland. He was much interested in geology, and literally filled the house with fossils from the pits and caves round where we dwelt. One morning he came home in a great state of excitement, and made me go with him to look at some ancient remains he had found at the bottom of a dried-up tarn. 'Look!' he cried, bending down and pointing at them, 'here is a human skeleton with a wolf's head. What do you make of it?' I told him I did not know, but supposed it must be some kind of monstrosity. 'It's a werwolf!' he rejoined, 'that's what it is. A werwolf! This island was once overrun with satyrs and werwolves! Help me carry it to the house.' I did as he bid me, and we placed it on the table in the back kitchen. That evening I was left alone in the house, my grandfather and the other members of the household having gone to the kirk. For some time I amused myself reading, and then, fancying I heard a noise in the back premises, I went into the kitchen. There was no one about, and becoming convinced that it could only have been a rat that had disturbed me, I sat on the table alongside the alleged remains of the werwolf, and waited to see if the noises would recommence. I was thus waiting in a listless sort of way, my back bent, my elbows on my knees, looking at the floor and thinking of nothing in particular, when there came a loud rat, tat, tat of knuckles on the window-pane. I immediately turned in the direction of the noise and encountered, to my alarm, a dark face looking in at me. At first dim and indistinct, it became more and more complete, until it developed into a very perfectly defined head of a wolf terminating in the neck of a human being. Though greatly shocked, my first act was to look in every direction for a possible reflection—but in vain. There was no light either without or within, other than that from the setting sun—nothing that could in any way have produced an illusion. I looked at the face and marked each feature intently. It was unmistakably a wolf's face, the jaws slightly distended; the lips wreathed in a savage snarl; the teeth sharp and white; the eyes light green; the ears pointed. The expression of the face was diabolically malignant, and as it gazed straight at me my horror was as intense as my wonder. This it seemed to notice, for a look of savage exultation crept into its eyes, and it raised one hand—a slender hand, like that of a woman, though with prodigiously long and curved finger-nails—menacingly, as if about to dash in the window-pane. Remembering what my grandfather

SECTION III

Philosophical and Theological Approaches to Metamorphosis

Introduction

Long regarded as the key theoretical text in the history of witch-craft and witchcraft persecution, the *Malleus Maleficarum* (1486–87) went into eight editions before the close of the fifteenth century. Its authors, Heinrich Kramer and James Sprenger (Dominicans), cre-ated a manual that served as the philosophical and theological basis for the legal judgments of jurists such as Bodin, Boguet, and Remy. (That the *Malleus Maleficarum* is strongly anti-feminine and is a manual of what Sydney Anglo calls "scholastic pornography" is not particularly rele-vant to the consideration of lycanthropy.)

Drawing on the philosophical and theological writings of au-thorities such as St. Thomas Aquinas, St. Augustine, St. Antoninus, Albertus Magnus, Vincent of Beauvais, the authors analyze the nature of matter, the nature of God, the nature of Satan; and, although they argue that only God can create and alter matter (substance), Satan can, by the permissive will of God, move "the inner perceptions and humours, effect changes in the actions and faculties, physical, mental, and emotional, working by means of any physical organ soever."

The two options that can account for the transformation of a human being into an animal form are these: (1) the Devil, entering into the imagination or dreams, creates the illusion of metamorphosis; (2) the Devil enters into actual wolves, making them ravenously de-structive. Obviously, the second option would give no opportunity for legal action, since natural wolves (even though demon-possessed) can-not easily be captured and are not subject to human legal processes. The first option, however, strengthens and enlarges the power of the demonic in all forms of human activity and makes the detection of lycanthropes (and witches) urgent.

In spite of the intricate arguments about the nature of matter, of God, and of Satan; in spite of the citing of authorities and the quoting of Scripture; the effect of the *Malleus Maleficarum* was to elevate and intensify the role of demons in human life. No reiteration of "the permissive will of God" could deflect the community from hunting down lycanthropes. Persecution, inhumane practices, and inquisitorial techniques followed hard upon a theory so heavily reliant on the continuing power of Satan to delude humans into metamorphosis, a deluded state in which they became instruments of his will.

Reginald Scot reacted to this treatise with refutations and denunciations; his vigorous opposition is found in this section of the *Reader.*[1]

Argument by argument, Reginald Scot in *The Discoverie of Witchcraft* (1584) works his way through the writings of Bodin, and of Kramer and Sprenger. He, too, knows how to engage in philosophical and theological discussions on the nature of matter, the nature of God, the nature of Satan, the nature of the spirit world. He, too, can cite authorities and quote Scripture. However emotional and impassioned he may become, his conclusions are based on sound reasoning, on refutation of evidence of transformation that simply would not stand up to empirical verification, and a fresh approach to contemporary intellectual issues and legal problems.

Scot's basic premise is that God is the creator and sustainer of His creation, and that to give power to the demons (as do Bodin and Kramer and Sprenger) is to relegate God to the role of "the Devil's drudge." From there he proceeds to examine and analyze human form and spirit form. *Human form:* "Our bodies are visible, sensitive, and passive, and are endued with many other excellent properties, which all the devils in hell are not able to alter." *Spirit form:* "The spirits themselves have their laws and limits prescribed." There is, then, no easy commerce between the human world and the spirit world, and no opportunity for demonic disruption of human tranquillity. Spirits, too, are created beings; they cannot alter even the perceptions of a human being.

After establishing these basic premises, Scot moves to a refutation of metamorphosis. Lycanthropy (he agrees with Wier) is a disease—it is not demon possession. Lycanthropes suffer from mental illness. They deserve compassion and healing, not persecution and death. (He refuses to credit the case of Gilles Garnier as demon-delusion.)

As throughout the *Malleus Maleficarum* the demonic emerges as the dominant force in human life, so throughout the *Discoverie of Witchcraft* the Providence of God is the shaping power in human life. No one can make the image-bearer of God assume the flesh of a beast. The God who cares for His creation will not let Satan alter his creatures. Like Hamlet, Scot defies augury; and would most surely agree with Hamlet that "There is special providence in the fall of a sparrow" (V. II. 220–1).

As Scot attacked Bodin, and Kramer and Sprenger, so King James I of England attacked Scot in the Preface to his *Daemonologie* for not believing in witchcraft: "an Englishman, [who] is not ashamed in pub-like print to deny, that ther can be such a thing as Witch-craft; and so mainteines the old error of the Sadducees, in denying of spirits." The second person he attacked for defending witches was Wier. James followed those thinkers of his day who defended their belief in God by admitting the power of the Devil in witchcraft, magic, necromancy, sorcery, disease. James hastened, however, to insist that the Devil's power is derivative: Satan serves God; he is not co-equal with God. James can account for the evil initiated and instigated by the Devil as God using evil for good: punishing the wicked, establishing justice, correcting the erring, instructing the faithful in patience. The *Daemonologie*, which reinforced the dominant philosophical and theological positions on witchcraft, was first published in Edinburgh in 1597, appeared in London editions in 1603, and was translated into Latin, French, and Dutch.

Not doubting the active presence of the spirit world in the human world, and not negating the power of Satan to intervene in human life, James nevertheless denied categorically that the Devil could transform humans into wolves. Human beings, he argued, who think they are wolves are insane. They are no more wolves with wolfskin and fur than those who think themselves Pitchers are made of glass. Lycanthropic insanity is caused by a "natural super-abundance of Melancholie." As for those lycanthropes who sincerely believe they are wolves and counterfeit wolf behavior, it is the Devil who spreads the rumors and lies of their actual physical metamorphosis. James, then, did not deny the power of the demonic in human life, but he could not accept a metaphysical change in substance.[2]

The name John Darrel was well known in ecclesiastical circles in England in the last decade of the sixteenth century. Darrel was a prominent Puritan exorcist who gained publicity from his exorcisms.

Attacked by fellow Puritans such as Deacon and Walker and brought to trial by Anglicans, Darrel was condemned as a counterfeit exorcist by the Anglican courts; his casting out of devils was allegedly supported by fraudulent testimony. Samuell Harsnett, Chaplain to the Bishop of London, throughout A Discovery called Darrel a juggler, devil-flinger, devil-driver, seducer, deceiver, imposter.[3]

It is in the context of exorcism that Deacon and Walker's writings on lycanthropy appeared. They denounced Darrel; Darrel counter-accused them of not believing in witches or witchcraft, of denying the existence of the demons, and, hence, of being atheists. What prompted Deacon and Walker to make pronouncements on lycanthropy was the basic question raised by Darrel on the nature of disease: is disease (including insanity) a form of demon-possession, or is it attributable to natural causes?

For Darrel, the Devil is active in all aspects of human life, including disease; for Deacon and Walker, demon-possession is a much-abused term to describe natural (though sometimes inexplicable) illnesses. Further, authentic demon-possession would require a miracle to exorcise, and miracles do not occur in the post-apostolic age. Deacon and Walker believed in God; and, following physicians such as Lemnius and Wier, believed that Lupina insania arose from a disordered, troubled brain. In a detailed description of how the brain and the melancholy humor cooperate to create the disease of lycanthropy, they persuade Lycanthropus in the dialogue that he is not actually a lycanthrope. And they urge preachers to use their pulpits "to strengthen the minds of their people against every such phantasticall and fond illusion of satan." The ultimate error in lycanthropy, they argued, is that "they doe therein attribute that power to a creature: which onely belongeth to God the creator of all things."[4]

A century before, the preacher Dr. Johannes Geiler von Kaiserberg had, on the third Sunday in Lent, preached a sermon on werewolves. "Do you ask me if I know aught about them? I answer, Yes. They are apparently wolves which eat men and children, and that happens on seven accounts: Hunger, Savageness, Old Age, Experience, Madness, The Devil, God." In all but one instance, Geiler is describing natural wolves; and when he speaks of the Devil, he refers only to medieval and ancient texts, and to the fantasy that a human being is a wolf. Like St. Francis, he was acutely aware of how wolves

Wolf (or werewolf) attacking humans. From Johannes Geiler von
Kaiserberg, *Die Emeis*, fol. XLI (1516). Courtesy of University of
Chicago Library, Department of Special Collections.

when they "find nothing to eat in the woods, they must come to people
and eat men when hunger drives them to it."[5]

Notes

1. For a study of the *Malleus Maleficarum*, see Sydney Anglo in *The Damned Art*, 1–31.

2. For a study of James's *Daemonologie*, see Stuart Clark in *The Damned Art*, 156–81.

3. Samuell Harsnett, *A Discovery* (London, 1599).

4. For a study of Deacon and Walker, see D. P. Walker, *Unclean Spirits* (Philadelphia: University of Pennsylvania Press, 1981).

5. Johannes Geiler von Kaiserberg, *Die Emeis* (Strassburg: 1516), fol. XLI.

11

The Malleus Maleficarum

HEINRICH KRAMER and JAMES SPRENGER

Question X

Whether Witches can by some Glamour Change Men into Beasts

Here we declare the truth as to whether and how witches transform men into beasts. And it is argued that this is not possible, from the following passage of *Episcopus* (XXVI, 5): Whoever believes that it is possible for any creature to be changed for the better or for the worse, or to be transformed into any other shape or likeness, except by the Creator Himself, Who made all things, and by Whom all things are created, is without doubt an infidel, and worse than a pagan.

And we will quote the arguments of S. Thomas in the *2nd Book of Sentences*, VIII: Whether devils can affect the bodily senses by the delusion of a glamour. There he argues first that they cannot. For though that shape of a beast which is seen must be somewhere, it cannot exist only in the senses; for the senses perceive no shape that is not received in actual matter, and there is no actual beast there; and he adduces the authority of the Canon. And again, that which seems to be, cannot really be; as in the case of a woman who seems to be a beast, for two substantial shapes cannot exist at one and the same time in the same matter. Therefore, since that shape of a beast which appears cannot exist anywhere, no glamour or illusion can exist in the eye of the beholder; for the sight must have some object in which it terminates.

And if it is argued that the shape exists in the surrounding atmosphere, this is not possible; both because the atmosphere is not capable of taking any shape or form, and also because the air around that person is not always constant, and cannot be so on account of its fluid nature, especially when it is moved. And again because in that case such a transformation would be visible to everyone; but this is not so,

Translated by Montague Summers (London: John Rodker, 1928); reprinted (New York: Dover, 1971), 61–65; first published 1486–87.

because the devils seem to be unable to deceive the sight of Holy Men in the least.

Besides, the sense of sight, or the faculty of vision, is a passive faculty, and every passive faculty is set in motion by the active agent that corresponds to it. Now the active agent corresponding to sight is twofold: one is the origin of the act, or the object; the other is the carrier, or medium. But that apparent shape cannot be the object of the sense, neither can it be the medium through which it is carried. First, it cannot be the object, since it cannot be taken hold of by anything, as was shown in the foregoing argument, since it does not exist in the senses received from an object, neither is it in the actual object, nor even in the air, as in a carrying medium, as was treated of above in the third argument.

Besides, if the devil moves the inner consciousness, he does so either by projecting himself into the cognitive faculty, or by changing it. But he does not do so by projecting himself; for he would either have to assume a body, and even so could not penetrate into the inner organ of imagination; for two bodies cannot be at the same time in the same place; or he would assume a phantasmal body; and this again would be impossible, since no phantasm is quite without substance.

Similarly also he cannot do it by changing the cognition. For he would either change it by alteration, which he does not seem able to do, since all alteration is caused by active qualities, in which the devils are lacking; or he would change it by transformation or local motion; and this does not seem feasible for two reasons. First, because a transformation of an organ cannot be effected without a sense of pain. Secondly, because in this case the devil would only make things of a known shape appear; but S. Augustine says that he creates shapes of this sort, both known and unknown. Therefore it seems that the devils can in no way deceive the imagination or senses of a man.

But against this, S. Augustine says (*de Civitate Dei*, XVIII) that the transmutations of men into brute animals, said to be done by the art of devils, are not actual but only apparent. But this would not be possible if devils were not able to transmute the human senses. The authority of S. Augustine is again to the point in Book LXXXIII, which has already been quoted: This evil of the devil creeps in through all the sensual approaches, etc.

Answer. If the reader wishes to refer to the method of transmutation, he will find in the Second Part of this work, chapter VI, various methods. But proceeding for the present in a scholastic manner, let us say in agreement with the opinions of the three Doctors, that the devil can deceive the human fancy so that a man really seems to be an animal. The last of those opinions, which is that of S. Thomas, is more subtle than the rest. But the first is that of S. Antoninus* in the first part of his *Summa*, V, 5, where he declares that the devil at times works to deceive a man's fancy, especially by an illusion of the senses; and he proves this by natural reasoning, by the authority of the Canon, and by a great number of examples.

And at first as follows: Our bodies naturally are subject to and obey the angelic nature as regards local motion. But the bad angels, although they have lost grace, have not lost their natural power, as has often been said before. And since the faculty of fancy or imagination is corporeal, that is, allied to a physical organ, it also is naturally subject to devils, so that they can transmute it, causing various phantasies, by the flow of the thoughts and perceptions to the original image received by them. So says S. Antoninus, and adds that it is proved by the following Canon (*Episcopus*, XXVI, 5): It must not be omitted that certain wicked women, perverted by Satan and seduced by the illusions and phantasms of devils, believe and profess that they ride in the night hours on certain beasts with Diana, the heathen goddess, or with Herodias, and with a countless number of women, and that in the untimely silence of night they travel over great distances of land. And later: Wherefore priests ought to preach to the people of God that they should know this to be altogether false, and that when such phantasms afflict the minds of the faithful, it is not of God, but of an evil spirit. For Satan himself transforms himself into the shape and likeness of different persons, and in dreams deluding the mind which he holds captive, leads it through devious ways.

Indeed the meaning of this Canon has been treated of in the First Question, as to the four things which are to be preached. But it would be to misunderstand its meaning to maintain that witches cannot be so transported, when they wish and God does not prevent it; for very often men who are not witches are unwillingly transported bodily over great distances of land.

But that these transmutations can be effected in both ways will be shown by the aforesaid *Summa*, and in the chapter where S. Augustine relates that it is read in the books of the Gentiles that a certain sor-ceress named Circe changed the companions of Ulysses into beasts; but that this was due to some glamour or illusion, rather than an actual accomplishment, by altering the fancies of men; and this is clearly proved by several examples.

For we read in the Lives of the Fathers, that a certain girl would not consent to a young man who was begging her to commit a shame-ful act with him. And the young man, being angry because of this, caused a certain Jew to work a charm against her, by which she was changed into a filly. But this metamorphosis was not an actual fact, but an illusion of the devil, who changed the fancy and senses of the girl herself, and of those who looked at her, so that she seemed to be a filly, who was really a girl. For when she was led to the Blessed Macarius, the devil could not so work as to deceive his senses as he had those of other people, on account of his sanctity; for to him she seemed a true girl, not a filly. And at length by his prayer she was set free from that illusion, and it is said that this had happened to her because she did not give her mind to holy things, or attend the Sacraments as she ought; therefore the devil had power over her, although she was in other respects honest.

Therefore the devil can, by moving the inner perceptions and humours, effect changes in the actions and faculties, physical, mental, and emotional, working by means of any physical organ soever; and this accords with S. Thomas, I, 91. And of this sort we may believe to have been the acts of Simon Magus in the incantations which are narrated of him. But the devil can do none of these things without the permission of God, Who with His good Angels often restrains the wickedness of him who seeks to deceive and hurt us. Wherefore S. Augustine, speaking of witches, says: These are they who, with the permission of God, stir up the elements, and confuse the minds of those who do not trust in God (XXVI, 5).

Also devils can by witchcraft cause a man to be unable to see his wife rightly, and the converse. And this comes from an affectation of the fancy, so that she is represented to him as an odious and horrible thing. The devil also suggests representations of loathsome things to the fancy of both the waking and the sleeping, to deceive them and lead them to sin. But because sin does not consist in the imagination but in the will, therefore man does not sin in these fancies suggested by the devil, and these various transformations, unless of his own will he consents to sin.

The second opinion of the modern Doctors is to the same effect, when they declare what is glamour, and in how many ways the devil can cause such illusions. Here we refer to what has already been said concerning the arguments of S. Antoninus, which there is no need to repeat.

The third opinion is that of S. Thomas, and is an answer to the argument where it is asked, Wherein lies the existence of the shape of a beast that is seen; in the senses, or in reality, or in the surrounding air? And his opinion is that the apparent shape of a beast only exists in the inner perception, which, through the force of imagination, sees it in some way as an exterior object. And the devil has two ways of effecting such a result.

In one way we may say that the forms of animals which are conserved in the treasury of the imagination pass by the operation of the devil into the organs of inner senses; and in this way it happens in dreams, as has been declared above. And so, when these forms are impressed on the organs of the outer senses, such as sight, they appear as if they were present as outer objects, and could actually be touched.

The other way results from a change in the inner organs of perception, through which the judgement is deceived; as is shown in the case of him who has his taste corrupted, so that everything sweet seems bitter; and this is not very different from the first method. Moreover, even men can accomplish this by the virtue of certain natural things, as when in the vapour of a certain smoke the beams of a house appear to be serpents; and many other instances of this are found, as has been mentioned above.

Solutions of the Arguments

As to the first argument, that text is often quoted, but is badly understood. For as to where it speaks of transformation into another shape or likeness, it has been made clear how this can be done by prestidigitatory art. And as to where it says that no creature can be made by the power of the devil, this is manifestly true if Made is understood to mean Created. But if the word Made is taken to refer to natural production, it is certain that devils can make some imperfect creatures. And S. Thomas shows how this may be done. For he says that all transmutations of bodily matters which can be effected by the forces of nature, in which the essential thing is the semen which is found in the elements of this world, on land or in the waters (as serpents and frogs and such things deposit their semen), can be effected by the work of devils who have acquired such semen. So also it is when anything is changed into serpents or frogs, which can be generated by putrefaction.

But those transmutations of bodily matters which cannot be effected by the forces of nature can in no way be truly effected by the work of the devils. For when the body of a man is changed into the body of a beast, or a dead body is brought to life, such things only seem to happen, and are a glamour or illusion; or else the devil appears before men in an assumed body.

These arguments are substantiated. For Blessed Albertus in his book *On Animals,* where he examines whether devils, or let us even say witches, can really make animals, says that they can, with God's permission, make imperfect animals. But they cannot do so in an instant, as God does, but by means of some motion, however sudden, as is clear in the case of witches. And touching the passage in *Exodus* vii, where Pharao called his wise men, he says: The devils run throughout the world and collect various germs, and by using them can evolve various species. And the gloss thereon says: When witches attempt to effect anything by the invocation of devils, they run about the world and bring the semen of those things which are in question, and by its means, with the permission of God, they produce new species. But this has been spoken of above.

Another difficulty may arise, whether such devils' works are to be deemed miraculous. The answer was made clear in the preceding arguments, that even the devils can perform certain miracles to which their natural powers are adapted. And although such things are true in fact, they are not done with a view to the knowledge of the truth; and in this sense the works of Antichrist may be said to be deceptions, since they are done with a view to the seduction of men.

The answer to the other argument, that concerning the shape, is also clear. The shape of a beast which is seen does not exist in the air, or in actual fact, as has been shown, but only in the perception of the senses, as has been demonstrated above from the opinion of S. Thomas.

For the argument that every passive is set in motion by its corresponding active, this is granted. But when it is inferred that the shape which is seen cannot be the original object which sets in motion the act of sight, since it arises from none of the senses, it is answered that it does not arise, since it originates from some sensible image conserved in the imagination, which the devil can draw out and present to the imagination or powers of perception, as has been said above.

For the last argument, it is to be said that the devil does not, as has been shown, change the perceptive and imaginative powers by projecting himself into them, but by transmuting them; not indeed by altering them, except in respect of local motion. For he cannot of himself induce new appearances, as has been said. But he changes them by transmutation, that is, local motion. And this again he does, not by dividing the substance of the organ of perception, since that would result in a sense of pain, but by a movement of the perceptions and humours.

But it may be further objected as follows: that according to this the devil cannot present to a man the appearance of anything new in respect of things seen. It is to be said that a new thing can be understood in two ways. In one way it may be entirely new both in itself and in its beginnings; and in this sense the devil cannot present anything new to a man's sense of vision: for he cannot cause one who is born blind to imagine colours, or a deaf man to imagine sounds. In another sense, a thing may be new as to the composition of its whole; as we may say that it is an imaginatively new thing if a man imagines that he sees mountains of gold, which he never saw; for he has seen gold, and he has seen a mountain, and can by some natural operation imagine the phantasm of a mountain of gold. And in this way the devil can present a new thing to the imagination.

What is to be Thought of Wolves
which sometimes Seize and Eat Men and Children out of their Cradles
Whether this also is a Glamour caused by Witches.

There is incidentally a question concerning Wolves, which sometimes snatch men and children out of their houses and eat them, and run about with such astuteness that by no skill or strength can they be hurt or captured. It is to be said that this sometimes has a natural cause, but is sometimes due to a glamour, when it is effected by witches. And as to the first, Blessed Albertus in his book *On Animals* says that it can arise from five causes. Sometimes on account of the fierceness of their strength, as in the case of dogs in cold regions. But this is nothing to the point; and we say that such things are caused by an illusion of devils, when God punishes some nation for sin. See *Leviticus xxvi*: If ye do not my commandments, I will send the beasts of the field against you, who shall consume you and your flocks. And again *Deuteronomy xxxvii*: I will also send the teeth of beasts upon them, etc.

As to the question whether they are true wolves, or devils appearing in that shape, we say that they are true wolves, but are possessed by devils; and they are so roused up in two ways. It may happen without the operation of witches: and so it was in the case of the two-and-forty boys who were devoured by two bears coming out of the woods, because they mocked the prophet Elisaus, saying, Go up, thou bald head, etc. Also in the case of the lion which slew the prophet who would not perform the commandment of God (*III Kings xiii*). And it is told that a Bishop of Vienna ordered the minor Litanies to be solemnly chanted on certain days before the Feast of the Ascension, because wolves were entering the city and publicly devouring men.

But in another way it may be an illusion caused by witches. For William of Paris tells of a certain man who thought that he was turned into a wolf,† and at certain times went hiding among the caves. For there he went at a certain time, and though he remained there all the time stationary, he believed that he was a wolf which went about devouring children; and though the devil, having possessed a wolf, was really doing this, he erroneously thought that he was prowling about in his sleep. And he was for so long thus out of his senses that he was at last found lying in the wood raving. The devil delights in such things, and caused the illusion of the pagans who believed that men and old women were changed into beasts. From this it is seen that such things only happen by the permission of God alone and through the operation of devils, and not through any natural defect; since by no art or strength can such wolves be injured or captured. In this connexion also Vincent of Beauvais (in *Spec. Hist.*, VI, 40) tells that in Gaul, before the Incarnation of Christ, and before the Punic War, a wolf snatched a sentry's sword out of its sheath.

Notes

*"S. Antoninus." The famous Dominican Archbishop of Florence, born at Florence, 1 March, 1389; died 2 May, 1459. His feast day is 10 May. His chief literary work is the "Summa Theologica Moralis, partibus IV distincta," written shortly before his death, and marking a very considerable development in moral theology. Crohns in his "Die Summa theologica des Antonin von Florenz und die Schätzung des Weibes im Hexenhammer," Helsingfors, 1903, has set out to show that the very pronounced misogyny which is apparent in the "Malleus Maleficarum" can be traced to the "Summa" of S. Antoninus. But Paulus, "Die Verachtung der Frau beim hl. Antonin," in "Historisch-Politische Blätter," 1904, pp. 812–30, has severely criticized this thesis, which he declares to be untenable.

Within fifty years after the first appearance of the "Summa" of S. Antoninus, fifteen editions were printed at various important centres of learning. Many other editions followed, and in 1740 it was issued at Verona in four volumes, folio, edited by P. Ballerini; in 1741 at Florence by two Dominicans, Mamachi and Remedelli.

†"A wolf." There are two kinds of werwolves, voluntary and involuntary. The voluntary were, of course, wizards, such as Gilles Garnier, who on 18 January, 1573, was condemned by the court of Dôle, Lyons, to be burned alive for "the abominable crimes of lycanthropy and witchcraft." More than fifty witnesses deposed that he had attacked and killed children in the fields and vineyards, devouring their raw flesh. He was sometimes seen in human shape, sometimes as a "loup-garou." During the sixteenth century in France lycanthropy was very prevalent, and numerous trials clearly show that murder and cannibalism were rife in many country districts.

12.

The Discoverie of Witchcraft

REGINALD SCOT

Booke V

Chapter I

Of transformations, ridiculous examples brought by the adversaries
for the confirmation of their foolish doctrine.

Now that I may with the verie absurdities, conteined in their owne
authors, and even in their principall doctors and last writers,
confound them that mainteine the transubstantiations of witches; I will
shew you certeine proper stuffe, which Bodin (their cheefe champion
of this age) hath gathered out of M. *Mal.* and others, whereby he
laboureth to establish this impossible, incredible, and supernaturall, or
rather unnaturall doctrine of transubstantiation.

First, as touching the divell (Bodin saith) that he dooth most
properlie and commonlie transforme himselfe into a gote, confirming
that opinion by the 33. and 34. of *Esaie:* where there is no one title
sounding to anie such purpose. Howbeit, he sometimes alloweth the
divell the shape of a blacke Moore, and as he saith he used to appeare
to Mawd Cruse, Kate Darey, and Jone Harviller. But I mervell, whether
the divell createth himselfe, when he appeareth in the likenesse of a
man; or whether God createth him, when the divell wisheth it. As for
witches, he saith they speciallie transubstantiate themselves into
wolves, and then whom they bewitch into asses: though else-where he
differ somewhat herein from himselfe. But though he affirme, that it
may be naturallie brought to passe, that a girle shall become a boie;
and that anie female may be turned into the male: yet he saith the same
hath no affinitie with *Lycanthropia;* wherein he saith also, that men are
wholie transformed, and citeth infinite examples hereof.

First, that one Garner in the shape of a woolfe killed a girle of the
age of twelve yeares, and did eat up hir armes and legges, and carried

Introduced by Hugh Ross Williamson (Arundel: Centaur Press, 1964), 92–102; first
published London, 1584.

the rest home to his wife. Item, that Peter Burget, and Michael Werdon, having turned themselves with an ointment into woolves, killed, and finallie did eate up an infinite number of people. Which lie Wierus dooth sufficientlie confute. But untill you see and read that, consider whether Peter could eate rawe flesh without surfetting, speciallie flesh of his owne kind. Item, that there was an arrowe shot into a woolves thigh, who afterwards being turned into his former shape of a man, was found in his bed, with the arrowe in his thigh, which the archer that shot it knew verie well. Item, that another being *Lycanthropus* in the forme of a woolfe, had his woolves feet cut off, and in a moment he became a man without hands or feete.

He accuseth also one of the mightiest princes in christendome, even of late daies, to be one of those kind of witches (so as he could, when he list, turne himselfe to a woolfe) affirming that he was espied and oftentimes seene to performe that villanie; bicause he would be counted the king of all witches. He saith that this transubstantiation is most common in Greece, and through out all Asia, as merchant strangers have reported to him. For Anno Domini, 1542, when Sultan Solimon reigned, there was such force and multitude of these kind of woolves in Constantinople, that the emperour drave togither in one flocke 150. of them, which departed out of the citie in the presence of all the people.

To persuade us the more throughlie heerein, he saith, that in Livonia, yearelie (about the end of December) a certeine knave or divell warneth all the witches in the countrie to come to a certeine place: if they faile, the divell commeth and whippeth them with an iron rod; so as the print of his lashes remaine upon their bodies for ever. The capteine witch leadeth the waie through a great pool of water: manie millians of witches swim after. They are no sooner passed through that water, but they are all transformed into woolves, and flie upon and devoure both men, women, cattell, etc. After twelve daies they returne through the same water, and so receive humane shape againe.

Item, that there was one Bajanus a Jew, being the sonne of Simeon, which could, when he list, turne himselfe into a woolfe; and by that meanes could escape the force and danger of a whole armie of men. Which thing (saith Bodin) is woonderfull: but yet (saith he) it is much more marvelous, that men will not beleeve it. For manie poets affirme it; yea, and if you looke well into the matter (saith he) you shall find it easie to doo. Item, he saith, that as naturall woolves persecute beasts; so doo these magicall woolves devoure men, women, and children. And yet God saith to the people (I trowe) and not to the cattell of Israell: If you observe not my commandements, I will send among you the beasts of the feeld, which shall devoure both you and your cattell. Item, I will send the teeth of beasts upon you. Where is Bodins distinction now become? He never saith, I will send witches in the likenes of wolves, etc.: to devoure you or your cattell. Nevertheles, Bodin saith it is a cleare case: for the matter was disputed upon before pope Leo the seventh, and by him all these matters were judged possible: and at that time (saith he) were the transformations of Lucian and Apuleius made canonicall.

Furthermore, he saith, that through this art they are so cunning that no man can apprehend them, but when they are a sleepe. Item, he nameth another witch, that (as *M. Mal.* saith) could not be caught, bicause he would transforme himselfe into a mouse, and runne into everie little hole, till at length he was killed comming out of the hole of a jamme in a windowe: which indeed is as possible, as a camell to go through a needels eie. Item, he saith, that diverse witches at Vernon turned themselves into cats, and both committed and received much hurt. But at Argentine there was a wonderfull matter done, by three witches of great wealth, who transforming themselves into three cats, assalted a faggot-maker: who having hurt them all with a faggot sticke, was like to have beene put to death. But he was miraculouslie delivered, and they worthilie punished; as the storie saith, from whence Bodin had it.

After a great manie other such beastlie fables, he inveieth against such physicians, as saie that *Lycanthropia* is a disease, and not a transformation. Item, he mainteineth, as sacred and true, all Homers fables of Circes and Ulysses his companions: inveieng against Chrysostome, who rightlie interpreteth Homers meaning to be, that Ulysses his people were by the harlot Circes made in their brutish maners to resemble swine.

But least some poets fables might be thought lies (whereby the witchmongers arguments should quaile) he mainteineth for true the most part of Ovids *Metamorphosis*, and the greatest absurdities and impossibilities in all that booke: marie he thinketh some one tale therein may be fained. Finallie, he confirmeth all these toies by the storie of Nabuchadnez-zar. And bicause (saith he) Nabuchadnez-zar continued seven yeres in the shape of a beast, therefore may witches remaine so long in the forme of a beast; having in all the meane time, the shape, haire, voice, strength, agilitie, swiftnes, food and excrements of beasts, and yet reserve the minds and soules of women or men. Howbeit, S. Augustine (whether to confute or confirme that opinion judge you) saith; *Non est credendum, humanun corpus daemonum arte vel potestate in bestialia lineamenta converti posse:* We may not beleeve that a mans bodie may be altered into the lineaments of a beast by the divels art or power. Item, Bodin saith, that the reason whie witches are most commonlie turned into woolves, is; bicause they usuallie eate children, as woolves eate cattell. Item, that the cause whie other are truelie turned into asses, is; for that such have beene desirous to understand the secrets of witches. Whie witches are turned into cats, he alledgeth no reason, and therefore (to helpe him foorth with that paraphrase) I saie, that witches are curst queanes, and manie times scratch one another, or their neighbors by the faces; and therefore perchance are turned into cats. But I have put twentie of these witchmongers to silence with this one question; to wit, Whether a witch that can turne a woman into a cat, &c: can also turne a cat into a woman?

Chapter II

Absurd reasons brought by Bodin, and such others, for confirmation of transformations.

These Examples, and reasons might put us in doubt, that everie asse, woolfe, or cat that we see, were a man, a woman, or a child. I marvell that no man useth this distinction in the definition of a man. But to what end should one dispute against these creations and recreations; when Bodin washeth away all our arguments with one word, confessing that none can create any thing but God; acknowledging also the force of the canons, and imbracing the opinions of such divines, as write against him in this behalfe? Yea he dooth now (contrarie to himselfe elsewhere) affirme, that the divell cannot alter his forme. And lo, this is his distinction, *Non essentialis forma (id est ratio) sed figura solùm pemutatur:* The essentiall forme (to wit, reason) is not changed, but the shape or figure. And thereby he prooveth it easie enough to create men or beasts with life, so as they remaine without reason. Howbeit, I thinke it is an easier matter, to turne Bodins reason into the reason of an asse, than his bodie into the shape of a sheepe: which he saith is an easie matter; bicause Lots wife was turned into a stone by the divell. Whereby he sheweth his grosse ignorance. As though God that commanded Lot upon paine of death not to looke backe, who also destroied the citie of Sodome at that instant, had not also turned hir into a salt stone. And as though all this while God had beene the divels drudge, to go about this businesse all the night before, and when a miracle should be wrought, the divell must be faine to doo it himselfe.

Item, he affirmeth, that these kind of transfigurations are more common with them in the west parts of the world, than with us here in the east. Howbeit, this note is given withall; that that is ment of the second persons, and not of the first: to wit, of the bewitched, and not of the witches. For they can transforme themselves in everie part of the world, whether it be east, west, north, or south. Marrie he saith, that spirits and divels vex men most in the north countries, as Norway, Finland, &c: and in the westerne islands, as in the west India: but among the heathen speciallie, and wheresoever Christ is not preached. And that is true, though not in so foolish, grosse, and corporall a sense as Bodin taketh it. One notable instance of a witches cunning in this behalfe touched by Bodin in the chapter aforesaid, I thought good in this place to repeat: he taketh it out of *M Mal.* which tale was delivered to Sprenger by a knight of the Rhods, being of the order of S. Jones at Jerusalem; and it followeth thus.

Chapter III

Of a man turned into an asse, and returned againe into a man
by one of Bodins witches: S. Augustines opinion thereof.

It happened in the city of Salamin, in the kingdome of Cyprus (wherein is a good haven) that a ship loaden with merchandize staied there for a short space. In the meane time many of the souldiers and mariners went to shoare, to provide fresh victuals. Among which number, a certaine English man being a sturdie yoong fellowe, went to a womans house, a little waie out of the citie, and not farre from the sea side, to see whether she had anie egs to sell. Who perceiving him to be a lustie yoong fellowe, a stranger, and farre from his countrie (so as upon the losse of him there would be the lesse misse or inquirie) she considered with hir selfe how to destroie him; and willed him to staie there awhile, whilest she went to fetch a few egs for him. But she tarried long, so as the yoong man called unto hir, desiring hir to make hast: for he told hir that the tide would be spent, and by that meanes his ship would be gone, and leave him behind. Howbeit, after some detracting of time, she brought him a few egs, willing him to returne to hir, if his ship were gone when he came. The young fellowe returned towards his ship; but before he went aboord, hee would needs eate an eg or twaine to satisfie his hunger, and within short space he became dumb and out of his wits (as he afterwards said). When he would have entred into the ship, the mariners beat him backe with a cudgell, saieng; What a murren lacks the asse? Whither the divell will this asse? The asse or yoong man (I cannot tell by which name I should terme him) being many times repelled, and understanding their words that called him asse, considering that he could speake never a word, and yet could understand everie bodie; he thought that he was bewitched by the woman, at whose house he was. And therefore, when by no means he could get into the boate, but was driven to tarrie and see hir departure; being also beaten from place to place, as an asse; he re-membred the witches words, and the words of his owne fellowes that called him asse, and returned to the witches house, in whose service hee remained by the space of three yeares, dooing nothing with his hands all that while, but carried such burthens as she laied on his backe; having onelie this comfort, that although he were reputed as asse among strangers and beasts, yet that both this witch, and all other witches knew him to be a man.

After three yeares were passed over, in a morning betimes he went to towne before his dame; who upon some occasion (of like to make water) staied a little behind. In the meane time being neere to a church, he heard a little saccaring bell ring to the elevation of a morrowe masse, and not daring to go into the church, least he should have beene beaten and driven out with cudgels, in great devotion he fell downe in the churchyard, upon the knees of his hinder legs, and did lift his forefeet over his head, as the preest doth hold the sacrament at the elevation. Which prodigious sight when certeine merchants of Genua espied, and with woonder beheld; anon commeth the witch with a cudgell in hir hand, beating foorth the asse. And bicause (as it hath beene said) such kinds of witchcrafts are verie usuall in those parts; the merchants aforesaid made such meanes, as both the asse and the witch were attached by the judge. And she being examined and set upon the racke, confessed the whole matter, and promised, that if she might have libertie to go home, she would restore him to his old shape; and being dismissed, she did accordinglie. So as notwithstanding they apprehended hir againe, and burned hir: and the young man returned into his countrie with a joifull and merrie hart.

Upon the advantage of this storie M. *Mal*. Bodin, residue of the witchmongers triumph; and speciallie bicause S. Augustine subscribeth thereunto; or at the least to the verie like. Which I must confesse I find too common in his books, insomuch as I judge them rather to be foisted in by some fond papist or witchmonger, than so learned a mans dooings. The best is, that he himselfe is no eiewitnesse to any of those his tales; but speaketh onelie by report; wherein he uttereth these words: to wit, that it were a point of great incivilitie, &c: to discredit so manie and so certeine reports. And in that respect he justifieth the corporall transfigurations of Ulysses his mates, throgh the witchcraft of Circes: and that foolish fable of Praestantius his father, who (he saith) did eate provender and haie among other horsses, being himselfe turned into an horsse. Yea he verifieth the starkest lie that ever was invented, of the two alewives that used to transforme all their ghests into horsses, and to sell them awaie to markets and faires. And therefore I saie with Cardanus, that how much Augustin saith he hath seen with his eies, so much I am content to beleeve. Howbeit S. Augustin concludeth against Bodin. For he affirmeth these transubstantiations to be but fantasticall, and that they are not according to the veritie, but according to the appearance. And yet I cannot allow of such appearances made by witches, or yet by divels: for I find no such power given by God to any creature. And I would wit of S. Augustine, where they became, whom Bodins transformed woolves devoured. But

        . . . ô quàm

Credula mens hominis, & erectoe fabulis aures!
    Good Lord! how light of credit is
    the wavering mind of man!
    How unto tales and lies his eares
    attentive all they can?

Generall councels, and the popes canons, which Bodin so regardeth, doo condemne and pronounce his opinions in this behalfe to be absurd; and the residue of the witchmongers, with himselfe in the number, to be woorsse than infidels. And these are the verie words of the canons, which else-where I have more largelie repeated; Whosoever beleeveth, that anie creature can be made or changed into better or woorsse, or transformed into anie other shape, or into anie other similitude, by anie other than by God himselfe the creator of all things, without all doubt is an infidell, and woorsse than a pagan. And therewithall this reason is rendered, to wit: bicause they attribute that to a creature, which onelie belongeth to God the creator of all things.

Chapter IV

A summarie of the former fable, with a refutation thereof,
after due examination of the same.

Concerning the veritie or probabilitie of this enterlude, betwixt Bodin, M. Mal. the witch, the asse, the masse, the merchants, the inquisitors, the tormentors, &c: First I woonder at the miracle of transubstantiation: Secondlie at the impudencie of Bodin and James Sprenger, for affirming so grosse a lie, devised beelike by the knight of the Rhodes, to make a foole of Sprenger, and an asse of Bodin: Thirdlie, that the asse had no more wit than to kneele downe and hold up his forefeete to a peece of starch or flowre, which neither would, nor could, nor did helpe him: Fourthlie, that the masse could not reforme that which the witch transformed: Fiftlie, that the merchants, the inquisitors, and the tormentors, could not either severallie or jointlie doo it, but referre the matter to the witches courtesie and good pleasure.

But where was the young mans owne shape all these three yeares, wherein he was made an asse? It is a certeine and a generall rule, that two substantiall formes cannot be in one subject *Simul & semel*, both at once: which is confessed by themselves. The forme of the beast occupied some place in the aire and so I thinke should the forme of a man doo also. For to bring the bodie of a man, without feeling, into such a thin airie nature, as that it can neither be seene or felt, it may well be unlikelie, but it is verie impossible: for the aire is inconstant, and continueth not in one place. So as this airie creature would soone be carried into another region: as else-where I have largelie prooved. But indeed our bodies are visible, sensitive, and passive, and are indued with manie other excellent properties, which all the divels in hell are not able to alter: neither can one haire of our head perish, or fall awaie, or be transformed, without the speciall providence of God almightie.

But to proceed unto the probabilitie of this storie. What lucke was it, that this yoong fellow of England, landing so latelie in those parts, and that old woman of Cyprus, being both of so base a condition, should both understand one anothers communication; England and Cyprus being so manie hundred miles distant, and their languages so farre differing? I am sure in these daies, wherein trafficke is more used, and learning in more price; few yong or old mariners in this realme can either speake or understand the language spoken at Salamin in Cyprus, which is a kind of Greeke; and as few old women there can speake our language. But Bodin will saie; You heare, that at the inquisitors commandement, and through the tormentors correction, she promised to restore him to his owne shape: and so she did, as being thereunto compelled. I answer, that as the whole storie is an impious fable; so this assertion is false, and disagreeable to their owne doctrine, which mainteineth, that the witch dooth nothing but by the permission and leave of God. For if she could doo or undoo such a thing at hir owne pleasure, or at the commandement of the inquisitors, or for feare of the tormentors, or for love of the partie, or for remorse of conscience: then is it not either by the extraordinarie leave, nor yet by the like direction of God; except you will make him a confederate with old witches. I for my part woonder most, how they can turne and tosse a mans bodie so, and make it smaller and greater, to wit, like a mowse, or like an asse, &c: and the man all this while to feele no paine. And I am not alone in this maze: for Danaeus a special mainteiner of their follies saith, that although Augustine and Apuleius doo write verie crediblie of these matters; yet will he never beleeve, that witches can change men into other formes; as asses, apes, wooolves, beares, mice, &c.

Chapter V

That the bodie of a man cannot be turned into the bodie of a beast by a witch, is prooved by strong reasons, scriptures, and authorities.

But was this man an asse all this while? Or was this asse a man? Bodin saith (his reason onelie reserved) he was trulie transubstantiated into an asse; so as there must be no part of a man, but reason remaining in this asse. And yet Hermes Trismegistus thinketh he hath good authoritie and reason to saie; *Aliud corpus quàm humanum non capere animam humanam; nec fas esse in corpus animae ratione carentis animam rationalem corruere;* that is; An humane soule cannot receive anie other than an humane bodie, nor yet canne light into a bodie that wanteth reason of mind. But S. James saith; the bodie without the spirit is dead. And surelie, when the soule is departed from the bodie, the life of man is dissolved: and therefore Paule wished to be dissolved, when he would have beene with Christ. The bodie of man is subject to divers kinds of agues, sicknesses, and infirmities, whereunto an asses bodie is not inclined: and mans bodie must be fed with bread, &c: and not with hay. Bodins asseheaded man must either eat haie, or nothing: as appeareth in the storie. Mans bodie also is subject unto death, and hath his daies numbred. If this fellowe had died in the meane time, as his houre might have beene come, for anie thing the divels, the witch, or Bodin knew; I mervell then what would have become of this asse, or how the witch could have restored him to shape, or whether he should have risen at the daie of judgement in an asses bodie and shape. For Paule saith, that that verie bodie which is sowne and buried a naturall bodie, is raised a spirituall bodie. The life of Jesus is made manifest in our mortall flesh, and not in the flesh of an asse.

God hath endued everie man and everie thing with his proper nature, substance, forme, qualities, and gifts, and directeth their waies. As for the waies of an asse, he taketh no such care: howbeit, they have also their properties and substance severall to themselves. For there is one flesh (saith Paule) of men, another flesh of beasts, another of fishes, another of birds. And therefore it is absolutelie against the ordinance of God (who hath made me a man) that I should flie like a bird, or swim like a fish, or creepe like a worme, or become an asse in shape: insomuch as if God would give me leave, I cannot doo it; for it were contrarie to his owne order and decree, and to the constitution of anie bodie which he hath made. Yea the spirits themselves have their lawes and limits prescribed, beyond the which they cannot passe one haires breadth; otherwise God should be contrarie to himselfe: which is farre from him. Neither is Gods omnipotence hereby qualified, but the divels importencie manifested, who hath none other power, but that which God from the beginning hath appointed unto him, conso-nant to his nature and substance. He may well be restreined from his power and will, but beyond the same he cannot passe, as being Gods minister, no further but in that which he hath from the beginning enabled him to doo: which is, that he being a spirit, may with Gods leave and ordinance viciat and corrupt the spirit and will of man: wherein he is verie diligent.

What a beastlie assertion is it, that a man, whom GOD hath made according to his owne similitude and likenes, should be by a witch turned into a beast? What an impietie is it to affirme, that an asses bodie is the temple of the Holy-ghost? Or an asse to be the child of God, and God to be his father; as it is said of man? Which Paule to the Corinthians so divinelie confuteth, who saith, that Our bodies are the members of Christ. In the which we are to glorifie God: for the bodie is for the Lord, and the Lord is for the bodie. Surelie he meaneth not for an asses bodie, as by this time I hope appeareth: in such wise as Bodin, may go hide him for shame; especiallie when he shall understand, that even into these our bodies, which God hath framed after his owne likenesse, he hath also brethed that spirit, which Bodin saith is now remaining within an asses bodie, which God hath so subjected in such servilitie under the foote of man; Of whom God is so mindfull, that he hath made him little lower than angels, yea than himselfe, and crowned him with glorie and worship, and made him to have dominion over the workes of his hands, as having put all things under his feete, all sheepe and oxen, yea woolves, asses, and all other beasts of the field, the foules of the aire, the fishes of the sea, &c. Bodins poet, Ovid, whose *Metamorphosis*, make so much for him, saith to the overthrow of this phantasticall imagination:

> *Os homini sublime dedit, coelúmque videre*
> *Jussit, & erectos ad sydera tollere vultus.*
>> The effect of which verses is this;
>> The Lord did set mans face so hie,
>> That he the heavens might behold,
>> And looke up to the starrie skie,
>> To see his woonders manifold.

Now, if a witch or a divell can so alter the shape of a man, as contrarilie to make him looke downe to hell, like a beast; Gods works should not onelie be defaced and disgraced, but his ordinance should be woonderfullie altered, and thereby confounded.

Chapter VI

The witchmongers objections, concerning Nabuchadnez-zar answered,
and their errour concerning *Lycanthropia* confuted.

Malleus Maleficarum, Bodin, and manie other of them that mainteine witchcraft, triumph upon the storie of Nabuchadnez-zar; as
though Circes had transformed him with her sorceries into an oxe, as
she did others into swine, &c. I answer, that he was neither in bodie
nor shape transformed at all, according to their grosse imagination; as
appeareth both by the plaine words of the text, and also by the opinions of the best interpretors thereof: but that he was, for his beastlie
government and conditions, throwne out of his kingdome and banished for a time, and driven to hide himselfe in the wildernesse, there
in exile to lead his life in beastlie sort, among beasts of the field, and
fowle of the aire (for by the waie I tell you it appeareth by the text, that
he was rather turned into the shape of a fowle than of a beast) untill he
rejecting his beastlie conditions, was upon his repentance and amend-
ment called home, and restored unto his kingdome. Howbeit, this (by
their confession) was neither divels nor witches dooing; but a miracle
wrought by God, whom alone I acknowledge to be able to bring to
passe such workes at his pleasure. Wherein I would know what our
witchmongers have gained.

I am not ignorant that some write, that after the death of
Nabuchadnez-zar, his sonne Eilumorodath gave his bodie to the ravens
to be devoured, least afterwards his father should arise from death,
who of a beast became a man againe. But this tale is meeter to have
place in the Cabalisticall art, to wit: among unwritten verities than
here. To conclude, I saie that the transformations, which these witchmongers doo so rave and rage upon, is (as all the learned sort of
physicians affirme) a disease proceeding partlie from melancholie,
wherebie manie suppose themselves to be woolves, or such ravening
beasts. For Lycanthropia is of the ancient physicians called *Lupina
melancholia,* or *Lupina insania.* J. Wierus declareth verie learnedlie, the
cause, the circumstance, and the cure of this disease. I have written the
more herein; bicause hereby great princes and potentates, as well as
poore women and innocents, have beene defamed and accounted
among the number of witches.

13.

Men-Woolfes

JAMES I OF ENGLAND

*f*or there is nothing in the bodies of the faithfull, more worthie of honour, or freer from corruption by nature, nor in these of the unfaithful, while time they be purged and glorified in the latter daie, as is dailie seene by the vilde diseases and corruptions, as yee will see clearelie proved, when I speake of the possessed and Daemoniacques.

PHI: Yet there are sundrie that affirmes to have haunted such places, where these spirites are alleaged to be: And coulde never heare nor see anie thing.

EPI: I thinke well: For that is onelie reserved to the secreete knowledge of God, whom he will permit to see such thinges, and whome not.

PHI: But where these spirites hauntes and troubles anie houses, what is the best waie to banishe them?

EPI: By two meanes may onelie the remeid of such things be procured: The one is ardent prayer to God, both of these persones that are troubled with them, and of that Church whereof they are. The other is the purging of themselves by amendement of life from such sinnes, as have procured that extraordinarie plague.

PHI: And what meanes then these kindes of spirites, when they appeare in the shaddow of a person newlie dead, or to die, to his friendes?

EPI: When they appeare upon that occasion, they are called Wraithes in our language. Amongst the Gentiles the Devill used that much, to make them beleeve that it was some good spirite that appeared to them then, ether to forewarne them of the death of their friend; or else to

Daemonologie (Edinburgh, 1597) 60–62.

discover unto them, the will of the defunct, or what was the way of his slauchter, as is written in the booke of the histories Prodigious. And this way hee easelie deceived the Gentiles, because they knew not God: And to that same effect is it, that he now appeares in that maner to some ignorant Christians. For he dare not so illude anie that knoweth that, neither can the spirite of the defunct returne to his friend, or yet an Angell use such formes.

PHI: And are not our war-woolfes one sorte of these spirits also, that hauntes and troubles some houses or dwelling places?

EPI: There hath indeed bene an old opinion of such like thinges; For by the Greekes they were called *lykanthropoi* which signifieth menwoolfes. But to tell you simplie my opinion in this, if anie such thing hath bene, I take it to have proceeded but of a naturall super-abundance of Melancholie, which as wee reade, that it hath made some thinke themselves Pitchers, and some horses, and some one kinde of beast or other: So suppose I that it hath so viciat the imagination and memorie of some, as *per lucida intervalla*, it hath so highlie occupied them, that they have thought themselves verrie Woolfes indeede at these times: and so have counterfeited their actiones in goeing on their handes and feete, preassing to devoure women and barnes, fighting and snatching with all the towne dogges, and in using such like other bruitish actiones, and so to become beastes by a strong apprehension, as Nebucad-netzar was seven yeares: but as to their having and hyding of their hard & schellie sloughes, I take that to be but eiked, by uncertaine report, the author of all lyes.

14

Spirits and Devils

JOHN DEACON and JOHN WALKER

𝕴f spirits and divels can truely and essentially transforme themselves into true naturall bodies: or but change themselves into the true shapes and formes of such bodies. And, this (I beleeve) doth break the very neck of those your supposed transformations of spirits and divels whatsoever.

Lycanthropus: This that you say is undoubtedly true, and yet still me thinke the divell should have power, so to transforme himselfe, either in substance, or appearance at least: although I my selfe am unable to render any one reason thereof.

Orthodoxus: It is verie ridiculous (saith one) for a man to leave manifest things, and such as even by naturall reason may soundly be prooved: and so, to seeke after unknowen things, which, by no likelyhood may be conceived, nor yet tried out by any rule of reason: but,

Good Lord, how light of credit is the wavering minde of man?
How unto lies and tales, his eares attentive all they can?

Lycanthropus: Good maister *Orthodoxus?* I am drawn (by the very force of your speech) into a marvelous perplexitie. For when I examine the weight of your reasons propounded, I am driven to denie the transformation of spirits and devils; but, so soone as I returne to the necessarie consideration of my present distressed estate, then, that former new-bredde conceit is cut in the necke, and squashed quite.

Orthodoxus: And why so I praie you?

Lycanthopus: Surely sir, because I my selfe am essentially transformed into a woolfe: I make no question, but that devils can also substantially change themselves into any true naturall bodie.

Dialogicall Discourses of Spirits and Divels (London, 1601), 158–62.

Orthodoxus: Verie true as you say: the one is every way as possible as is the other.

Lycanthropus: Why, then alas, the Lord be mercifull to us: for what man in the world may possiblie be free from their malice?

Philologus: How now *Lycanthropus*, are you indeed in good earnest? doe you verilie imagine you are essentially transformed into a woolfe? now surely, this is the oddest jest that ever I heard.

Lycanthropus: Nay, nay (alas) it passeth a jest: for I finde it and feele it to be true by experience.

Physiologus: Well said Lycanthropus, now I perceive your name was not given you for nought: it being so proportionablie answerable to your phantasticall nature. You are called *Lycanthropus*: that is, a man transformed to a woolfe: which name is verie fitlie derived from the verie disease it selfe that disorders your braine, called *Lycanthropia*. Which worde, some Physitions do translate *Daemonium Lupinum*, that is, a woolvish Demoniacke: others *Lupina melancholica*, and *Lupina insania*, that is a woolvish melancholie, or a woolvish furie and madnes. And it is nothing else in effect, but an infirmitie arising upon such phantasticall imaginations, as do mightily disorder and trouble the braine.

Lycanthropus: An infirmitie say you? It is a verie strange and fearefull infirmitie, that can so essentially transforme a man into a verie naturall woolfe? God blesse every good man from such kind of infirmities.

Physiologus: Had you lived in such a time, as beasts, and beares and woolves were supposed to speake like men: it had beene an easie matter (I perceive) to persuade you that you are a woolfe.

Lycanthropus: Yea, but how are you able to persuade me the contrarie?

Physiologus: That may easily be done, by describing briefly unto you, the verie true nature of that the aforesaid diseases, which so fearefully affecteth your minde, with these phantasticall imaginations and fond conceits.

Lycanthropus: I praie you then describe it plainly unto me.

Physiologus: With verie good will. Wherein you must principally consider, that the verie first matter which causeth *Lycanthropie,* or this woolvish Demoniacke: consisteth in the very selfesame matter of stuffe that maketh in any other man else, a melancholike humour, for either of both are melancholike persons. Howbeit, the peculiar cause it selfe which more especially procureth *Lycanthropie,* is either that kinde of melancholy which ariseth properly of *choler adust:* or that which comes of a simple and naturall melancholie. Sometimes also it proceedes of an impostume of bloud in the braine: but verie seldome of bloud adust. Now then, that Lycanthropie which ariseth onely of the abundance of a simple melancholie, as it is (for the most part) the verie woorst of all, & therefore is called *Lupina insania,* a woolvish furie or madnes: so is it commonly seated in the exteriour parts of the braine, and hath an operation not unlike to the matter of a disease, called *Karabitus,* which is a hotte impostume of the head, seated in the verie ventricle of the braine it selfe, causing *choller adust,* and the melancholike matter verie much to abound. Whose vaporous humors (vitiating and corrupting the braine,) doe procure the patient unto a verie deepe sleepe. Wherein his phantasie is fearefully troubled with the dailie impression of such fearefull and strange imaginations as do cause the interiour spirits of the braine to waxe verie wilde and fearfull: by reason of those blacke and cloudie representations: which were received before in the phantasie. And heereof it is, that some unskilfull Physitions, do so rashly ascribe this humorous disease to the operation of the divell: and that the ignorant people do absurdly imagine the partie thus affected, to be undoubtedly possessed of devils. Howbeit, they should certeinly know, that a cholerike humour (so soone as an extreme adustion affecteth the same) is foorthwith converted to furie or madnes: neither is it then satisfied with an onely simple melancholike affection. This disease, it hapneth to men especially in Autumne through the malitiousnes of the humors abounding, and eftsoones is encreased in the spring, & in summer: yea, & it is then the extreamest of all when the north-winde blowes, by reason of the drines [dryness] thereof. The signes that commonly fall foorth in the beginning of this disease, are these, namely, strange conceits and feares, a pronesse to anger: the partie affecting solitarinesses, having a fearefull swimming and turning about of the braine. Howbeit, when the disease is once growne to perfection: then there folowes verie fearefull and strange effects. For, some are afraide the heavens will overwhelme them forthwith: some feare the earth will swallow them quicke: some stand in continuall dread of theeves: and others againe, that woolves will enter into them. Some imagine themselves to be divels, birds, and vessels of earth: yea, and that they be truely transformed into woolves, and therefore they do counterfeit their voices, & wander about in the fields. This undoubtedly is your present disease: & this is that which makes you so resolute concerning the supposed possession of spirits and divels. All which you may plainely perceive, is nothing else in effect, but a phantasticall conceit, occasioned only upon those disordered humours which hurt and trouble your braine. That which any further concerneth the nature, the causes, the circumstances, and cure of *Lycanthropie*: you may see more at large in Wierus his workes.

Lycanthropus: This is very strange I assure you, and more then ever I heard: albeit I have felt the experience thereof in my selfe.

Physiologus: Not so strange as true: and therefore, forsake your folly in time.

Orthodoxus: I pray you hartely doe so, and that so much the rather: by how much the divel (in working upon that disordered humour) will be ready eftsoones to abuse you afresh. In consideration whereof, I will shew you what the Ancyran councell and others have carefully decreed against such humerous persons, saying thus. Wereas certeine gracelesse women (seduced wholly by satans illusions) doe verely imagine themselves (for certeine howers in the night) to be riding upon woolves and beasts with Diana the pagane Goddesse, and to passe through sundry countries: through which erronious conceite, they (being grossly abused) doe verely beleeve those things to be true, yea, and (in beleeving the same) do fearefully straggle from the true saving faith. It appertaineth therefore to the ministers (in every their severall churches) to publish and confute the falshood hereof: and withall, to strengthen the minds of their people against every such phantasticall and fond illusion of satan. Who eftsoones assailing the minds of humerous women, and (through infidelity) coupling them sure to him-

selfe, deludes their said minds with dreames and visions: making them
sometimes mery, and sometimes sad: shewing them sundry persons,
both knowne and unknown: yea, and leading them dangerous bie-
waies to their owne destruction. Thus you see the councels decree
against these roving conceites, wherewith yourselfe (at this present) is
fearefullie tainted: and therefore, forethinke you thereof in time.

Lycanthropus: Are there then no essentiall transformations at all?

Orthodoxus: No verily, whatsoever they seeme in shewe, they are but
illusions and sleights of the divel to deceive: and therefore (I advise
you to winde your selfe from them with speede, for feare of a further
mischiefe. And, because you shall not imagine this councell I give, to
be but a dreaming devise of my owne: therefore, (besides that which
was spoken before) I will yet further make knowen unto you, how
generall councels, many good writers, yea, and the Popes owne canons
do all jointly condemne and pronounce this peevish opinion concerning the supposed transformation of divels, to be impious, absurd and
divellish, and the maintainers thereof to be woorse then Infidels, saying thus: Whosoever beleeveth that any one creature can be made or
changed into better or woorse, or to be transformed into any other
shape, or into any other similitude, by any other then by God himselfe
the creator of all things: without doubt, he is but an Infidell, and
woorse then a Pagane. And therewithall, this reason is rendred. Because (say they) they doe therein attribute that power to a creature:
which onely belongeth to God the creator of all things. By this you
may plainely perceive, of what reckoning these your supposed transformations have beene in former times.

Philologus: Lycanthropus? Your opinion (it appeareth) is plainely condemned of all: and therefore, forsake it for shame.

Lycanthropus: So I do I assure you: praising the Lord with all my hart,
for bringing me thus to behold the folly thereof: yea, and am hartely
sory, for being bewitched therewith so long, being also ashamed now
of my odious name.

SECTION IV
Critical Essays on Lycanthropy

Introduction

𝕴f lycanthropy were only a stale memory in the racial consciousness, it would not be attracting the attention of anthropologists, historians, medical historians, and others. Two papers on werewolves were read at a conference in 1976 of the Folklore Society of Great Britain and of the Department of Sociology of the University of Reading. H. R. Ellis Davidson, whose essay is included in the *Reader*, focused on "Shape-Changing in the Old Norse Sagas," and W. M. S. Russell and Claire Russell researched "The Social Biology of Werewolves."

Davidson, approaching Norse sagas from the standpoint of narratology, concludes that the sagas reveal the "complex relationship between myth, magic ritual and folktales, and how the existence of all three could keep alive the sense of a close relationship between man and animal."

Many strains of werewolf lore can be detected in the Norse sagas. There is a fascination with the power, swiftness, cunning, and valor of wolves; there is a transfer of those qualities to warriors (especially kings' sons) who put on wolfskins in order to sustain courage in battle (and sometimes after battle cannot remove the wolfskins); there are girdles and belts and magic ointments as instruments of transformation; there are spirits who leave human bodies and enter into wolves while the human body remains in a trance; there are dreams of animal guardians; there are wolf names that charm and defy the forces of evil. Obviously, there is a blending of many elements in the werewolf folklore, and the werewolf emerges as a paradoxical figure who can be benevolent as well as malevolent, a symbol and a symptom, a nudge into reality or an escape from it.

Although the werewolf element in folklore can be explained on an elementary level—animals and humans in early Norse civilization lived in close proximity and both were threatening to each other—on the deeper levels of myth the elemental clash between good and evil (both external and internal to humans) is expressed. The shape-changing may indicate that evil was not always regarded as external: that humans in the shape of wolves were responsible for the terrorizings in their communities. On the other hand, the shape-changing can indicate the need to acquire strength and courage from an animal noted for both those traits and can prove a stimulant to the heroic.

The Russells, on the other hand, look for origins and valid explanations in a non-mystical reading of lycanthropy. They begin with historical events which focus on the werewolf; from an analysis of these historically verified events, they make rational judgments and draw conclusions.

Dividing their survey into wolves, humans, and human-wolves, they place actual wolves in a sociological context. Marauding wolves that attacked and destroyed cattle and ravaged villages can be accounted for as starving or as suffering from rabies. The terror which these wolves struck in the hearts of humans is reflected in the accounts. Turning to trial records, the authors analyze humans who were apprehended for mass murders and cannibalism, and offer several explanations, including hunger, sadism, and pathological states induced by hallucinogens and inadvertent poisoning by ergot. As for werewolf epidemics and trials in the historical records, the authors regard these as evidence of "two successive crises of overpopulation."[1] In this approach the werewolf has been demythologized.

The historians who appear in this section of the *Reader* approach lycanthropy in two different ways: Monter's approach is through comparative analyses (internal and external), Clark's is through philosophical and scientific arguments. Monter works with regional statistics, with an examination of trial records, judicial theory, theological treatises, and religious distribution of the population; Clark works with "epistemological puzzles" raised in the basic demonological treatises.

Monter's essay examines popular and official demonology. Monter provides information on the number of treatises on lycanthropy that appeared in a given period; for example, between 1595 and 1615 "treatises on lycanthropy were written by a monk, a nobleman, and a physician"; after 1650 nine works on lycanthropy appeared in the Holy Roman Empire, but in Switzerland and France no further works on lycanthropy appeared.

Monter concludes that Protestant demonologists battled both judicial and popular opinion and they "got results, at least among judges of their religion." The trials of werewolves in the Protestant areas which Monter studied became as extinct as werewolves themselves.

Re-examining assumptions about natural processes, the occult, and witchcraft, Clark attempts to get into the mind of the Renaissance. His survey of the writing of the demonologists and his philosophical analysis of the underlying assumptions of these treatises show how essential it is for the twentieth century to reshape its questions about demons, the occult, witchcraft, werewolves, and nature in the Renaissance.

Clark's approach is through epistemology: How do we know? How do we perceive? And how did the thinkers of the Renaissance know the natural, the preternatural, the supernatural? And how did they perceive natural, preternatural, supernatural phenomena?

Clark cites Francis Bacon to illustrate the need to understand how a seventeenth-century scientist could use aberrations in nature to understand nature; could use speculation on the preternatural or supernatural to understand the natural:

> Neither am I of opinion in this history of marvels, that superstitious narratives of sorceries, witchcrafts, charms, dreams, divinations, and the like, where there is an assurance and clear evidence of the fact, should be altogether excluded. For it is not yet known in what cases, and how far, effects attributed to superstition participate of natural causes; and therefore howsoever the use and practice of such arts is to be condemned, yet from the speculation and consideration of them (if they be diligently unravelled) a useful light may be gained, not only for the true judgment of the offences of persons charged with such practices, but likewise for the further disclosing of the secrets of nature.

Clark concludes with a whole new set of questions: "The question we have to ask, therefore, is not the one prompted by rationalism (Why were intelligent men able to accept so much that was supernatural?), but simply the one prompted by the history of science (What concept of nature did they share?)." He calls for a reconsideration of "the validity of these phenomena and of the criteria for understanding them."

The medical historians in this section of the *Reader* are both working with hypotheses: Illis with congenital porphyria as a diagnostic option for lycanthropy, and Estes with the medical revolution in the Renaissance as a factor in promoting witchcraft as a diagnostic entity in mental illness.

Illis's detailed description of the symptoms of porphyria allows him to draw the following conclusions about lycanthropy:

> such a person, because of photosensitivity and the resultant dis-
> figurement, may choose only to wander about at night. The pale,
> yellowish, excoriated skin may be explained by the haemolytic
> anaemia, jaundice, and pruritus. These features, together with
> hypertrichosis and pigmentation, fit well with the descriptions, in
> older literature, of werewolves. The unhappy person may be men-
> tally disturbed, and show some type or degree of abnormal be-
> haviour. In ancient times this would be accentuated by the phys-
> ical and social treatment he received from the other villagers,
> whose instincts would be to explain the apparition in terms of
> witchcraft or Satanic possession.

Estes suggests that the new intellectual forms that medicine was taking in the Renaissance could not account for widespread mental illness:

> Yet the increasing attention that the medical profession was pay-
> ing to specific pathological states, linked with the inability of
> medical theory to expand or change fast enough to provide ade-
> quate explanations for all of the new facts that were emerging,
> meant that the individual physician would certainly encounter
> many ailments whose symptomatology was so unusual or so irreg-
> ular that he could not offer an intelligible remedy. . . . Fernell
> argued, and most physicians for the next century followed him in
> this . . . that such diseases had an unnatural or supernatural
> cause, and were probably the result of the intervention of the
> Devil.

On the basis of this hypothesis, physicians, by relegating lycanthropy (as a form of witchcraft) to the realm of the supernatural, could legitimately abandon the impossible search for a medical cure.

Notes

1. W. M. S. Russell and Claire Russell, "The Social Biology of Werewolves," in *Animals in Folklore,* edited by J. R. Porter and W. M. S. Russell (London: Published by D. S. Brewer, Ltd., and Totowa: Rowman & Littlefield for the Folklore Society, 1978), 163–64, 166–67.

Shape-changing in the Old Norse Sagas

H. R. ELLIS DAVIDSON

It is impossible to get very far in the study of Old Norse literature without meeting the phenomenon of the change from human to animal shape. In the myths, stories and poems, men and women appear in animal form, and gods and goddesses manifest themselves in the shape of animals, birds and fishes, while the art of the pre-Christian period is full of animal symbolism, and gives some evidence for the use of animal masks and of men in animal disguises. Faced with so much and such varied material, the problem is where to begin.

It might be as well to start with words. In Old Icelandic the word *hamr*, 'shape', can be used for an animal skin, the wings and feathers of a bird, and also for a non-human shape assumed by someone with special powers. A man with supernatural gifts may be called *hamrammr*, 'shape-strong', while the verb *hamask* means to fall into a state of wild fury, an animal rage, and one in such a state may be called *hamslauss*, 'out of his shape'. We find also the word *hamhleypa*, 'shape-leaper', 'leaper out of his skin', used of someone with powers of magic, and in later times for a man with unusual powers of energy and strength. It is said in *Eyrbyggja Saga* 61 that a certain individual was *eigi einhamr*, 'not of one shape', until he was converted to Christianity. Particularly interesting is the term *hamfarir* (in the plural), 'shape-journeys', used in the sagas to denote the sending out of the spirit in animal form while the man's body rests in a state of sleep or trance. The use of these terms indicates that magic powers and powers beyond the ordinary were associated in some way with a change of form and possibly with the taking on of animal shape, but it is not easy to know how far this is metaphorical use of language and how far belief in an actual change of appearance is involved.

These terms come from Icelandic literature, since nearly all early

In *Animals in Folklore*, edited by J. R. Porter and W. M. S. Russell (London: Published by D. S. Brewer, Ltd., and Totowa: Rowman & Littlefield for the Folklore Society, 1978), 126–42, 258–59. Copyright © 1978 by H. R. Ellis Davidson.

Norse material from about the eleventh century onwards comes from Iceland. The sources of this may be native oral tradition, or tales brought in from abroad and retold in Iceland, or written sources in Latin or other languages introduced after the conversion. The Icelanders accepted Christianity in the year AD 1000, and their written literature must therefore be later than this, since it is derived from manuscripts produced in monasteries; nevertheless it may include material current before the conversion, since the Icelanders were immensely proud of the early traditions from what they regarded as an heroic period and a golden age, and they were anxious to preserve them. All this has to be borne in mind in attempting to assess ideas about magic in the Icelandic sagas. Moreover the Icelandic storytellers were so skilful in welding together their diverse material that it is no easy task to detect the source of inspiration behind any particular episode. There is a rich background of mixed tradition behind the tales of shape-changers which seem so spontaneous and naive, and I want to suggest what some of the main influences behind them may be.

Animals which play a part in shape-changing stories are bears, wolves, walrus and pigs, and occasionally cattle, goats, dogs and fishes. An example of how vigorous and yet how elusive such accounts may be is a story from the saga of Hrolf kraki, an early king of Denmark. This belongs to a group known as sagas of old-time, or 'lying sagas', and is a tale based on old heroic traditions skilfully retold, popular folklore, and strange happenings set in the pagan past. The central figure is not so much King Hrolf—who like King Arthur collected many celebrated champions around him—but one of his loyal followers, Bodvar Biarki. Bodvar's father Biorn had been changed into a bear by a wicked stepmother when he rejected her advances, and he was finally hunted to his death by men and dogs. During his time as a bear, he was able to resume his human form at night, and a girl called Bera joined him in his cave. Before he was killed he warned her never to eat bear's flesh, but the wicked queen forced her to swallow a mouthful. Bera bore three sons at a birth after Biorn's death; the first was half man and half elk; the second had dog's feet; and the third was Bodvar Biarki, who at first appeared wholly human. But when the time came for King Hrolf to fight his final battle against overwhelming odds, since he was being attacked by evil supernatural powers, Bodvar showed that he too had characteristics beyond the ordinary. He was unaccountably missing from the forefront of the battle, but a wonderful event took place there: [1]

> Men saw that a great bear went before King Hrolf's men, keeping always near the king. He slew more men with his forepaw than any five of the king's champions. Blades and weapons glanced off him, and he brought down both men and horses in King Hjorvard's forces, and everything which came in his path he crushed to death with his teeth, so that panic and terror swept through King Hjorvard's army. . . .

Meanwhile Bodvar's friend Hjalti had gone to look for him, and when he found the champion sitting motionless in his tent, he railed on him for his desertion of the king in time of need. At last Bodvar rose and went out, saying that now he could help the king far less than he could have done had he been left where he was. When he reached the battlefield, the bear had gone, and from this point the tide of battle turned against Hrolf and his followers, and they went down fighting round their king. This powerful image of a mighty bear wreaking terror and destruction upon an army has recently been used again with great effect in Richard Adams' novel *Shardik.*

The implication here is clear: Bodvar fights in bear form while his body remains motionless in his tent. The battle in which he fought was one famous in Danish heroic tradition, and we have an account of it by Saxo Grammaticus in Latin, written at the beginning of the thirteenth century, based apparently on an old poem *Biarkamál,* of which some Icelandic fragments survive. It seems that Biarki (the name used by Saxo) was the original one borne by the hero, and Bodvar (*bǫð,* a poetic word for battle) was really a nickname: he was the Biarki of battle, that is, a warrior. [2] There is however no indication that Saxo knew the story of the bear, or that this came into the original poem. Biarki means Little Bear, while Biorn, his father's name, means Bear, and Bera, his mother's name, She-Bear. The story of his birth in the saga indeed follows a well-established folktale pattern, that of the Bear Mother. [3]

The story is that of a human girl who becomes the wife of a bear, and whose children are half bear and half human, and are thus able to form a link between man and the animal world. The Lapp Turi, whose account of his own people and their beliefs was written down in 1910, clearly knew of such a tale, at least in an incomplete form:[4]

> I have heard that there was once a girl who spent a whole winter in a bear's house . . . and she slept very well through the winter . . . and the bear was a he-bear and he got the girl with child. And the child was a boy, and its one hand was a bear's paw, and the other a human hand, and the one hand he never left uncovered. And once a man wanted him to show it to him, although he said that he could not show it because it was dangerous. But the man didn't believe him and insisted . . . And when he had uncovered it for the man, then he couldn't control himself, but tore the man's face to pieces. And then folk saw that it was true, what he said about his hand.

In the seventeenth century Edward Topsell, in his delightful *Historie of Fourefooted Beastes*[5] refers to a tale which a man from Constance 'did most confidently tell' to him, of a bear in the mountains of Savoy which carried off a young girl to his den. He brought apples each day for her to eat, and treated her very lovingly; in the end she was rescued by her parents, but there is no mention of children born of the union, or of whether the bear was killed. The tale is indeed found as far away as Mongolia, and is also illustrated on totem poles and carvings made at the end of the last century by American Indian artists, some of whose names are known, among tribes on the north Pacific coast and in the northern Rockies.[6] In this region the tale is a myth, told to account for the origin of the bear-hunting ritual. It was said that after the father bear had been killed, the children of the bear mother taught the hunters of the tribe how to catch bears, and how to sing the correct dirges over those which they killed. Barbeau published a number of these carvings, which show great skill and powerful imaginative treatment; some had spread to areas like Queen Charlotte Island, where there were no bears. He claimed that the tradition must have reached North America from eastern Asia. His examples remind us of the complex relationship between myth, magic ritual and folktales, and how the existence of all three could keep alive the sense of a close relationship between man and animal. When the hunting magic no longer retains its power, and the bear becomes a creature remote from the life of the community, the traditions finally degenerate into tales for children.

The bear was the most powerful and dangerous animal in the Scandinavian north, likely to leave a vivid impression on those who hunted him for food. Bearskins were evidently used as something on which the dead could be laid, or perhaps wrapped round them in the grave, as is shown by traces of the claws surviving in graves in Norway and Sweden in the period before the Viking Age.[7] Snorri Sturluson in the introduction to the *Prose Edda* has a reference to the youthful Thor proving his strength by lifting 12 bearskins from the ground at once; this may be no more than a simple trial of physical prowess, but it is unlikely to have arisen in a purely Icelandic context, and the association with the young god is interesting. In a search for traces of initiation ceremonial in the Icelandic sagas, Mary Danielli[8] quotes a number of tales where the hero has to encounter a bear as proof of his manhood; in one of these a youth wears a bearskin cloak until he comes back with the bear's snout to prove that he has overcome it; in another the fur cloak is thrown at the bear by the leader of a band of men 'testing' the young hero, and he has to recover it and to cut off the bear's paw. Moreover in several of the stories the company of men (sometimes specified as berserks) is twelve in number, and the leader is called Biorn; it is therefore possible that the twelve bearskins lifted by Thor have some special significance, and that behind such confused traditions lies the memory of testing young warriors entering a company of berserks by arranging an encounter with a bear, real or simulated, and that the warriors put on bearskins for such ceremonies.

Among the Lapps in later times we know that the bear was honoured by special names and elaborate ceremonies, which have been well recorded in a number of different regions.[9] The word *saivo* used of a slain bear is the same as that used for the spirits of men who have died, and at the bear-feast it may be noted that the hunter who had killed the bear put on the head and skin of the dead animal.[10] There was a well-established custom also of drinking the blood of the bear, in order to obtain something of its strength and courage.[11] Such practices form a promising basis for tales of shape-changing between men and bears. Those who have studied the bear cult among the Lapps and other northern peoples emphasize that it was the enormous strength of the animal and its strange habits which distinguished it from other wild beasts, above all the ability to survive the winter without food, which caused wonder, and made the bear specially revered by those who hunted it. Although highly dangerous and a formidable adversary, the bear was not thought to be an evil beast, like the wolf. Its flesh was of great benefit to men, and many parts of the body, especially the fat, were believed to possess special powers of healing. It was felt to have a close link with men, partly because of its tendency to rear itself on its hind legs, and to strike a victim with its forepaw, or to hug him to death; its footprints resembled those of men, and it was thought to look like a human being when skinned. [12] It was also felt that the bear had no natural antagonism towards human beings. To quote again from Turi: [13]

> The bear is a wonderful animal who lives through the winter without eating. And he is not angry with a person who comes up to him and does not do anything to him. . . .
>
> The bear's law is this, if he kills a human being then he may not sleep in peace through the winter. And the oldtime Lapps thought that the bear had a conscience; and for another thing, if the Uldas (spirits) are his providers during the winter, then they wouldn't bother any more with a bear who had besmirched himself with human blood.

It was also believed by the Lapps that a bear would not willingly attack a woman, and one meeting a bear had only to hold up her skirt to show that she was one for him to leave her alone. [14]

Since there were no bears in Iceland and the largest land animal was the Arctic fox, it seems probable that the detailed story of Biarki's birth and appearance in bear form came in from Norway. A more homely story of a man who fought in the form of a bear comes from *Landnámabók*, the thirteenth-century account of the settlement of Iceland at the end of the ninth century, based on what was remembered of the early settlers. Among these were two men called Dufthak and Storolf, who were neighbours. Dufthak was a slave who had gained his freedom and bought land, while Storolf came from a distinguished family in northern Norway. It was said of Dufthak: [15]

> He was very shapestrong (*hamrammr*), and so also was Storolf Hœngsson, who lived at Hval at that time; they quarrelled over grazing rights. One evening about sunset a man with the gift of

second sight saw a great bear go out from Hval and a bull from Dufthak's farm, and they met at Storolfvellir and fought furiously, and the bear had the best of it. In the morning a hollow could be seen in the place where they had met, as though the earth had been turned over, and this is now called Oldugrof. Both were wearied out.

The man who took bear shape was a son of the famous Ketil Hœng, who came from a region where the Lapps dwelt and where there must have been abundance of bear lore. Another piece of bear tradition is linked with one of Ketil's descendants, Örvar-Odd. [16] When marooned with his crew on an island off the Baltic coast, he was threatened by hostile people from the mainland, and he set up the head and skin of a bear, supported across a stick. When a giantess was sent to attack them, he put embers into the beast's mouth, and then drove her back with his magic arrows. The setting up of a bear skin in this way is found among the rites associated with bear-slaying among the Lapps and other peoples. [17]

A practice which may have helped to keep up the tradition of a close link between man and bear in Scandinavia was the use of animal names for men of distinguished families. There has been much argument as to the origin of this custom, and how far it was based on pre-Christian beliefs in the Germanic world. [18] It is clear that the two most popular names of this type were those based on the bear and the wolf, either in a simple form (Biorn, Ulf) or with an additional syllable (Arnbiorn, Kveldulf). In Germanic uage both names are used together with words for battle, as in the names Hildewolf and Guthbeorn, or for weapons and armour. There seems little doubt that both bear and wolf were associated with an important form of magic, that concerned with battle, the ritual which sought to establish good luck and victory for warriors. This was current among both German and Scandinavian fighting men, and was linked closely with the God Wodan or Odin. The northern sagas have many allusions to the men called berserks who were among Odin's followers. As described by Snorri Sturluson in the thirteenth century in *Ynglinga Saga* 6:

His (Odin's) men went without their mailcoats and were mad as hounds or wolves, bit their shields and were as strong as bears or bulls. They slew men, but neither fire nor iron had effect upon them. This is called 'going berserk' (*berserkgangr*).

The term *berserk* may have been based on the wearing of a bearskin (*serkr* = shirt), and this is suggested by the alternate name given to them: *úlfheðnar*, 'wolf-coats'. Alternately, the first part of the word might have come from *berr*, meaning 'bare', 'naked', and Snorri appears to take it in this way, since he stresses their practice of fighting without mailcoats; they may well have been accustomed to fling off protective armour when the berserk fury came upon them. The latter interpretation was that given in the early dictionaries, but since about 1860 the link with the bear has been the accepted derivation as in the *Old Icelandic Dictionary* by Vigfusson and Cleasby. Noreen defends the earlier theory in an article published in 1932,[19] but I do not find his arguments altogether convincing. We are told in *Vatnsdœla Saga* 9 that

> . . . those berserks who were called *úlfheðnar* had wolf shirts (*vargstakkar*) for mailcoats.

The term wolf-coats is used again as an alternate name for berserks in an early poem, *Hrafnsmál*, composed about AD 900,[20] and here the noise made by the warriors is also emphasized: 'the berserks bayed . . . the wolf-coats howled'. In the same poem there is a description of such warriors at the court of King Harald Fairhair, who ruled in the second half of the ninth century:

> Wolf-coats they are called, those who carry
> bloodstained swords to battle;
> they redden spears when they come to the slaughter,
> acting together as one.

We do not have any detailed descriptions of these savage fighters wearing bearskins or wolfskins, but on the other hand we find what appear to be human figures with heads of bears or wolves, dressed in the skin but with human feet; they are depicted on helmet plates or scabbards, mainly from the pre-Viking period in Sweden.[21] It is perhaps worth noting that in a paper on werewolves by Nils Lid stress is laid on the importance of the belt of wolfskin in shape changing tales;

such a belt was put on by a man or woman who wanted to turn into a wolf, or put into the bed at night, and is mentioned in a number of Norwegian witch-trials. [22] It is possible that the popular motif of a little dancing warrior with a horned helmet, wearing nothing except a belt but armed with a spear or sword, might possibly represent the warrior in his belt of bear or wolfskin; I have suggested for other reasons that such figures represent the champions of Odin. [23] The belt, as Lid makes clear from later evidence, was held to stand for the skin as a whole.

The link with bear or wolf was a logical one for professional warriors or warrior leaders in the Viking Age. The difference between the two animals is clear. The bear is a lone fighter, an independent champion of tremendous power, with a certain nobility in his behaviour, although when carried away by rage he will strike down anyone in his way. The wolf, however, fights as one of a pack, closely linked with his companions, cunning and utterly ruthless, sparing none. They thus represent two ways of doing battle in the Viking Age and the period before it. The outstanding champion established his reputation by prowess in single combat and courage above the ordinary; he would fight in the forefront of the army against champions of the opposing side, and would scorn to attack an unarmed or weak opponent. The raiding party of Vikings or small force of mercenaries would act as a fierce gang, ruthless in attack, greedy for plunder, supporting one another with loyalty and determination (although also apt to quarrel among themselves) and letting nothing stand in their way. There is plenty of evidence from outside observers that the German warriors and the Vikings after them fought with a savage intensity, an animal ferocity and wildness, which shocked Romans and Byzantines. As late as the tenth century Leo the Deacon watched some of the eastern Vikings fighting with Svyatoslav on the Danube against the Emperor, and commented with disapproval on their methods of fighting, so different from those of the Greeks, who, he said, relied on the arts of war. These men seemed, he claimed, to be driven by ferocity and blind madness, and fought like wild beasts, 'howling in a strange and disagreeable manner.'[24]

There is a vivid account of what might be called a retired berserk in the opening chapter of *Egils Saga*. The grandfather of the famous adventurer and poet, Egil Skallagrimsson, who lived in northern Norway, was called Kveldulf, literally 'Evening-Wolf', and was the son of a man called Bialfi, which means an animal skin. The saga-teller accounts for his name by the fact that he grew sleepy and bad-tempered in the evening; this might seem natural in an aging man who used to get up very early to do smithying, as we are told Kveldulf did, but here it is clearly associated with shape-changing, for he is said to be *hamrammr*. Although there is no indication that he was ever seen in wolf form, he and his son Skallagrim were at times subject to terrible fits of rage which left them shaken and weak, and when these fits were upon them they would attack anyone they encountered; Egil himself as a young boy narrowly escaped death from his father's violence during a ball game. Egil in his turn showed some berserk tendencies; he attacked a boatload of enemies in Norway in a state of furious anger, and on another occasion bit the throat of his opponent, also said to be a berserk, in a duel. [25]

It may be assumed that those who lived a warrior's life in Scandinavia must have received some kind of training, and we know that there were special spells to be used in battle, and some indication of ceremonial in which fighting men took part; possible suggestions of initiation ceremonies when the troop of berserks admitted a new recruit have already been noted. Another story which might preserve a memory of training of this kind is found in *Vǫlsunga Saga*, a thirteenth century saga which tells the history of the Volsung family, and seems to have made use of earlier sources now lost. In the opening chapters we have the story of how Sigmund reared his son Sinfjotli, training him for the task of vengeance on the king who had killed Sigmund's father and brothers: [26]

One day they went into the forest to look for plunder, and they found a house, and in the house two men were asleep with thick gold rings on their arms; an evil fate had been wrought upon them, for wolfskins hung above them; they could take off the skins every tenth day, and they were kings' sons. Sigmund and Sinfjotli put on the wolfskins, and were unable to take them off. With the wearing of them went the same nature as before: they spoke with the voice of wolves, and yet each understood what was uttered. They stayed out in the wilds, each going his own way; they made an agreement that each would take on as many as seven men but no more, and that he who was attacked first should cry out as a wolf does. 'We must not depart from this', said Sigmund,

'for you are young and full of reckless courage, and men will want
to hunt you down.' Now they went their several ways, and while
they were apart, Sigmund encountered some men, and howled,
and when Sinfjotli heard him he came at once and slew them all;
they parted once more, and before he (Sinfjotli) had gone far in
the forest, he met with eleven men and fought them and managed
to slay them all.

Sigmund was very angry that Sinfjotli had not called for help:

Sigmund leapt on him with such force that he staggered and fell,
and Sigmund bit him in the throat. That day they could not get
out of their wolfskins, and Sigmund picked up Sinfjotli on his
back and carried him to the hut and sat over him, cursing the
wolfskins.

However Sigmund saw a weasel carrying a leaf which it used to cure
another which had been bitten in the throat, and so he healed Sinfjotli
in the same way. Finally the time came when they could take the skins
off and they burned them, praying that no harm should come to
anyone else through them. The story ends:

But in these shapes of bewitchment they wrought many famous
deeds in the kingdom of King Siggeir.

This tale contains some of the elements of folktales, but in the
agreement about taking on enemies and the reference to warlike
achievements in the wolfskins, there seems to be a hint of a different
tradition, one associated with young heroes living like wolves in the
forest and learning how to support themselves by robbery and killing.
Wolves were also identified with outlaws, and the word *vargr*, wolf, was
used as a legal term for an outlaw. It may be noted that the Lapp Turi
also associated wolves with thieves: he says that in the old days the
shamans turned themselves into wolves, and it was easier to do this
when they had slain innocent people, like certain Russians who robbed
and killed in Lapp territory, until finally with the help of the Uldas or
spirits they became wolves and were driven out: [27]

. . . and they went back to Russia, and that is why there are so
many wolves in Russia, and wolves so fierce that they eat human
beings.

It is interesting that here there is a reversal of the usual rule, and the spirit of evil men enters into the beasts instead of the animal spirit entering a man. Turi declared that there was proof that some wolves had once been men:

> . . . Such proof as finding under certain wolves' hides (while flaying them) things belonging to the people they used to be . . . flint and steel and tinder, and sulphur-cups too.

Whereas the bear is a noble adversary, the wolf is a mean and cunning one. Turi believed that he could do magic on a bullet, so that it missed its mark, and could cause those watching for him to fall asleep. He has, says Turi, one man's strength and nine men's cunning, and to hunt him successfully it was necessary to know all his names in the Lapp dialects, and to think of nine different ways of trapping him, using the last in the list.

This picture of the wolf is characteristic of the herdsman and hunter, threatened by invasions on their reindeer and cattle, so that it seems natural to identify a cunning thief and outlaw with a wolf, and the further step of seeing a particularly cunning wolf as a man in wolf shape is not a very difficult one. In the Viking Age the wolf haunted the battlefield, and was one of those which along with birds of prey feasted on the dead, so that he was an even more sinister figure; it was a great compliment to a successful leader to claim that he gave food to the wolves. This helps to explain the symbol of the wolf in dreams in the sagas. To dream of a number of wolves signified an enemy company about to attack, and sometimes a bear was included as a leader. There was much interest in the meaning of dreams in the Middle Ages, and Latin dream-books were known in Iceland. [28] However when a host of attackers is described as a troop of eighteen wolves led by a cunning vixen (a witch in the party), or when a huge bear is seen leaving a house together with two cubs, such symbolism seems likely to be based on native dream lore. The wolf shapes in a dream in *Havarðar Saga* are said to be *hugir* of men. The bear, described as a noble beast with no equal, is said in *Njáls Saga* to be the *fylgja* of Gunnar, the noble hero who was Njall's close friend. In *Ljosvetninga Saga* the brother of the powerful chief Gudmund the mighty dreamed that a splendid ox walked into Gudmund's hall and fell down dead by the high seat, presaging Gudmund's death, and again the word *fylgja* is used for the symbolic animal shape. The most entertaining account of this kind of animal form, visible in dreams or to someone with the power of second sight, is probably told as a jest. It comes in the story of a boy abandoned as a baby and brought up by simple folk.[29] One day he visited the hall where his true parents lived, and a wise old man, the father of the householder, was sitting there. The boy Thorstein

> . . . came in with a great rush, as children usually do. He slipped on the hall floor, and when Geitir saw this, he burst out laughing. . . . The boy went up to Geitir and said 'Why did it seem funny to you when I fell just now?' Geitir answered 'Because indeed I could see what you could not.' 'What was that?' asked Thorstein. 'I will tell you. When you came into the hall, a white bear cub came behind you and ran along the floor in front of you. Now when he saw me, he stopped, but you were going rather fast, and you fell over him—and it is my belief that you are not the son of Krum and Thorgunna but must be of greater parentage.'

It seems likely that such a story is based on popular belief, introduced as a humorous episode by someone who does not take it too seriously. Another example of the use of popular tradition is found in *Njáls Saga* 41, this time the belief that as a man's death draws near he has special powers of perception, and can receive warning of its approach:

> It happened one time that Njall and Thord were sitting outside. A goat used to wander in the home meadow, and no one would drive it away. Thord began to speak: 'Now, that is a strange thing', said he. 'What do you see that you find so strange?' asked Njall. 'It seems to me that I can see the goat lying here in the hollow, all covered in blood.' Njall said that there was no goat there, nor anything else. 'Then what can it be?' asked Thord. 'You are a doomed man', said Njall, 'for it must be your *fylgja* which you have seen; take care of yourself.' 'That will do me little good', said Thord, 'if this is my doom.'

Close parallels to this conception of an animal guardian or companion, to be seen by those with special powers, or in a dream, are to be found in the beliefs concerning the soul or spirit among the Lapps in pre-Christian times, and various other Finno-Ugrian peoples in northern Europe and Asia.[30] In the seventeenth century Forbus, in his account of the Lapps and their beliefs, refers to a *Nemoqvelle*, said to be passed on to a child at baptism, which belonged to his father and grandfather before him:

> . . . and with the name the child also receives the Nemoqvelle, which can often reveal itself and walks before the Lapp near marshes and seas.

This comes from a Lapp word *Namma-Guelle*, meaning 'namefish', and is used of the name given to a child, which was believed to protect it against evil powers during its life. The reference to marshes and seas suggests a fish which can be seen by the water, but the Lapps also had a tradition of animal spirits of the same kind. A missionary writing in 1726 stated that such spirits were not held to belong to all Lapps, but to a few only, and it seems that the belief was more common among the eastern Lapps. Other names for the accompanying spirit are found among other northern peoples; the Ostyaks had the *jepil*, said to be a visible shadow spirit, the Vogul and Ziryen the *urt* or *ort*, said to dwell as a guardian with the man to whom it belonged; the Skolt Lapps had the *kadz*, and believed that every family, though not necessarily every member of it, possessed such a spirit. Among the Norwegian Lapps the guardian spirit seems to have belonged to the *noidi* or shaman, and might take the form of animal, fish or bird. Here we have something very close to the conception of the *fylgja* in the sagas. It has been suggested that the word is related to ON *fulga*, meaning a thin covering or membrane, and that it may have been used for the afterbirth, as it is in modern Icelandic.[31] The word *ham* in Norwegian dialects can also be used for the afterbirth as well as for a skin. The obvious meaning of *fylgja* however would be 'to follow', and whatever the original significance, this no doubt influenced the meaning, and strengthened the conception of a spirit which followed its owner wherever he went. The connection with the afterbirth would help to account for the idea of a double soul or spirit. Jónasson, writing of Icelandic superstitions, pointed out that the afterbirth was popularly believed to contain some part of the child's soul, so that it must be disposed of with great care and buried in a safe place, such as the threshold of the house, rather than burned or thrown away.[32] The word *hugr*, used of the animal form seen in dreams, seems rather to emphasize the purpose of the person which it represents, since the term can be used with the sense of 'mind', 'wish', or 'foreboding'. Wolves in a dream appear to symbolize the hostile intention of certain men at a particular time rather than to represent their guardian spirits, but obviously it was not difficult for the two conceptions to overlap.

Shamanistic lore from the Lapps and other Finno-Ugrian peoples contains a wealth of stories in which the guardian spirits of the shamans fight in animal form. Among the Lapps these are generally thought to be reindeer, but they might be pictured as bulls, whales, fishes or other creatures, and it is not possible to be sure whether these are the spirits of the shamans themselves, visiting the Other World while their human forms lie in a condition of trance, or whether they should be thought of as the tutelary spirits of the shamans. [33] The episode of the bear in *Hrólfs Saga*, which fought on the battlefield while Bodvar sat in his tent, is an example of such an animal spirit. It was believed that these spirits could be used to work harm to others, and the Skolt Lapps are said still to believe that an evil *noidi* could assume the form of bear, wolf, snake or bird of prey, and be sent out against a victim. [34] We have episodes in the legendary sagas where two men fight in animal form; in one case a Lapp fights another man, and they battle first in the shape of dogs, then as two eagles; in another a man takes on the shape of a walrus and attacks a ship, and he in turn is attacked by a man and a woman in the shapes of a porpoise and a sword-fish. [35] In the second story the importance of the name of the shape-changer is emphasized, recalling the Lapp reference to the 'name-fish'; the man who becomes a sword-fish lies down in the ship under a heap of clothes and forbids anyone to utter his name aloud. The return of the spirit to the body may be a difficult and dangerous process; the girl who took the shape of a porpoise was found afterwards unconscious and very weak, and had to be revived with wine. In another story in *Kormáks Saga* 18 a hostile witch is said to have threatened a boat in the shape of a walrus, and to have been recognized by her eyes; the walrus was hit with a spear and submerged, and afterwards it was said that the witch was seriously ill and that in the end she died from the injury.

The more impressive shape-changing stories seem to be associated with wild creatures rather than domesticated ones. Sometimes men and women take the shape of pigs, but such episodes are of a rather different nature from those concerned with wolves and bears. The wild boar, an animal of great strength and savagery, was certainly associated with battle, and the boar symbol used on helmets, scabbards and swords, while the name of the wedge formation in battle was known among Germans and Scandinavians as the swine formation or the boar's head: *svínfylking* or *caput porci*; it took its name from the tapering head of the boar, with the section in front, where two champions usually headed the attack, known as the *rani* or snout.[36] However the man who takes on boar form seems to do so as a disguise or a means of protection, in the same way as the wearing of a boar helmet appears to be thought of as a means of protection in battle.[37] In the saga stories, the change into a boar or pig is generally used as a means of disguise to avoid attack by enemies, as in the tale of a witch who kept watch in the form of a boar, and woke up those in the house with the news that enemies were approaching, or in that of a man and woman who tried to escape from a burning house in the forms of a boar and a sow.[38] Such stories are of a more conventional kind, and have not the convincing force of the tales of shape-changing discussed earlier.

It is perhaps worth mentioning that there are no stories of shape-changers appearing as horses. Loki was capable of this,[39] but a suggestion that a man might follow his example would be considered a deadly insult, a suggestion of unpleasant and anti-social practices; such as an insult might be offered by erecting a 'scorn-pole' (*niðstǫng*) on which a horse's head was fixed or the shape of a horse carved, along with baleful runes, to bring shame and possibly hurt upon the evil doer.[40] The reasons for this practice are too complex to be discussed here, and although relevant to the subject of animal magic, take us outside the realm of shape-changing.

It would seem that on the whole the tales of shape-changers in the sagas are not told 'for true'. Their background may be realistic, but the tales themselves are not; they serve an artistic purpose, bringing in a touch of fantasy, excitement, humour or horror into the saga according to the desire of the teller. They must however have their roots in popular tradition. Werner, discussing the problem of Germanic personal names based on animals and birds, mentions two opposing theories: first, that the names were thought to be lucky, because of the special qualities of the creature chosen; and secondly, because of the important part played by animal names in the diction of heroic poetry.[41]

These could not, he said, both be true, but I do not myself see why not. Clearly a long tradition of animal names in poetry helped to emphasize certain qualities associated with the wild creatures which were felt to be proper also to the warrior, so that the bestowal of such names would be felt to bring in an element of power and luck. The background of warrior lore and also that of hunting magic went back into the Germanic past, and it is the wild animals native to the North which inspire the best stories of shape-changing, while the widespread conception of the guardian spirit and of twin souls, found among all the Finno-Ugric peoples and much farther afield, must have extended the popular tales about men appearing as animals still further. Expressions with a metaphorical or psychological significance could easily be given a literal interpretation in a story; similarly a naive popular belief could be used by a skilful story-teller to give his story a deeper meaning. Such expressions and popular traditions have their roots in an assumption of a close link between man and the animal world, and a widespread knowledge and keen observation of wild creatures, such as is natural to hunting peoples. Because of these deep roots, men were prepared to be frightened, amused or mystified by tales of people becoming animals and as always with popular literature, the saga-tellers provided their audiences with what they knew they wanted.

Notes

1. *Hrólfs Saga Kraka*, p. 50

2. In the history of Saxo Grammaticus (Bk. ii, 64) Bjarke declares that he won the name *belliger* (warlike) from a previous exploit. This is presumably Saxo's Latin translation of *boðvar*, genitive of *bǫð*, a poetic word for battle.

3. M. Barbeau, 'Bear Mother', *Journal of American Folklore* 59 (1946), pp. 1ff.

4. J. Turi, *Turi's Book of Lapland*, edited by E. D. Hatt, translated from the Danish by E. G. Nash (1931), p. 124.

5. E. Topsell, *The Historie of Foure-Footed Beastes* (1607), p. 27.

6. Barbeau (note 3 above), pp. 4ff.

7. H. Vierck, 'Zum Fernverkehr über See im 6 Jahrhundert,' in K. Hauck, *Goldbrakteaten aus Sievern* (Munich, 1970), p. 385.

8. M. Danielli, 'Initiation Ceremonial from Norse Literature', *Folklore* 56 (1945), pp. 229–45.

9. A. Irving Hallowell, 'Bear Ceremonialism in the Northern Hemisphere', *American Anthropologist* (N.S.28), 1926, pp. 2ff.; R. Karsten, *The Religion of the Samek* (Leiden, 1955), and references there given.

10. *Ibid.*, p. 114; cf. Hallowell (see above), pp. 104, 132.

11. *Ibid.*, pp. 104, 130; A. V. Ström, 'Die Hauptriten des Wikingert zeitlichen nordischen Opfers', *Festschrift Walter Baetke* (Weimar, 1966), p. 336.

12. Hallowell (note 9 above), p. 149.

13. Turi (note 4 above), pp. 123, 125.

14. *Ibid.*, p. 245, note 41*.

15. *Landnámabók* (Isl.Forn., Reykjavik, 1968), S. 350, I, ii. pp. 355–6.

16. *Örvar-Odds Saga*, 5; cf. *Faereyinga Saga*, 12, where the bear is propped up after being killed, and a piece of wood put between its jaws to keep them open.

17. Hallowell (note 9 above), p. 85.

18. G. Müller, *Studier zu der theriophoren Personennamen der Germanen* (*Niederdeutsche Studier* 17, Vienna, 1970); cf. H. Beck, *Das Ebersignum im Germanischen* (*Quellen u. Forschungen zur Sprachund Kulturgeschichte der Germ. Völker*, N.F. 16, 1965), pp. 70ff.

19. E. Noreen, 'Ordet Bärsärk', *Arkiv f. Nord Filologi* (series 3) 4 (1932), pp. 242–54.

20. Also known as *Haraldskvœði* (F. Jonnson, *Den Norsk-Islandske Skjaldedigtning* (Copenhagen, 1912), p. 23, verse 8; p. 25, verse 21; cf. N. Kershaw, *Anglo-Saxon and Norse Poems* (1922), pp. 76ff.

21. E.g. The dies from Ölund (H. R. E. Davidson, *Pagan Scandinavia*, 1967, pl. 41). Cf. P. Paulsen, *Alamannische Adelsgräber von Niederstotzingen* (Stuttgart, 1967), pp. 96ff.

22. N. Lid, 'Til Varulvens Historie', *Trolldom* (Oslo 1950), pp. 82–108, esp. pp. 91ff.

23. H. R. E. Davidson, 'The Significance of the Man in the Horned Helmet,' *Antiquity* 39 (1965), pp. 23ff.

24. H. R. E. Davidson, *The Viking Road to Byzantium* (1976), pp. 113ff.

25. *Egils Saga*, chapters 27, 40, 57, 65.

26. *Völsunga Saga* 8.

27. Turi (note 4 above), pp. 130ff.

28. G. Turville-Petre, 'Dream Symbols in Old Icelandic Literature', *Festschrift Walter Baetke* (Weimar, 1966), pp. 348ff.; cf. *Folklore* 69 (1958), pp. 93ff.

29. *Flateyjarbók* (Christiania, 1860) I, pp. 205, 253.

30. O. Pettersson, *Jabmek and Jabmeaimo* (*Lunds Univ. Aarskrift* N.F.1, 52) (1956), pp. 64ff.

31. H. Falk and A. Torp, *Etymologisk Ordbog* (Oslo, 1903), *fylgje*; cf. Turville-Petre, 'Liggja Fylgjur þinar til Islands', *Viking Society Saga Book* 12 (1940), pp. 119–26.

32. J. Jonasson, *Islenzkir Þjóðh ættir* (Reykjavik, 1934), p. 261.

33. A. Hultkranz, 'Spirit Lodge', *Studies in Shamanism*, ed. Edsman (Stockholm, 1967), pp. 59–60; cf. Karsten (note 9 above), pp. 76ff.

34. *Ibid.*, p. 79.

35. *Sturlaugs Saga Starsfsama* 12; *Hjálmðérs Saga ok Olvés* 20; cf. H. R. E. Davidson, 'Hostile Magic in the Icelandic Sagas', *The Witch Figure*, ed. Newall (1973), pp. 29ff.

36. Beck (note 18 above), pp. 41ff.

37. H. R. E. Davidson, *Gods and Myths of Northern Europe* (1964), pp. 98ff.

38. *Þorskfirðinga Saga* 10, 17; cf. *Harðar Saga* 26; *Eyrbyggja Saga* 20.

39. In Snorri Sturluson's account of the building of a wall round Asgard, in the *Prose Edda*, Loki becomes a mare in order to lure away the giant's horse which had been acting as his helper.

40. The fullest study of the practice of *níð* is B. Almqvust, *Norrön Niddiktning* (Uppsala, 1965); cf. F. Ström, 'Nið, ergi and Old Norse moral attitudes', Dorothea Coke Lecture, University College, London, 1973 (1974).

41. J. Werner, 'Tiergestaltige Heilsbilder und germanische Personennamen', *Deutsche Vierteljahrsschrift f. Literaturwissenschaft* 37 (Stuttgart, 1963), pp. 379ff.

Witchcraft in France and Switzerland

E. WILLIAM MONTER

Official Theory versus Popular Belief

The belief that sorcerers can transform themselves into animals is probably nearly as universal in "primitive" societies as is the belief in magical healing. Of course animal transformations can take many forms, but the animals chosen will often include those most feared by a given society. Over much of western Christendom the wolf was such an animal, and the most sinister possible transformation was the man-wolf or werewolf. He was accordingly found in legends, in published treatises, and in legal records of the sixteenth and seventeenth centuries. [1]

But popular belief and demonology differed somewhat about werewolves. The demonologist was usually convinced that such beliefs were superstitious. Nobody denied the truth of the adage *homo homini lupus*, nobody denied that men (or women) could disguise themselves as wolves and wreak havoc, and nobody denied that the Devil could assume the shape of a wolf. What most demonologists (with the important exception of Jean Bodin) denied was that anyone could really become a wolf through witchcraft. The issue was whether a sorcerer could transform himself body and soul into a wolf through black magic, i.e., whether the Devil could transubstantiate; and the demonological mainstream clearly answered "no," condemning the vulgar opinion to the contrary as superstitious. The demonologists never disputed that people could pretend to be wolves, or that such man-wolves should be killed when discovered; they had a subtler explanation but a similar conclusion.

The best-known Jura demonologist, Henri Boguet, treated this topic in a fairly long chapter, at a time (1602) when the kingdom of France was undergoing a wave of special interest in werewolves: between 1595 and 1615 treatises on lycanthropy were written by a monk,

Witchcraft in France and Switzerland (Ithaca and London: Cornell University Press, 1976), 145–51.

a nobleman, and a physician; three werewolves were discovered in Anjou in 1598, and in 1603 the Parlement of Bordeaux sentenced a teenage werewolf to life imprisonment in a monastery.[2] Boguet typifies not only the special interest of his time and place, but also its ordinary demonological explanation. There are ample grounds, he says, both for affirming and for denying that men can be changed into beasts. His evidence for the former is entirely empirical: Boguet fills pages with illustrations from classical authors, from his neighbors in Franche-Comté, and finally from the Bible. Then he shifts ground: "nevertheless, it has always been my opinion that lycanthropy is an illusion, and that the metamorphosis of a man into a beast is impossible."[3] Here his reasons are primarily theological. If a man is metamorphosed, either his soul enters an animal's body, or else he loses his soul and recovers it later, which implies that the Devil can work true miracles: both are impossible.

Boguet finds it difficult to explain lycanthropy away after he has admitted its empirical reality. He sees two possibilities. Sometimes Satan turns himself into a wolf and persuades the sleeping witch that he (the witch) has done the resulting *maleficia*. But more often the witch himself runs around killing livestock and children—"not that he is metamorphosed into a wolf, but it appears to him that he is; this comes from the Devil's confusing the four humors of which he is composed."[4] Finally, after a long discussion of exactly how Satan manipulates the witch's imagination in such cases, Boguet sternly reminds his readers that "it is the witches themselves who run about and kill people . . . and even if they were guilty in nothing but their damnable intentions, they would still be worthy of death"[5] because of the legal maxim that a complete attempt to commit a capital crime is equivalent to the crime itself.

Boguet's reasonings may seem extremely tortuous, and virtually every demonologist treated this subject slightly differently, although all agreed that werewolves should be put to death. Boguet had himself condemned at least four of them, while two others "were hurried too quickly to their deaths" before they could give complete details about their crimes. Considering that Boguet had tried fewer than thirty witches when he composed his demonology,[6] we might conclude that werewolves were a common aspect of European witchcraft, fully deserving the attention which many writers lavished on them.

But another feature of demonological literature leads us to think otherwise. The same werewolves appear over and over again in the literature about lycanthropy. Boguet listed four werewolves from Franche-Comté who had been captured between 1520 and 1575: the first three were already known to Johann Weyer in 1563, while the fourth was a sadistic hermit named Gilles Garnier, the subject of a 1574 pamphlet, who was so notorious that another expert remarked in 1608 that "it would be a waste of time to say anything more about him."[7] Franche-Comté in general and Boguet's home district of St. Claude in particular were heavily forested, mountainous, and underpopulated: ideal wolf country. Franche-Comté was unusually full of wolves and its records contain an unusually rich series of werewolves, including the earliest European examples.[8] The provincial parlement was visibly worried about werewolves when it organized wolf-hunts in several *bailliages* in the 1630s; after 1650, a parlementaire still defended the reasonableness of the belief in werewolves by the peasants of St. Claude—even though he and his colleagues no longer convicted anyone for this crime.

Available evidence indicates that in most parts of Christendom werewolves were extremely rare. Just north of Franche-Comté was Lorraine, slightly larger and just as heavily forested: it had only five recorded werewolves.[9] Most other places had no more than one apiece. Alsace seems to have had no werewolves;[10] and Montbéliard, an enclave within Franche-Comté, also apparently had none.[11] Peter Stump, the notorious werewolf of the Bishopric of Cologne and, like Garnier, the subject of a well-known pamphlet, seems to have been a unique instance in his territory.[12] Several other German territories also seem to have had only one werewolf apiece.[13] Throughout the kingdom of England, where wolves had been eliminated by 1500, there were very few tales about werewolves; even King James VI of Scotland, composing his demonology in 1597, knew of no cases of lycanthropy first-hand.[14]

On the Swiss side of the Jura werewolves were not very common. There are two interesting cases from Neuchâtel's Val de Travers, which is one of the few passes into Franche-Comté: in 1580 a woman confessed that she had kidnapped two children, "being like a wolf to the sight" and took them to the Sabbat to be eaten; ten years later, a man confessed that he had become a wolf "seven or eight times" after lubricating himself with an ointment given to him by the Devil, but had never eaten any children despite two botched attempts to kidnap some.[15] South of Neuchâtel, in the Pays de Vaud, we find a region where child-eating werewolves date back at least to 1448.[16] Some confessions from 1602 indicate that both werewolves and cannibalism had survived the Reformation intact here: three women, changed into wolves by the Devil's ointment, kidnapped a child and ate him at the Sabbat—all except his right hand, "which God hadn't permitted."[17] As late as 1624 a man confessed that he had become a wolf and entered a stable in an unsuccessful attempt to kill the livestock.[18] However, the only Vaud demonology, published in 1653 by a pastor, argued flatly that lycanthropy was merely a form of melancholia, purely illusory, and that it had nothing at all to do with witchcraft.[19] The only subsequent reference to a werewolf in Vaud, in 1670, came from a twelve-year-old boy who claimed that he and his mother could turn themselves into wolves, but he was not taken seriously. Under questioning, he admitted that he had stopped all forms of witchcraft "ever since they had installed a new schoolmaster."[20]

The series of Vaud werewolves is too short to demonstrate a simple cause-and-effect relationship between demonology and the disappearance of werewolves from its witch trials. But there is an interesting counter-example to it. The only part of Europe that showed a vigorous continuing interest in werewolves after 1650 was the Holy Roman Empire, where at least nine works on lycanthropy were printed between 1649 and 1679.[21] And only in the Empire or its eastern extensions could werewolves be found after 1650.[22] In some places, like the Austrian Alps, they continued to be found well into the eighteenth century, while in east Prussia they took such odd forms as a werewolf who did only good deeds![23] By that time werewolves had long since been relegated to the status of a mere superstition in most other corners of Christendom.

Do the counter-examples of post-1650 Vaud and Germany indicate that demonologists determined whether or not people would be tried as werewolves, that theory determined practice? Perhaps; but they also suggest a more important line of questioning. The Vaud demonologist was a Calvinist, and he followed an important principle of Huguenot demonology, namely that such wonders of the Devil as turning men into wolves were always illusions, *mira* rather than *miracula*.

(Catholics did not stress this point and were left struggling, like Boguet, with the intricacies of humoral theory.) Protestant demonologists battled not only against the illusion of man-wolves but also against such *mira* as the witch's ability to raise hailstorms—and they got results, at least among judges of their religion.

Werewolves were rare in fifteenth-century demonologies and trials; the *Malleus*, for instance, has nothing to say about them, although its authors had worked in the mountainous and forested diocese of Constance.[24]

Notes

1. Despite his well-known prejudices, which render so much of his work completely useless, Montague Summers managed to compose a book on *The Werewolf* (London, 1933) which is quite valuable, both for its discussion of various demonological theories and for its listings of literary sources, including some trials.

2. In addition to Summers, *Werewolf*, ch. 5 (212–35), there are some valuable pieces of information in Robert Mandrou, *Magistrats et sorciers en France au XVIIe siècle* (Paris, 1968), 157, 185–88, 301.

3. Boguet, *Discours*, ch. 47 (Ashwin, 143). Consider how Judge Nicholas Remy, his neighbor in Lorraine, had handled this point seven years earlier: "It is, therefore, absurd and incredible that anyone can truly be changed from a man into a wolf or other animal. Yet there must be some foundation for the opinion so obstinately held by so many." *Demonolatry* (Lyon, 1595), Bk. II, ch. 5; English translation by E. A. Ashwin with an introduction by Montague Summers (London, 1930), 111.

4. Boguet, *Discours*, ch. 47 (Ashwin, 146).

5. *Ibid.* (Ashwin 154–55).

6. See F. Bavoux, *Boguet, Grand-juge de la terre de St. Claude* (Besançon, 1956), 12, for the best discussion on this point.

7. Quoted in Summers, *Werewolf*, 240; the pamphlet itself is translated on 226–28.

8. Francis Bavoux left copious notes at the ADD from a talk about werewolves which he delivered to the *Société d'Emulation du Doubs* in 1952, drawing on cases from the *bailliages* of Dôle (1573 and 1605), Baume (1599) and Orgelet (1610) in addition to St. Claude; he also included some fascinating information about the parlement's visible hesitations in the 1630s when the judges repeatedly rewrote the phrases dealing with werewolves in their wolf-hunting edicts.

9. See Etienne Delcambre, *Le concept de la sorcellerie dans le duché de Lorraine au XVIe et au XVIIe siècle*, 3 vols. (Nancy, 1948–51), 2: 222ff. Remy, *Demonolatry*, Bk. II, ch. 5, cited two cases from his own large experience, plus Gilles Garnier.

10. R. Reuss, *La sorcellerie au seizième et au dix-septième siècles, particulièrement en Alsace* (Paris, 1871), 83.

11. F. Bavoux, "Less caractères originaux de la sorcellerie dans le pays de Montbéliard," *Mém. de la Société pour l'Histoire du Droit et des Institutions des anciens pays bourgignons, comtois et romands*, 20 (1958/59), 95 n. 1.

12. The English translation of a German pamphlet about him, from 1590, is reprinted in Summers, *Werewolf*, 253–59. Like Garnier, he appears in many treatises on lycanthropy; like Garnier, he was a sadistic mass killer, with thirteen victims.

13. For example, the Bishopric of Münster in 1615: D. B. Niehues, *Zur Geschichte des Hexenglaubens und der Hexenprozesse, vornehmlich im ehemaligen Fürstbistum Münster* (1875), 77ff; Wildenburg in 1617: O. Rinscheid, "Die Hexenwahn in Wildenburger Lande," *Mitt. der Westdeutschen Gesellschaft für Familienkunde*, 21 (1963), 208; or the city of Hamburg, in 1631: cited by Heberling (see above, n. 1), 205. Only one suspected "loupwaroux" was found among many Namur trials: E. Brouette, "La Sorcellerie dans le Comté de Namur au début de l'époque moderne (1509–1646)," *Annales de la Société archéologique de Namur*, 47 (1953), 374.

14. See the thorough account by Summers, *Werewolf*, ch. 4 (182–211).

15. AEN, P.C. du Val de Travers, vol. I (unpaginated), procès Guyetta Bugnon (8–7–1580); procès Michel Jaques (22–6–1590).

16. ACV, Ac 29/5–28 (Jacques de Panissière).

17. ACV, Bh 10, vol. III, procès Michée Bauloz (22–4–1602) and Jeanne de la Pierre (same date); condemned with them was Suzanne Prevost, who had helped to eat the child but not to kidnap him. The whole case was sufficiently famous to be mentioned in a 1615 treatise on lycanthropy by the French physician Nynauld: see Summers, *Werewolf*, 234–35.

18. ACV, Bh 20, vol. II, procès Isaac du Roussel (6–2–1624).

19. François Perreaud, *Demonologie, ou Traitté des Demons et sorciers* (Geneva, 1653), 113–15 (ch. 7). Lambert Daneau, *Les Sorciers*, 2d. ed. (Geneva, 1579), ch. 3, also came to the conclusion that lycanthropy was impossible.

20. ACV, Bd 62/255–59, fully described by Eugène Olivier, *Médecine et santé dans le Pays de Vaud*, Part 1, *Des origines à la fin du XVIIe siècle*, 2 v. (Lausanne, 1962), 2: 649–51.

21. A full list of these titles in Summers, *Werewolf*, x–xi.

22. For instance, in the Electorate of Trier in 1652: W. Krämer, *Kurtrierische Hexenprozessen im 16. und 17. Jahrbundert* (Munich, 1959), 19–31; in Hesse in 1656 and 1683: Karl-Heinz Spielmann, *Die Hexenprozessen in Kurhessen* (Marburg, 1932), 103–4, 125.

23. See F. Byloff, *Hexenglauben und Hexenverfolgungen in den Österreichischen Alpenländern* (Berlin-Leipzig, 1934), 146–52. The "good" werewolf of Lithuania in 1692 is discussed by Carlo Ginzburg, *I benandanti: Richerche sulla stregonerie e culti agrari fra Cinque e Seicento* (Turin, 1966), 37–39.

24. One of the earliest werewolves was tried at Basel in 1407: Joseph Hansen,

Zauberwahn, Inquisition und Hexenprozess im Mittelalter (Munich, 1900), 382–83. But in German Switzerland the usual belief was different, namely. that witches rode around on wolves' backs.

Abbreviations

France
ADD   Archives Départementales du Doubs, Besançon

Switzerland
ACV   Archives Cantonales Vaudoises, Lausanne
AEN   Archives de l'Etat, Neuchâtel

The Scientific Status of Demonology

STUART CLARK

We use the word "supernatural" when speaking of some native belief, because that is what it would mean for us, but far from increasing our understanding of it, we are likely by the use of this word to misunderstand it. We have the concept of natural law, and the word "supernatural" conveys to us something outside the ordinary operation of cause and effect, but it may not at all have that sense for primitive man. For instance, many peoples are convinced that deaths are caused by witchcraft. To speak of witchcraft being for these peoples a supernatural agency hardly reflects their own view of the matter, since from their point of view nothing could be more natural. [1]

𝔍n a treatise on witchcraft first published in Trier in 1589 a German bishop explained that all apparently occult operations that were not in fact miracles could be ascribed in principle to physical causes. For whether or not any particular instance was actually demonic in inspiration, "magic" was simply the art of producing wonderful natural effects outside the usual course of things and above the common understanding of men. It followed that "if this part of philosophy was practised in the schools in the manner of the other ordinary sciences . . . it would lose the name of 'magic' and would be assigned to physics and natural science [*et Physicae naturalique scientiae asscriberetur*]." Likewise, in a set of theses on magical operations and witchcraft published a year later in Helmstädt, a natural philosopher and physician began by arguing that "magical actions and motions are reducible to considerations of physics [*Ad Physicam considerationem reducuntur motus et actiones magicae*]." We might be tempted to read into such statements intimations of that scepticism which (it is said) ultimately undermined the learned belief in the reality of demonic effects, especially those associated with witchcraft, by accounting for them just as adequately in natural scientific terms. But

In *Occult and Scientific Mentalities in the Renaissance*, edited by Brian Vickers (Cambridge: Cambridge University Press, 1984), 351–73.

the bishop was in fact Peter Binsfeld, and the notable contribution of his *Tractatus de confessionibus maleficorum et sagarum* to classic demonology, as well as its association with vigorous witch hunting, make it inconceivable that he could have meant to convey any general form of doubt.[2] The more obscure proposer of theses, Martin Biermann, although anxious to refute some of the extreme demonological opinions of Bodin, was no less traditional in his belief in the possibility of limited demonic activity in the world and in the reality of pacts between demons and both magicians and witches.[3]

It seems that insofar as they depend on an assumed disjunction between the "occult" and the "scientific," our expectations about belief and disbelief in such texts may be misleading. Understanding what sort of scepticism was most threatening to orthodox demonology depends on grasping its central intellectual defenses. But since these appear to *include* the use of natural scientific explanations, we need to look again at our assumptions about what it made sense for demonologists to accept as an account of the natural world and its processes. There is still a tendency to think that the flourishing of the debate about demonism and witchcraft somehow contradicted the general cultural, and especially scientific, achievements of the sixteenth and seventeenth centuries. If, however, this debate was not isolated from, or even antagonistic to, other aspects of Renaissance thought, including its science, then the contradiction becomes artificial. It is this wider issue of rationality, as well as the question of what was meant by arguments such as those of Binsfeld and Biermann, that involve us in reconsidering the status of demonology as an attempt to offer an ordered construction of natural reality.

A beginning might be made with those individual scientists who concerned themselves with demonology without any sense of incongruity or of the compromising of their criteria of rational inquiry: from Agostino Nifo, Giovanni d'Anania, and Andrea Cesalpino in sixteenth-century Italy to Henry More, Joseph Glanvill, and Robert Boyle in later seventeenth-century England. Others not primarily concerned with natural philosophy nevertheless combined it with demonology without intellectual embarrassment: for example, Jean Bodin, Lambert Daneau, and the Dutchman Andrea Gerhard (Hyperius). In perhaps the largest group there were the many physicians who made special studies of demonic pathology: the Italian Giovanni Battista Codronchi, the Germans Wilhelm Schreiber and Johann Wier, the Swiss Thomas Erastus, the Englishman John Cotta, and the many French doctors involved in cases of possession, among them Jacques Fontaine, Michel Marescot, and Pierre Yvelin. [4]

Intellectual biography would, however, only drive us back to issues. Some of these were, of course, merely practical. Arguments about the etiology and treatment of the various conditions associated with melancholia provided a general context for many medical incursions into demonology. [5] In the further case of the investigation of demoniacs it has even been suggested that exorcists, possibly displaying an empiricism beyond that of their medical colleagues, carried out what amounted to controlled experiments in order to test for the marks of true possession. [6] Other issues brought theorizing about demons, along with narratives of witchcraft, indirectly into scientific debate, as in the arguments over incorporeal substance in Restoration England. If, for instance, we can now see that Glanvill's demonology was inseparable from his experimental philosophy, it is because behind both lay the perception of a threat to Anglican theology posed by the Sadducism of scientific "materialists" and others. [7] Glanvill thought that the study of spirits could be recommended to the Royal Society without contradicting its standards of inquiry. Nevertheless, in this context the spirits entered scientific investigation, as another natural philosopher and demonologist, George Sinclair, remarked, primarily as "one of the *Outworks of Religion*."[8] The resulting blend of the newest scientific ideals with the oldest witchcraft beliefs was achieved at a key moment in both their histories. Yet the understandable interest shown in this example should not obscure the real novelty involved. What had changed was not the idea that the devil could be retained in a perfectly natural account of the world; it was the view of nature presupposed by this enterprise.

This can be illustrated if we consider a further set of issues, certainly not unrelated to theological questions (or indeed to Baconian elements in the activities of the Royal Society), but generated directly by what was regarded as the central ontological characteristic of demonic phenomena: the fact that they were extraordinary. The principal themes of sixteenth- and seventeenth-century demonology were the qualities and powers of demonic agents and the effects produced by their activity in the world. These were not merely moral effects: They were either real, physical operations, or they appeared to be, for demons were consummate deceivers. Yet neither were they commonplace. At the very least they were, as Glanvill himself put it, "somewhat varying from the common *Road of Nature*."[9] In fact, for the most part they were prodigious in character and, therefore, often confused with other apparently aberrant phenomena. The key questions faced by demonologists were thus of a causal and criterial kind: What was the exact causal status of demonic effects? What laws did they obey or disobey? What were the criteria for distinguishing between their true and illusory aspects? Along what point on the axis from miracles through natural wonders to ordinary natural contingencies were they to be placed? Tackling such questions involved making distinctions that were critical for any explanation of phenomena, whether demonic or not—distinctions between what was possible and impossible, or really and falsely perceived, and between both supernature and nature, and nature and artifice. It had to be decided what were the boundary conditions governing miracles, prodigies, marvels, and "prestiges"; how to define and use categories such as "magic" and "occult"; and how to relate the explanatory languages of theology and natural philosophy. However bizarre the resulting discussions may sometimes seem, they were genuine attempts to establish criteria of intelligibility for the understanding of a very wide range of what were taken to be puzzling events, that is, events which were said to have "no certain cause in nature."

This concentration on the interpretation of essentially perverse phenomena is not easily related to any narrowly conceived "scientific revolution" in the same period.[10] But this does not mean that it was peculiar to demonologists. What helped to give the debate about demonism and witchcraft such a general currency toward the end of the sixteenth century was the extent to which its interest in the eccentric in nature was a shared intellectual preoccupation. In his remarkable study, *La Nature et les prodiges: l'insolite au XVIᵉ siècle, en France*, Jean Céard has indicated both the range of the literature dealing with monsters, prodigies, and marvels (as well as with the more general features of "variety" and "vicissitude"), and the fundamental character of the conceptual problems it raised in the overlapping territories of philosophy, theology, and science. More recently the specific case of the monstrous has been canvassed as an important individual indicator of changes in explanatory models in early modern France and England.[11] Demonologists often considered an identical teratology—for example, the monsters generated by incubus or succubus devils—and they usually located demonic prodigies semiologically within a broadly apocalyptic account of God's intentions. On the other hand, their stress on demonic manipulation of the natural world was rather oblique to the theme of nature's own generosity or fecundity in producing forms, which emerges strongly from the literature of the "unusual." The important point, however, is not that they may have given different answers to those engaged in the wider enterprise, but that they confronted the same epistemological puzzles. Wherever and to what extent the devil and witches were actually situated in the causation of irregular events are less significant than the broader identity of purpose. It is in this sense that Céard's work enables us to think of demonology as continuous and not discontinuous with Renaissance natural philosophy.[12]

Moreover, the nature of this link does seem to have been recognized from within the "great tradition" of early modern scientific thought. Francis Bacon's proposal (in his *De augmentis scientiarum*) for a natural history of "pretergenerations"—"the Heteroclites or Irregulars of nature"—has often been cited in the context of prodigy literature, but the general relevance of Bacon's project for demonology is thought to have been negligible. In both its theoretical stance and its actual influence on the early program of the Royal Society, this proposal certainly made the marvelous a central rather than a peripheral category of investigation. Bacon's argument was partly technological—that rarities in nature would lead men to rarities in art—but it was also epistemological; hence, the repetition of the suggestion in Book 2 of the *Novum organum*, at the heart of what we have of his actual logic of inquiry. Singularities and aberrations in nature were not merely correctives to the partiality of generalizations built on commonplace examples; as deviations from the norm they were especially revealing of nature's ordinary forms and processes. This makes the example on which Bacon chose to concentrate in the *De augmentis scientiarum* all the more striking:

Neither am I of opinion in this history of marvels, that super-stitious narratives of sorceries, witchcrafts, charms, dreams, divinations, and the like, where there is an assurance and clear evidence of the fact, should be altogether excluded. For it is not yet known in what cases, and how far, effects attributed to super-stition participate of natural causes; and therefore howsoever the use and practice of such arts is to be condemned, yet from the speculation and consideration of them (if they be diligently un-ravelled) a useful light may be gained, not only for the true judgment of the offences of persons charged with such practices, but likewise for the further disclosing of the secrets of nature.[13]

It would not be totally implausible to transpose even Bacon's point about the technological potential of knowledge of "erring" nature into a demonological context and to ask, for instance, whether the treatment of demoniacs was regarded as offering particularly decisive tests of the efficacy of medical (as well as exorcistic) practices. Howev-er, it is the fact that he thought of witchcraft narratives in connection with the epistemological benefits of this knowledge that is so sug-gestive. For in effect this not only made demonism and witchcraft fit subjects for natural philosophy, but elevated them to the rank of Baco-nian "prerogative instances," that is, areas of empirical inquiry es-pecially privileged by their unusual capacity to disclose natural pro-cesses. This idea surely helps us to understand the role of European demonology in the wider setting. Its appeal in the scientific context was undoubtedly its ability, together with that of prodigy literature in general, to tackle one of the most intractable subject matters known to the period. Adapting Bacon's argument somewhat, we might say it was able to confront empirical and, more so, conceptual issues that, though fundamental to all systematic investigation, were laid bare in an es-pecially illuminating manner by the very waywardness of the phe-nomena dealt with and the struggle to understand them. In this broader sense demonology was one of the "prerogative instances" of early mod-ern science.

What matters here, again, is not that Bacon should eventually have arrived at the same interpretation of these phenomena as the demonologists. His principle that extraordinary events were worth more attention than ordinary ones had a formal truth, whether it was decided that they were all natural or all demonic. However, if, as we have seen, this was not in fact the nature of the choice that had to be made, then the real intellectual distance between a figure like Bacon and the world of demonology may not in any case be as great as it appears. In the *De augmentis* and the *Novum organum*, Bacon talked as though it was a personified nature itself which erred, not a nature acted on by demonic forces. In the *Sylva sylvarum* he also suggested that it was popular credulity which was responsible for the attribution of purely natural operations to some sort of efficacy in witchcraft. An example was the way the hallucinogenic effects of the "opiate and soporiferous" qualities of magical ointments were mistaken for the (supposedly real) transvections and metamorphoses that appeared in witches' confessions.[14] Above all, Bacon insisted that the only phenomena which were nonnatural were true miracles. It is not surprising that these views have been associated with outright naturalism and, therefore, with philosophical indifference to the problems raised by witchcraft beliefs. Yet all of them can be found in the writings of the demonologists, and the second and third might even be said to be presuppositions of their inquiry. The relative importance of demonically and nondemonically caused events remains the only really contentious issue, and here even Bacon allowed for the first when he remarked that "the experiments of witchcraft are no clear proofs [i.e., of the power of the imagination on other bodies]; for that they may be by a tacit operation of malign spirits."[15] Once again we are faced with the artificiality of bringing the modern notion that there is a difference of kind between the "scientific" and the "occult" to the investigation of what were simply differences of degree between varying conceptions of nature.

That the literature of demonology had any meaning at all in this wider context has been obscured by two misapprehensions about the intentions of its authors. Because the sensational aspects of witchcraft belief—the demonic pact, the sabbat, the reality of *maleficium*, and so on—have caught the modern attention, this has suggested, first of all, that the original texts concentrated narrowly and moralistically on the description of these particular crimes and the appropriate judicial and penal response. Of course, these topics were important, and some—notably the alleged transvection of witches to sabbats and their transmutation into animals—raised just those issues that demanded serious epistemological consideration. But the intention was to examine any phenomenon of sufficiently dubious credentials to warrant the suspicion that it was demonically caused. This led demonologists way beyond the range of topics and attitudes that have been traditionally associated with witchcraft beliefs. Martin Del Rio defined *magia* as "an art or technique which by using the power in creation rather than a supernatural power produces various things of a marvellous and unusual kind, the reason for which escapes the senses and ordinary comprehension." Within literally a few pages we find him tackling the validity of whole sciences such as natural magic, astrology, mathematics, and alchemy, as well as such questions as whether there is any physical efficacy in the innate qualities of magical practitioners, or in the imagination, or in the use of ritual touching, looking, speaking, breathing, and kissing, and whether characters, sigils, arithmetical and musical notation, words, charms, and amulets have any intrinsic powers.[16]

What is striking in his *Disquisitionum magicarum* and in other demonologies of similar scale, such as Francisco Torreblanca's *Daemonologia* and Giovanni Gastaldi's *De potestate angelica*, is the enormous variety of the subjects examined for their standing in reality and knowledge as well as in morals. At the end of his second volume Gastaldi, having already considered natural and other forms of magic, the traditional topics of witchcraft theory, the arts and prodigies of Antichrist, the healing power of the kings of France, the question of bodily transmutation, and the power of demons over magicians, sorcerers, and evil doers, adds a "Disputatio unica" in which he asks of particular wonders whether they are "natural" or "superstitious." These include the movements of the tides, the possibility of speaking statues, the effects of words and music on animal behavior, the power of fascination, the extraction of solid objects from the human body, and the proper cure for tarantism. Even modest monographs tried to cover the same borderland between the naturally marvelous and the magically specious. Thus, if we turn from Pierre de Lancre's best-known work on the witch trials in Labourd, the *Tableau de l'inconstance des mauvais anges et démons*, to one of his other demonological writings, *L'Incredulité et mescreance du sortilege plainement con-*

vaincue, we find another typical range of topics: the reality of sorcery, fascination, whether touching itself can harm or heal, divination, and how to distinguish between good and evil apparitions. [17]

The repetition of this pattern in many other texts rules out the view that it was random or haphazard; yet witchcraft itself was clearly not the only point of departure. Conversely, such topics and many of the same strategies of argument occur in accounts of curious natural and human behaviors that are not ostensibly demonological at all; for instance, in André du Laurens's treatise on the royal touch, where the idea that this form of ritual healing might be demonic has to be overcome, [18] or in more general surveys of the marvelous such as Claude Rapine (Caelestinus), *De his quae mundo mirabiliter eveniunt;* Scipion Dupleix, *La Curiosité naturelle;* and Gaspar Schott, *Physica curiosa.* [19] Demonology was not, then, anchored only to the question of witchcraft and witch trials. It meshed with other discussions with which it shared common intentions, whether or not its conclusions were the same. This enables us to see more easily how demonology could have been a genuine vehicle for what may be called a scientific debate—a debate concerning the exact status of a variety of extremely questionable phenomena. Indeed, it was this guiding issue that, despite the apparently disparate choice of themes, gave demonology real unity of purpose.

The second misapprehension has more seriously affected our understanding of the intentions behind this literature because it has prevented us from seeing the literature as a contribution to a debate at all, or at least to one of any complexity. This is the idea stemming from such early commentators as G. L. Burr and H. C. Lea, that (again on the issue of the reality of witchcraft) demonology could be divided into *either* belief *or* scepticism, with the assumption that belief was a cut-and-dried affair committing a writer to accepting the whole structure of what was alleged. [20] In fact, what is striking is how few examples there are at each end of the spectrum ranging from total acceptance of all demonic claims—where we find only Bodin and perhaps Rémy (in some passages from his *Daemonolatreiae*)—to total rejection—where we find only Reginald Scot and his English followers. This leaves a vast middle ground occupied by hundreds of texts where genuine attempts are made to discriminate between what is to be accepted and what rejected, where authors are familiar with a number of sceptical positions,[21] and where scepticism as well as belief is evident in their own views as demonologists. Repeatedly we are warned that the subject is controversial and obscure and that, faced with the question of the reality of demonic magic, no rational man would insist that it was all illusory or all true. This is the position adopted by Del Rio, Philipp Ludwig Elich, Francesco Maria Guazzo, Benito Pereira, James VI and I, John Cotta, Noël Taillepied (in the allied field of apparitions), and many others.[22] The example of Henri Boguet's *Discours des sorciers*, often singled out as an especially dogmatic work, shows just how carefully witchcraft confessions might be tested against assumptions about real and spurious causal efficacy. What governed his attitude was not any blanket credulity, but, as Lucien Febvre recognized, the application of standards of what was both possible *and impossible* for human and demonic agents to effect.[23]

Demonologists did not simply pile up the positive evidence for the guilt of demonic witchcraft. They tried to separate phenomena correctly attributed to demonic agency from phenomena incorrectly so attributed, and to both they applied a second set of criteria dealing with truth and illusion. They therefore had at their disposal four categories of explanation, or four explanatory languages, dealing, respectively, with real demonic effects, illusory demonic effects, real nondemonic effects, and illusory nondemonic effects. And they were well aware, without this compromising their general acceptance of demonic agency, of the category errors that could occur when (say) confessions contained nonetheless impossible feats, when the illusions of the devil were mistaken for reality, when unfamiliar but quite undemonic natural contingencies or startling technological achievements were blamed by the uninformed on demonism, or (above all) when hallucinatory experiences stemming from ordinary diseases or narcotic substances were attributed to witchcraft. This is clear, for instance, in Pierre Le Loyer's *Quatres Livres des spectres ou apparitions*, where in the context of a defense of the reality of demonism against the arguments of "naturalists," a variety of almost Pyrrhonist objections are marshaled against accepting either the evidence of the senses or the promptings of reason in cases of apparently aberrant phenomena.[24] Likewise, François Perrault's *Demonologie*, after typical emphasis on the dangers of both outright scepticism *and* outright credulity, consigns reputedly demonic effects such as *ignis fatuum* and *ephialtes* to the category of the purely natural.[25] We shall find the same features in discussions of natural magical instances in demonological contexts. The fact that a range of explanations was open to the great majority of writers enabled them to probe the conceptual puzzles of their subject matter to an extent that would have been impossible if, as is often assumed, their options had been limited to supporting or criticizing witchcraft trials.

This can be illustrated in more detail if we take the central topic of demonic power and consider the implications of the ways its effects could be explained. For despite their anxiety to warn readers of the threat of demonism and witchcraft in the world—and this is, of course, the tonality that we have tended to recognize most readily—demonologists were also, without exception, committed to exposing the limitations, weaknesses, and deceptions of the devil. In both a theologically and evangelically critical sense they were attempting to demystify and deflate demonic pretensions: theological, because of the paramount need (in the age of Reformation claims and counterclaims) to distinguish between the genuinely and the quasi miraculous; evangelical, because of an audience thought to be prone to believe anything about demonism and to overreact with "superstitious" countermeasures. It was always granted that demons had not lost their physical powers after their fall from grace and that their cumulative experience since the Creation, their subtle, airy, and refined quality, and their capacity for enormous speed, strength, and agility enabled them to achieve real effects beyond human ability. Nevertheless, it was also invariably insisted that such effects were within the boundaries of secondary or natural causation. They were either forms of local motion or alterations wrought by the application of actives on passives, even if both types of operation were (say) enormously accelerated. Explanations of this are found everywhere in demonology; here they are summarized by John Cotta:

> Though the divel indeed, as a Spirit, may do, and doth many things above and beyond the course of some particular natures: yet doth hee not, nor is able to rule or commaund over generall Nature, or infringe or alter her inviolable decrees in the perpetuall and never-interrupted order of all generations; neither is he generally Master of universall Nature, but Nature Master and Commaunder of him. For Nature is nothing els but the ordinary power

of God in al things created, among which the Divell being a creature, is contained, and therefore subject to that universall power. [26]

Satan might, of course, interfere with the initial specific conditions of natural events, but he could not dispense with the general laws governing their occurrence. [27]

This situation was not changed, only complicated, by the fact that where his power to produce real effects gave out, his ingenuity in camouflaging weaknesses by illusory phenomena took over. He could corrupt sensory perception, charm the internal faculties with "ecstasies" or "frenzies," use his extraordinary powers over local motion to displace one object with another so quickly that transmutation appeared to occur, present illusory objects to the senses by influencing the air or wrapping fantastic shapes around real bodies, and, finally, delude all the third parties involved so that no testimony damaging to his reputation as an agent was available. The devil was, therefore, severely limited in what he could really effect (for, as Boguet pointed out, even his delusions were species of natural action), but there was nothing that he might not *appear* to effect. [28] Demonologists consequently went to considerable lengths to expose such *glaucomata* or "lying wonders" in order to reveal the ontological and epistemological as well as the moral duplicity involved. The debate focused on the most spectacular claims—that witches could attend sabbats in noncorporeal form, that demonic sexuality could result in generation, and, above all, that humans could be changed into animals—for in these cases a manifest demonic incompetence to create the real effects that were claimed without breaking natural laws led to complicated strategies of deception on his part, none more involved than the last. Discussions of the possibility of lycanthropy in fact contain some of the most interesting examples of demonologists trying, in what I have suggested was a scientific way, to explain a particularly refractory set of claims.

In Jean de Nynauld's *De la Lycanthropy*, for example, we find the gamut of explanatory languages. He writes to disabuse the ignorant on a subject that surmounts the expectations of the senses but that nevertheless has its causes. Bound by the "divinely instituted course of nature," the devil cannot create fresh forms or change the essential character of existing forms. He can therefore only simulate transmutation of witches into wolves by troubling their imaginations, taking advantage of physiologically induced dream experiences, adding demonic efficacy to the ordinary strength of hallucinogenic unguents, and superimposing the required shapes and properties on their bodies in order to deceive any spectators. Thus while real transmutation cannot occur either nondemonically or demonically, there are real effects resulting from natural conditions and substances that lead to all the required sensory experiences, and that, because they are natural, the devil can manipulate. It might seem tempting to recruit Nynauld as a "sceptic." Yet he does not doubt the existence of witches or their use of potions made from slain infants. What he does is analyze all such phenomena on naturalistic lines in order to reveal the causal relationships between the chemical composition of the narcotic elements in such potions, the sensation of being "transmuted," and the psychosomatic effects of folly and credulity. Similarly, he argues that while no unguent can physically effect transvection to sabbats, this is not always an illusion either, since the devil can achieve it by means of local motion. None of this sets Nynauld apart from a supposed "believer" like Boguet, who accounted in exactly the same terms for the phenomena mistakenly thought to result from real lycanthropy and attendance at the sabbat in spirit only.[29]

This is only the briefest summary of a debate that appears in virtually every text. Although some of its features have attracted attention before, its implications for the scientific status of demonology have, I think, been neglected.[30] At the very least, we cannot go on ascribing to the category of the "supernatural" discussions whose purpose was to establish precisely what was supernatural and what was not. Demonism was said to be part of the realm of the natural, for it lacked just those powers to overrule the laws of nature that constituted truly miraculous agency. It must be stressed, therefore, that demonic intervention did not turn natural into supernatural causation. It is the case that its effects were sometimes labeled "nonnatural" or declared to be not attributable to natural causes. But in context this rarely meant more than either their going beyond what might normally have been expected from the ordinary "flow" of causes and effects, or their unfamiliarity or impossibility in relation to the nature known to and practiced upon by men or (less often) their reflection of the devil's desire to break the restraints he was under.[31] The distinguishing criterion of demonic, and indeed all forms of magic, was not that it was supernatural but that it was *unusual*. Even Nicolas Rémy's contradictory statements might be reconciled along these lines. While appearing to follow Bodin in his view that demonism was irreconcilable with any standard of what was natural, he nevertheless qualified this with several comparisons with what were merely the normal limitations and processes.[32] The danger in this situation of preempting meanings by thinking of the "supernatural" only in its modern sense is well shown by the case of John Cotta, who, after using the term several times in his *The Triall of Witch-Craft*, explained that

> although . . . the Divell as a Spirit doth many things, which in respect of our nature are supernaturall, yet in respect of the power of Nature in universall, they are but naturall unto himselfe and other Spirits, who also are a kinde of creature contained within the generall nature of things created: Opposite therefore, contrary, against or above the generall power of Nature, hee can do nothing.

Cotta's tract is of particular importance in this context because it is dominated by his awareness of the epistemological issue of how one could speak of acquiring "naturall knowledge"—by sense experience, reasoning, or conjecture—of such difficult and inaccessible phenomena. Yet William Perkins had also argued that demonic effects only seemed wonderful because they transcended both the "ordinarie bounds and precincts of nature" and the capacities of men, "especially such as are ignorant of Satans habilitie, and the hidden causes in nature, whereby things are brought to passe."[33]

Others reflected this relativism in preferring to use such terms as "quasi-natural"[34] or "hyperphysical."[35] And Del Rio captured it exactly when he proposed the category of the "preternatural" to describe prodigious effects that seemed miraculous only because they were "natural" in a wider than familiar sense.[36] But whatever terms were used, demonic effects were in principle part of natural processes, and in this sense demonology was from the outset a natural science: that is, a study of a natural order in which demonic actions and effects were presupposed. In fact, despite its reputation for intellectual confusion, demonology derived considerable coherence from a notion that there were limits to nature. As Perkins explained: "What strange workes and wonders may be truely effected by the power of nature, (though they be not ordinarily brought to passe in the course of nature) those the devill can do, and so farr forth as the power of nature will permit, he is able to worke true wonders."[37] This was also, necessarily, the standard in terms of which aspects of witchcraft beliefs could be rejected as illusory. The unity of Boguet's treatise and of his views about the inadmissibility of many demonic phenomena was a function of precisely this criterion. And the same intention in James VI and I's *Daemonologie* to link an account of what was possible in magic, sorcery, and witchcraft with the question "by what naturall causes they may be" drew a special commendation from Bacon.[38] The general application of this principle did not mean that demonologists always ended up locating the boundaries of nature in the same place. It was the fact that there was such uncertainty on this issue at the end of the sixteenth century that made demonology both a debate within itself and a contribution to a wider controversy among philosophers, theologians, and scientists. What is significant is the very adoption of the criterion itself. Beyond nature lay only miracles, which no one claimed devils could perform. The question we have to ask, therefore, is not the one prompted by rationalism (Why were intelligent men able to accept so much that was supernatural?), but simply the one prompted by the history of science (What concept of nature did they share?). And as Kuhn and others have shown, this is not something that can be settled in advance.

For these reasons P. H. Kocher was surely mistaken when he suggested that bringing Satan into nature was a prelude to exiling him from scientific inquiry altogether, and that in the English context it was in effect the first step toward the penetration of demonology by that rationalism which produced the radical scepticism of Reginald Scot. This was to prejudge just what was meant by "scientific" in sixteenth-century science. The reason why so many physicians, including Nynauld and, for that matter, a "sceptic" like Johann Wier himself, felt no incongruity in examining the demonic as well as the ordinary causes of lycanthropy and other aspects of witchcraft was because they were *both* natural forms of causation. Guazzo cited Codronchi, Cesalpino, Valesius, and Fernel in support of the view that a sickness could be both natural and instigated by the devil; to this list might be added

Jean Taxil, Jourdain Guibelet, and Giano Matteo Durastante. In these circumstances any choice between one explanation and the other was a matter of emphasis, not of principle. [39]

Demonic effects were not, then, qualitatively different from natural effects, but their causation was obscure and hidden from men. They were, in a word, occult, and this alerts us to another important aspect of the relationship between demonology and science. This is the exactly analogous epistemological stance taken up by demonologists and natural magicians. It has been assumed that the subject of natural magic entered demonological discussions in only two guises. It could be totally assimilated to demonism and then cited in order to further blacken the moral reputation of all forms of magic. Here the literature of witchcraft simply added a further layer of denunciations to a very old tradition of Christian hostility to the magical arts. [40] More significantly, it existed as a threatening source of potentially corrosive scepticism because it could explain mysterious natural effects in a way that usurped the accounts given by demonologists. The suggestion is that, like the other sciences of the "occult" tradition, natural magic had greater explanatory power than Aristotelian natural philosophy in this area. [41] There is, of course, evidence for both these stances, but they were not the only ones, and they may not have been the most typical. [42] In the light of what has been said about the naturalism inherent in quite orthodox demonology, the distinction involved in the second may turn out to be rather overdrawn, at least before 1677 when John Webster made it the foundation of his *The Displaying of Supposed Witchcraft*. Most writers wished to downgrade demonic effects by insisting on their ultimately natural (or more strictly, preternatural) character, while at the same time recognizing their occult appearance to the layman. This suggests a much more positive role for the idea of natural magic in their arguments, one which, far from undermining their belief in demonism, actually enabled them to sustain it.

This is, in fact, just what we find. Natural and demonic magic were at opposite ends of the moral spectrum, but they were epistemologically indistinguishable. The devil was therefore portrayed as a supremely gifted natural magician, the ultimate natural scientist. Paolo Grillandi said that he knew "more of natural things and the secrets of nature than all the men in the world put together," including those of "the elements, metals, stones, herbs, plants, reptiles, birds, fish and the movements of the heavens." King James agreed that he was "farre cunningner [sic] then man in the knowledge of all the occult proprieties of nature." In Rémy's view, demons had "a perfect knowledge of the secret and hidden properties of natural things." To Perkins, the devil had "great understanding, knowledge, and capacitie in all naturall things, of what sort, qualitie, and condition soever, whether they be causes or effects, whether of a simple or mixt nature."[43] Such characterizations suggest that even the merely commonplace dismissal of natural magic as satanic was more than a chapter in the history of a reputation. When Benito Pereira explained that it was actually learned from incredibly well-informed demons, this tells us as much about assumptions concerning what devils could know as about any suspicion of the "occult."[44] Moreover, the repeatedly expressed idea that the devil was the most expert natural philosopher put the demonologist in much the same intellectual predicament as the natural magician, or indeed the Aristotelian, when he discussed occult (as opposed to manifest) qualities: that of coming to terms with effects which could be experienced but whose causes might be unknowable. A remark of Perkins put the epistemological challenge posed by the devil rather effectively:

> Whereas in nature there be some properties, causes, and effects, which man never imagined to be; others, that men did once know, but are now forgot; some which men knewe not, but might know; and thousands which can hardly, or not at all be known; all these are most familiar unto him, because in themselvs they be no wonders, but only misteries and secrets, the vertue and effect whereof he hath sometime observed since his creation.[45]

In these circumstances the fact that demonologists often used the possibility of a natural magic to buttress some of their own central arguments becomes much less surprising than it seems at first. To begin with, there were occasions when writers who in no way doubted the general reality of witchcraft phenomena cited instances from natural magic to suggest that, nevertheless, there were many occult effects in nature which were wrongly confused with demonism simply because their causes were unknown or uncertain. We can see an example in the *De sagarum natura et potestate* of Wilhelm Schreiber (Scribonius), famous for his defense of the water ordeal in witch trials. Schreiber expressed plenty of the ordinary alarmism about witches and their guilt, but he took up a typical position between ascribing too little and too much to them, extremes which (he said) only a proper knowledge of natural philosophy could avoid. By this he meant knowledge both of the ability of unaided nature to generate its own marvels (here he used the play imagery—*lusus naturae*—common in the prodigy literature and in Bacon), and of the capacity of a mimetic and licit natural magic to repeat such marvels artificially. The latter he described traditionally as the most perfect philosophy in its knowledge of the mysteries and secrets of nature and as practiced by the Persian and Egyptian magi and by Moses, Solomon, and Daniel.[46]

A second case arose when demonologists, accepting without question that demonism and witchcraft had *some* sort of efficacy, wished to expose the claim that it lay in the actual means used, where this was (say) a ritual incantation or conjuration or some spurious physical means. This could be done by citing the natural but hidden causal links involved, recognizable only in terms of a knowledge of naturally magical effects. An example here would be De Lancre's attempt to discredit the idea that touching itself had an inherent efficacy. He argued that apparently supportive instances drawn from the unusual behavior of animals, plants, or metals—the torpedo fish, the *echeneis* or remora—or from natural magnetism could be explained in terms of various secret but perfectly natural properties and "antipathies." There were some such effects of which the causes were so hidden that they would never be known, and here men ought to be content with doubt and not strive, in the manner of "naturalists," for explanations at any risk to plausibility. But in other cases the reader might be referred to the works of the natural magicians, to Levinus Lemnius for the bleeding of corpses in the presence of the murderer, and to Jerome Fracastor for the *echeneis*.[47]

Third and most commonly, demonologists cited the science of the occult characteristics of natural things when they wished to reduce the status of demonic operations from the apparently miraculous to the merely wonderful. And this was in fact the context for Peter Binsfeld's remark that magic was just an esoteric form of physics. Because ordinary men were unaware of all nature's secrets, they attributed to the realm of the miraculous demonic effects that originated in natural powers, however elevated. And to this same distinction between popular superstition and learned science could be traced the reputation of natural magic, which appeared equally strange but was really only "a certain hidden and more secret part of Natural Philosophy teaching how to effect things worthy of the highest admiration . . . by the mutual application of natural actives and passives." Examining marvels from this source, such as the salamander, the volcano, and the magnet, would, Binsfeld thought, put the devil's works into proper focus. [48]

Fourth and finally, any remaining strangeness in the character of real demonic effects could be dissipated by the suggestion that they were in fact no more difficult to accept than the parallel claims made by natural magicians for what Boguet called "Nature . . . assisted and helped forward by Art." The speed to which demons accelerated ordinary processes like generation by corruption might (he admitted) invite scepticism. But if alchemists were to be believed, they too could "by a turn of the hand create gold, although in the process of Nature this takes a thousand years." Nor was there any reason to doubt that Satan could make a man appear like a wolf, for "naturalists" such as Albertus Magnus, Cardan, and Della Porta had shown how it was possible to effect similar "prestigitations." Somewhat similarly, Sébastien Michaelis compared demonic effects with the marvels described by Mercurius Trismegistus in his *Asclepius* to show that "there are many effects . . . against and above" the ordinary causation of things. For Rémy the yardstick offered by natural magic was what it revealed of nature itself rather than of art. When he came to consider the question of the reality of the objects supposedly ejected from the bodies of demoniacs, he cited the natural explanations for this being a true phenomenon given by Lemnius and Ambrose Paré (in his *Des Monstres et prodiges*), with the following comment: "If then Nature, without transgressing the limits which she had imposed upon herself can by her own working either generate or admit such objects, what must we think that the Demons will do."[49]

Naturally these arguments were often blended together. Elements of the second and third can be found in Lambert Daneau's dialogue, *De veneficis*, where the apparent (but spurious) efficacy of the forms of words and symbols used in witchcraft is explained away in terms of the natural means (like poisons) interpolated by demons. These are often very strange but never miraculous; instead, they are comparable with technical achievements like the flying wooden dove of Archytas. This reference to one of the classic marvels of the magical tradition (it is also discussed by Agrippa, Campanella, Dee, and Fludd) would not have been lost on Daneau's readers.[50] The idea of natural magic did not therefore always weaken demonology by implying some challenge to theories of demonic agency; on the contrary, it could provide important strengthening points of reference whenever there was a need to contrast or equate this agency with something comparably natural yet occult. Many repeated the standard indictment that the historical natural magic of the Persians and Egyptians had degenerated in time and was now indistinguishable from diabolism. Some, like Pereira and De Lancre, cautioned about the publication of natural magical works on the grounds that free access to such secrets was dangerous. But there was a sense in which the sort of scientific inquiry represented by them—that is, the concept itself of natural magic—remained an intrinsic part of their theories of knowledge. Given the frequency with which it is dealt with in the texts, it may even have been a necessary part of the intellectual structure of demonology.[51] From one direction this may still seem to constitute the debasement of what was undoubtedly a form of science by its association with satanism. The point to be reemphasized is that, considered from a different direction, it illustrates how closely demonological and scientific interests in certain interpretive issues can be identified with each other. Nor must it be forgotten that, conversely, natural magicians were led to a consideration of demonism by the questions raised in their discipline. Della Porta's examination of the powers of the witches' unguent, though excluded from later editions of his *Magiae naturalis*, was widely cited. Georg Pictor's *De illorum daemonum qui sub lunari collimitio versantur* was thought to be sufficiently cognate with the suppositious works of Agrippa for them to be published together in translation in England in 1665. Even Lemnius, who was reputed then and has been since as an outright "sceptic," did not exclude demons from the physical world. In his *De miraculis occultis naturae* they appear among the "accidents" of diseases, insinuating themselves "closely into men's bodies" and mingling with "food, humours, spirits, with the ayre and breath" as well as with violent and destructive tempests. They do not, of course, bulk large in Lemnius's natural philosophy; but neither are they ignored.[52]

This leads one to a final reflection on the entire range of attitudes to demonic magic and witchcraft phenomena in the Renaissance and Reformation period. By establishing that it was (in part) an epistemological debate—a debate about the grounds for ordered knowledge of nature and natural causation—which occupied the middle ground in demonology, we should be in a better position to interpret the views at the extremes. We can see, for instance, why Reginald Scot's radical scepticism stemmed not, as is sometimes suggested, from his espousal of the principles of natural magic, or in particular from the idea that, since miracles had ceased and all created things were left with only their natural capacities, all causation must also be natural. For this only begged the more fundamental question of what *counted* as a natural capacity; and since demonologists themselves endowed devils with such capacities, this was not a sceptical stance that posed any threat.[53] Scot's most telling argument was his reduction (in an Appendix to his *Discoverie of Witchcraft* of 1584) of all demonic agents to a noncorporeal condition, thus removing them from physical nature altogether. When demonologists attacked "naturalism," it was this step which they often had in mind—that is, not merely the commitment to a naturally caused world, but the denial of a devil capable of using such causation for evil ends. It was the fact that the principle of demonic agency's naturalness was not *itself* in doubt which, in other cases of supposedly damaging objections, enabled them to turn sceptical arguments to their own use. At the other extreme we can see that Bodin's reluctance to doubt anything in this area resulted from his view that it was impious to place any advance limits on what was possible in nature. To apply the language of physical events to metaphysical operations was a fundamental category error. Since aspects of magic and witchcraft belonged to this metaphysical reality, there was no criterion for accepting or rejecting them, other than trust. This obliterated the distinction that enabled most other demonologists to make sense of the world. But their case was the case of natural science as a whole. As Jean de Nynauld remarked, Bodin's position made all learning impossible, for "all the means for separating the false from the true would be taken away" if it was admitted that tomorrow the world might (with God's permission) be qualitatively different.[54]

Such issues were not, of course, discussed only at the time of the European "witch craze". Demonologists owed the foundations of their arguments to accounts of broadly the same range of phenomena given by Augustine and Aquinas. The question of what significance was to be given to the marvelous in nature had a very long history indeed. What may be suggested is that the need to reconsider the validity of these phenomena and of the criteria for understanding them was felt especially keenly in the sixteenth and seventeenth centuries, after which consensus was again established. No doubt the witchcraft trials themselves contributed to this. More importantly, the urgency stemmed from the unprecedented intensity of theological controversies concerned with the status and prevalence of miracles, the exact properties of religous objects and forms of words, the possibility of divination in a divinely ordained world, the apocalyptic meaning of prodigies, and so on. It may also be related to the fresh impetus given by disputes about the fundamentals of scientific and philosophical thought to the consideration of problems of epistemology—problems that came to be pursued with special vigor in the various parallel areas of the extraordinary in nature and art. The fact that they were also dealt with in discussions of incubus and succubus devils, flights to the sabbat, and werewolves should not deter us from accepting these, too, as contributions to scientific discourse.

Notes

1. E. E. Evans-Pritchard, *Theories of Primitive Religion* (Oxford, 1965), pp. 109–10.

2. Peter Binsfeld, *Tractatus de confessionibus maleficorum et sagarum*, 2nd ed. (Trier, 1591), pp. 174–6. In this argument Binsfeld follows Francisco Victoria, *Relectiones theologicae* (Lyons, 1587), relectio XII, "De arte magica," pp. 452–3.

3. Martin Biermann (propos.), *De magicis actionibus exetasis succincta* (Helmstädt, 1590), theorem I; cf. theorems XIII and LXXII, sigs. A3ʳ⁻ᵛ, D2ʳ.

4. Further details of medical interest in demonology, in the context of a supposed "slow progress to an enlightened attitude," are given by Oskar Diethelm, "The Medical Teaching of Demonology in the 17th and 18th Centuries," *Journal of the History of the Behavioural Sciences*, 6 (1970), pp. 3–15.

5. Sydney Anglo, "Melancholia and Witchcraft: The Debate between Wier, Bodin and Scot," and, emphasizing medical viewpoints, Jean Céard, "Folie et démon-

ologie au XVIe siècle," both in *Folie et dèraison à la Renaissance*, ed. A. Gerlo (Brussels, 1976), pp. 209–22, 129–43. Evidence of a general affinity of attitudes and methods between demonology and the "new science" is offered by Irving Kirsch, "Demonology and Science During the Scientific Revolution," *Journal of the History of the Behavioural Sciences*, 16 (1980), pp. 359–68. The same author's "Demonology and the Rise of Science: An Example of the Misperception of Historical Data," *Journal of the History of the Behavioural Sciences*, 14 (1978), pp. 149–57, merely points to coincidences in the timing of new interests in both fields.

6. D. P. Walker, *Unclean Spirits: Possession and Exorcism in France and England in the Late Sixteenth and Early Seventeenth Centuries* (London, 1981), p. 13 and passim; he calls this "an aspect of early modern science that has not yet . . . been investigated." H. C. Erik Midelfort, "Sin, Folly, Madness, Obsession: The Social Distribution of Insanity in Sixteenth-Century Germany," in *Understanding Popular Culture: Europe from the Middle Ages to the Nineteenth Century*, ed. Steven L. Kaplan (forthcoming).

7. Moody E. Prior, "Joseph Glanvill, Witchcraft, and Seventeenth-Century Science," *Modern Philology*, 30 (1930), pp. 167–93; T. H. Jobe, "The Devil in Restoration Science: The Glanvill-Webster Witchcraft Debate," *Isis*, 72 (1981), pp. 343–56.

8. George Sinclair, *Satan's Invisible World Discovered* (Edinburgh, 1685), p. xv.

9. Joseph Glanvill, *Sadducismus triumphatus*, 4th ed. (London, 1726), p. 8.

10. Hence the somewhat artificial linking of the debates of the witch hunt with the classic "revolution" in science in Brian Easlea, *Witch-Hunting, Magic and the New Philosophy: An Introduction to Debates of the Scientific Revolution 1450–1750* (Brighton, 1980), pp. 1–44 and passim.

11. Katharine Park and Lorraine J. Daston, "Unnatural Conceptions: The Study of Monsters in Sixteenth- and Seventeenth-Century France and England," *Past and Present*, no. 92 (1981), pp. 20–54.

12. Jean Céard, *La Nature et les prodiges: l'insolite au XVIe siècle, en France* (Geneva, 1977), passim, esp. pp. 352–64; cf. Lynn Thorndike, *A History of Magic and Experimental Science*, 8 vols. (New York, 1934–58), which, despite its astonishing range, is decidedly unsympathetic to the literature of witchcraft. For Thorndike's distaste for the subject, see V, 69–70; and for a characteristic judgment on a respectable Aristotelian whose demonology involves a "deluded mixture of theology and gross superstition," see his remarks on Cesalpino's *Daemonum investigatio peripatetica* (Florence, 1580), in VI, 325–8.

13. Francis Bacon, *De augmentis scientiarum*, bk. II, chap. 2, in *The Works of Francis Bacon*, ed. J. Spedding, R. L. Ellis, and D. D. Heath, 14 vols. (London, 1857–74), IV, 296; cited hereafter as *Works*. Cf. *Novum organum*, bk. II, aphorisms 28–9, in *Works*, IV, 168–9; *The Advancement of Learning*, bk. II, in *Works*, III, 330–2; *Parasceve ad historiam naturalem et experimentalem*, aphorisms 1–4, in *Works*, IV, 253–7 (all references are to the English trans.). Thomas Sprat, *The History of the Royal Society of London*, 3rd ed. (London, 1722), pp. 214–15, defends the study of "the most unusual and monstrous Forces and Motions of Matter," without mentioning witchcraft. For Boyle and Glanvill on witchcraft and marvels, see Prior, pp. 183–4.

14. Francis Bacon, *Sylva sylvarum: or a Natural History in Ten Centuries*, century X, no. 903; cf. no. 975; in *Works*, II, 642, 664.

15. Ibid., century X, no. 950, in *Works*, II, 658. For an "experiment solitary touching maleficiating," see century IX, no. 888, in *Works*, II, 634.

16. Martin Del Rio, *Disquisitionum magicarum* (Lyons, 1608), bk. I, chaps. 2–5.

17. Giovanni Tommaso Gastaldi, *De potestate angelica sive de potentia motrice, ac mirandis operibus angelorum atque daemonum*, 3 vols. (Rome, 1650–2); cf. Francesco Torreblanca (Villalpandus), *Daemonologia sive de magia naturali, daemoniaca, licita, et illicita, deque aperta et occulta, interventione et invocatione daemonis* (Mainz, 1623), bk. II, pp. 176–403; Pierre de Lancre, *L'Incredulité et mescreance du sortilege plainement convaincüe* (Paris, 1622).

18. André du Laurens, *De mirabili strumas sanandi vi solis Galliae Regibus Christianissimus divinitus concessa* (Paris, 1609), chap. 9.

19. I have used the French trans.: Claude Rapine (Caelestinus), *Des Chóses merveilleuses en la nature où est traicté des erreurs des sens, des puissances de l'âme, et des influences des cieux*, trans. Jacques Giraud (Lyons, 1557), chap. 8, pp. 113–30 ("On the Operation of Evil Spirits"); Scipion Dupleix, *La Curiosité naturelle rédigée en questions selon l'ordre alphabétique* (Rouen, 1635), pp. 393–4; Gaspar Schott, *Physica curiosa, sive mirabilia naturae et artis* (Würzburg, 1667), bk. I, pp. 1–195. Schott also deals with ghosts, miraculous races, demoniacs, monsters, portents, animal marvels, and meteors.

20. G. L. Burr, "The Literature of Witchcraft," in *George Lincoln Burr*, ed. R. H. Bainton and L. O. Gibbons (New York, 1943), pp. 166–89; H. C. Lea, *Materials Toward a History of Witchcraft*, ed. A. C. Howland, 3 vols. (Philadelphia, 1939; New York, 1957).

21. For a striking example of the presentation of sceptical arguments in a discussion nonetheless committed to the reality of demonism, see Loys le Caron (Charondas), *Questions divers et discours* (Paris, 1579), quest. VIII, ("Si par incantations, parolles ou autres semblables sortileges l'homme peult estre ensorcelé et offensé en ses actions et forces naturelles"), fols. 31ᵛ–43ᵛ; cf. the same author's *Responses du droict françois* (Paris, 1579–82), bk. IX, response 43 ("Si les sorciers et sorcières sont dignes de dernier supplice"), pp. 445–50. For the flexibility and variety in theories of witchcraft, see H. C. Erik Midelfort, *Witch Hunting in Southwestern Germany, 1562–1684: The Social and Intellectual Foundations* (Stanford, 1972), pp. 10–29.

22. Del Rio, bk. II, quaest. 6, p. 61; Philipp Ludwig Elich, *Daemonomagia* (Frankfurt, 1607), chap. 5, pp. 60–1; Francesco Maria Guazzo, *Compendium maleficarum*, trans. and ed. Montague Summers (London, 1929), bk. I, chap. 3, p. 7; Benito Pereira, *De magia, de observatione somniorum, et de divinatione astrologia* (Cologne, 1598), bk. I, chap. 1, pp. 4–5; James VI and I, *Daemonologie, in the Forme of a Dialogue* (Edinburgh, 1597), p. 42; John Cotta, *The Triall of Witch-Craft* (London, 1616), dedicatory epistle, sigs. A2–A3ᵛ; Noël Taillepied, *Traité de l'apparition des esprits* (Rouen, 1600), trans. and ed. Montague Summers as *A Treatise of Ghosts* (London, 1933), pp. xvi–xvii, 39–40.

23. Lucien Febvre, "Sorcellerie: sottise ou révolution mentale?" *Annales E.S.C.*, 3 (1948); trans. K. Folca as "Witchcraft: Nonsense or a Mental Revolution?" in *A New Kind of History from the Writings of Febvre*, ed. Peter Burke (London, 1973), pp. 185–92.

24. Pierre Le Loyer, *IIII Livres des spectres, ou apparitions et visions d'esprits, anges et Démons se monstrans sensiblement aux hommes* (Angers, 1586), partly trans. Z. Jones as *A*

Treatise of Specters or Straunge Sights, Visions and Apparitions Appearing Sensibly Unto Men (London, 1605).

25. François Perrault, *Demonologie ou discours en general touchant l'existence puissance impuissance des demons et sorciers* (Geneva, 1656), chaps. 1–3, pp. 1–52.

26. Cotta, chap. 6, p. 34.

27. For standard accounts of demonic power and knowledge and their limitations, see Silvestro da Prierio (Mazzolini), *De strigimagarum daemonumque mirandis* (Rome, 1575), bk. I, chaps. 13–15, pp. 95–126; Otto Casmann, *Angelographia* (Frankfurt, 1597), pt. 2 ("De malis angelis"), chaps. 12–14, 18–20, pp. 428–57, 508–82; Johann Wier, *De praestigiis daemonum et incantationibus ac veneficiis* (Basel, 1568), bk. I, chaps. 10–18; Torreblanca, bk. II, chaps. 5–10, pp. 191–220; Guazzo, bk. I, chaps. 3–4, 16, pp. 7–11, 57; Gervasio Pizzurini, *Enchiridion exorcisticum* (Lyons, 1668), praeludium, chap. 6, pp. 14–16. For a typical analysis of the devil's powers over local motion, see Leonardo Vairo, *De fascino* (Paris, 1583), bk. II, chap. 13. For a discussion of his interference in the conditions of natural combustion, see Adam Tanner, *De potentia loco motiva angelorum*, quaest. 6, in *Diversi tractatus*, ed. Constantine Munich (Cologne, 1629), pp. 90–1.

28. Descriptions of the range of illusion techniques are again in most standard demonologies; e.g., Guazzo, bk. I, chap. 4, p. 9. But see full accounts in Anthoine de Morry, *Discours d'un miracle avenu en la Basse Normandie* (Paris, 1598), pp. 39–56; Andrea Gerhard (Hyperius), "Whether That the Devils Have Bene the Shewers of Magicall Artes," in *Two Commonplaces Taken Out of Andreas Hyperius*, trans. R. V. (London, 1581), pp. 47–81; and André Valladier, "Des Charmes et sortileges, ligatures, philtres d'amour, ecstases diaboliques, horribles, et extraordinaires tentations de Satan . . . ," sermon for Third Sunday in Advent 1612, in his *La Saincte Philosophie de l'ame* (Paris, 1614), pp. 619–41. For the fact that demonic delusions were also naturally caused, see Henri Boguet, *Discours des sorciers*, trans. and ed. Montague Summers and E. A. Ashwin as *An Examen of Witches* (London, 1929), p. xliii.

29. Jean de Nynauld, *De la Lycanthropie, transformation, et extase des sorciers* (Paris, 1615), passim; cf. Boguet, chaps. 17, 47, pp. 46–51, 145–8.

30. P. H. Kocher, *Science and Religion in Elizabethan England* (San Marino, Calif., 1953; New York, 1969), pp. 119–45; Wayne Shumaker, *The Occult Sciences in the Renaissance* (London, 1972), pp. 70–85.

31. This last idea is in Jacob Heerbrand (praeses.), *De magia dissertatio* (Tübingen, 1570), prop. 6, p. 2.

32. Nicolas Rémy, *Daemonolatreiae* (Lyons, 1595), bk. III, chap. 12; bk. I, chap. 6; bk. III, chap. 1; trans. and ed. E. A. Ashwin and Montague Summers as *Demonolatry* (London, 1930), pp. 181–2; cf. pp. xii, 11, 141.

33. Cotta, p. 34; William Perkins, *A Discourse of the Damned Art of Witchcraft* (Cambridge, 1610), epistle; cf. pp. 18–21, 27–8, 159.

34. Paolo Grillandi, *Tractatus de hereticis et sortilegiis* (Frankfurt, 1592), quaest. 7, p. 96.

35. Johann Georg Godelmann, *Tractatus de magis, veneficis et lamiis recte cognoscendis et*

puniendis (Frankfurt, 1591), bk. I, chap. 8 ("De curatóribus morborum hyperphysicorum praestigiosis").

36. Del Rio, bk. I, chap. 4, quaest. 3, p. 25; cf. Rémy, bk. II, chap. 5, p. 113.

37. Perkins, p. 23.

38. James VI and I, "To the Reader," cf. p. 42; Bacon, *De augmentis scientiarum*, bk. II, chap. 2, in *Works*, IV, 296. See also Elich, chap. 6, pp. 75ff.

39. Guazzo, bk. II, chap. 8, p. 105; for Taxil and Guibelet, see Céard, "Folie et démonologie," pp. 129–43. Janus Matthaeus Durastantes, *Problemata . . . I, Daemones an sint, et an morborum sint causae* (Venice, 1567), fols. I–83ᵛ.

40. For a recent survey of this tradition, see Edward Peters, *The Magician, the Witch, and the Law* (Brighton, 1978), passim.

41. H. R. Trevor-Roper, *The European Witch Craze of the Sixteenth and Seventeenth Centuries*, rev. ed. (London, 1978), pp. 58–9; K. V. Thomas, *Religion and the Decline of Magic* (London, 1971), pp. 579, 646; P. W. Elmer, "Medicine, Medical Reform and the Puritan Revolution," unpublished Ph.D. thesis, University of Wales, 1980, pp. 289–302; Jobe, pp. 343–4.

42. For entirely negative accounts of magic, see James VI and I, *Daemonologie*, and Niels Hemmingsen, *Admonitio de superstitionibus magicis vitandis* (Copenhagen, 1575). There is an excellent example of the fully sceptical use of natural magical evidence in Michel Marescot et al., *Discours véritable sur le faict de Marthe Brossier de Romorrantin prétendue démoniaque* (Paris, 1599), pp. 29–30; trans. A. Hartwell as *A True Discourse . . .* (London, 1599), pp. 22–3. The authors do not, however, rule out the possibility of demonic possession in principle. Nor was the argument that only extraordinary effects above the laws of nature could be attributed to the devil (those of the Brossier case not being of this sort), a very telling piece of antidemonology, for the devil was conventionally placed within such laws.

43. Grillandi, quaest. 6, pp. 59, 68–9; these remarks are found in many other texts. James VI and I, p. 44; Rémy, bk. II, chap. 4, p. 107; Perkins, p. 19.

44. Pereira, bk. I, chap. 3, pp. 21–2.

45. Perkins, p. 20; for the epistemological problems posed by occult qualities in the wider context of scientific and philosophical controversy, see Keith Hutchison, "What Happened to Occult Qualities in the Scientific Revolution?" *Isis*, 83 (1982), pp. 233–53.

46. William Adolf Schreiber (Scribonius), *De sagarum natura et potestate* (Marburg, 1588), pp. 29–35; for the presence of demons in Schreiber's natural philosophy, see his *Rerum naturalium doctrina* (Basel, 1583).

47. Pierre de Lancre, disc. III ("De l'Attouchement"), fols. 113–77, esp. fols. 124–57. In the same way Boguet referred to Della Porta for the real natural effects of the witches' unguent, and Perkins discussed the well-known natural magical instance of the basilisk or cockatrice, concluding that fascination by breathing or looking alone was either fabulous or the indirect result of natural causes like contagion. There are arguments very similar to De Lancre's in Vairo, bk. II, chap. 10.

48. Binsfeld, pp. 173–8.

49. Boguet, pp. 64, 148–9; Sébastien Michaelis, *Pneumologie, ou discours des esprits*, 2nd ed. (Paris, 1613), trans. W. B. as *Pneumology or Discourse of Spirits* (London, 1613), pp. 5–6; Rémy, bk. III, chap. 1, pp. 139–41.

50. Lambert Daneau, *De veneficis* (Cologne, 1575), pp. 94–5, trans. R. W. as *A Dialogue of Witches* (London, 1575), sigs. H6v–I6v. For the dove of Archytas, see Frances Yates, *Giordano Bruno and the Hermetic Tradition* (London, 1964), pp. 147–9, and *The Rosicrucian Enlightenment* (London, 1972), p. 76.

51. A point perhaps insufficiently realized by D. P. Walker, *Spiritual and Demonic Magic from Ficino to Campanella* (London, 1958), pp. 145–85, for even Del Rio thought that to avoid attributing all unusual effects to demonism one had to know of the many things surpassing ordinary scientific inquiry (bk. II, quaest. 5, pp. 60–1).

52. Giovanni della Porta, *Magiae naturalis, sive de miraculis rerum naturalium* (Naples, 1558), bk. II, chap. 26, p. 102; *Henry Cornelius Agrippa: His Fourth Book of Occult Philosophy*, trans. R. Turner (London, 1655), pp. 109–53; Levinus Lemnius, *Occulta naturae miracula* (Antwerp, 1561), fols. 83–87v, quotations from the English trans., *The Secret Miracles of Nature* (London, 1658), pp. 86–90, 385.

53. In this respect it is instructive to compare Reginald Scot, *The Discoverie of Witchcraft* (London, 1584), bk. I, chap. 7, pp. 14–15, with Le Caron, *Questions divers*, fol. 32r, where the point is absorbed into conventional demonology.

54. Nynauld, p. 77; the argument is in fact identical to that of Rapine, p. 121. Cf. Jean Bodin, *De la Démonomanie des sorciers* (Paris, 1580), preface and "Refutation des opinions de Jean Wier," fols. 239v–40r, 244r, 247v, 251r–v.

On Porphyria and the Aetiology of Werwolves

L. ILLIS

Congenital porphyria is a rare disease, due to a recessive gene, in which there is an inability to convert porphobilinogen to porphyrin in the bone marrow. The condition is characterized by:

1. Severe photosensitivity in which a vesicular erythema is produced by the action of light. This may be especially noticeable during the summer or in a mountainous region (Vannotti 1954).

2. The urine is often reddish-brown as a result of the presence of large quantities of porphyrins.

3. There is a tendency for the skin lesions to ulcerate, and these ulcers may attack cartilage and bone. Over a period of years structures such as nose, ears, eyelids, and fingers, undergo progressive mutilation.

4. On the photosensitive areas hypertrichosis and pigmentation may develop.

5. The teeth may be red or reddish-brown due to the deposition of porphyrins.

6. The bone marrow is hyperplastic, usually in association with splenomegaly and haemolytic anaemia.

Porphyria cutanea tarda ("mixed porphyria") is another manifestation of disturbed porphyrin metabolism (Fig. 1).

This also, is familial, but of a dominant genetic trait. The age of onset of its manifestations is later and there is a marked sex difference in favour of males. Photosensitivity is less marked but does occur, and skin lesions are not so severe and do not usually progress to scarring and mutilation. A brownish pigmentation is common and the face may present a peculiar violaceous colour and show injection of the conjunctivae (Brunsting et al. 1951). Exposure to heat or light may be followed by pruritus in which case the affected parts may show excoria-

Excerpted from *Proceedings of the Royal Society of Medicine* 57 (1964): 23–26.

tion. Hirsuties occurs but is less common than in the congenital form. Jaundice, related to hepatic dysfunction, may be present (MacGregor et al. 1952).

Nervous manifestations are most common in the acute intermittent variety of porphyria. They do, however, occur in porphyria cutanea tarda (MacGregor et al. 1952) or the "mixed" type of hepatic porphyria. Although congenital and idiopathic porphyrias are separable on clinical and genetic grounds, Vannotti (1954) is of the opinion that there are "points of contact [which] could give rise to these mixed forms".

The nervous manifestations may be referable to any part of the nervous system, and include mental disorders ranging from mild hysteria to manic-depressive psychoses and delirium. Epilepsy may occur.

Both Waldenstrom (1937) and Vannotti have shown that, at least in idiopathic porphyria, there is an important geographic factor, and these cases often occur, in Sweden and in Switzerland, "in certain districts and especially along certain valleys" (Vannotti 1954). This also reflects the hereditary factor in the development of the disease.

It is possible, then, to paint a picture of a porphyric which, though not necessarily characteristic or typical, will fit with all the available evidence in the literature of porphyria: such a person, because of photosensitivity and the resultant disfigurement, may choose only to wander about at night. The pale, yellowish, excoriated skin may be explained by the haemolytic anaemia, jaundice, and pruritus. These features, together with hypertrichosis and pigmentation, fit well with the descriptions, in older literature, of werwolves. The unhappy person may be mentally disturbed, and show some type or degree of abnormal behaviour. In ancient times this would be accentuated by the physical and social treatment he received from the other villagers, whose instincts would be to explain the apparition in terms of witchcraft or Satanic possession.

The red teeth, the passage of red urine, the nocturnal wanderings, the mutilation of face and hands, the deranged behaviour: what could these suggest to a primitive, fear-ridden, and relatively isolated community? Figure 2 gives an obvious answer.

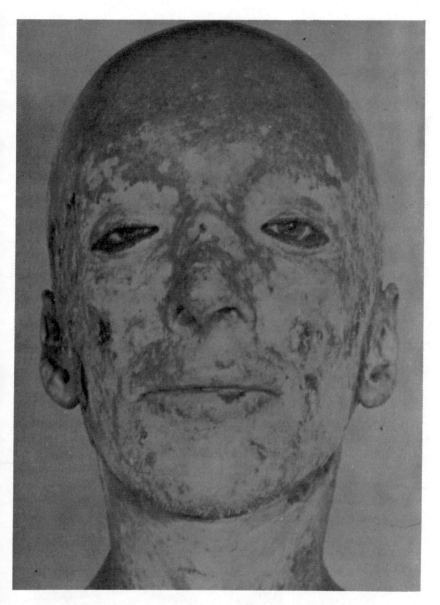

Patient with severe cutaneous hepatic porphyria with facial lesions. From A. Goldberg and C. Rimington, *Diseases of Porphyrin Metabolism*, 1962. Courtesy of Charles C. Thomas, Publisher, Springfield, Illinois, and A. Goldberg and C. Rimington.

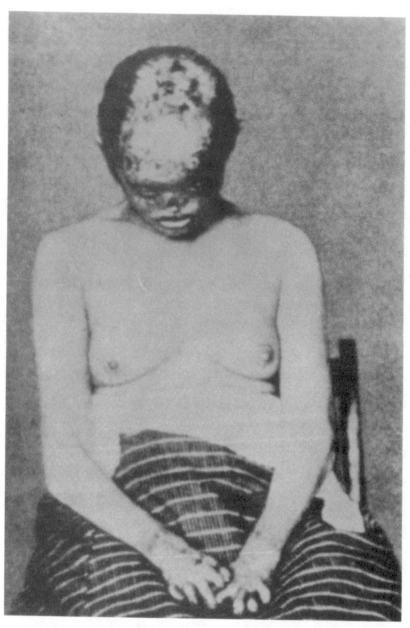

Congenital porphyria showing photosensitization, scarring, and mutilation. From W. Hausmann, *Strahlentherapie*, Suppl. 8 (1923). Courtesy of *Strahlentherapie*.

References

Brunsting L A, Mason H L & Aldrich R A
(1951) *Journal of the American Medical Association* 146, 1207.

Goldberg A & Rimington C
(1962) *Diseases of Porphyrin Metabolism.* Springfield, Ill.

Hausmann W (1923) *Strahlentherapie* Suppl. 8.

MacGregor A G, Nicholas R E H, & Rimington C
(1952) *Archives of Internal Medicine* 90, 483.

Vannotti A (1954) *Porphyrins.* Trans. C Rimington. London.

Waldenstrom J (1937) *Acta Medica Scandinavica Supplement* 82.

The Medical Origins of the
European Witch Craze: A Hypothesis

LELAND L. ESTES

𝕴t has usually been assumed by historians that the witch hunts of the sixteenth and seventeenth centuries were, at least in part, the result of beliefs that found their origins in the Middle Ages, or even in some earlier epoch.[1] This assumption should surprise no one since most scholars have been educated to regard the history of early modern culture as essentially a tale of the emergence of secular humanism and the rise of science. Yet the tendency of recent research has been to, slowly but steadily, whittle away the props that once firmly supported the belief that the witch craze was the last, corrupt efflorescence of the medieval spirit.[2] Increasingly, scholars have sought the origin of the craze among the practitioners of witch hunting rather than among their ancestors. However, research and thinking on the early modern source of witch hunting have been limited mostly to its social ramifications. Researchers have been concerned with how people used witchcraft accusations to attack certain social groups rather than with why they believed that certain types of misfortunes could be properly attributed to the malice of witches.[3] In the following pages I wish to address the second of these two problems and to propose tentatively that the revolution in scientific and particularly medical thought that characterized the late Renaissance, and which has heretofore been thought to be fundamentally inimical to a belief in witches, actually proved the intellectual basis, indeed the mainspring of witch hunting in the two centuries when the craze and the "new science" flourished together so extravagantly.

How might a medical revolution spark a hunt for witches? For a possible answer to this question we must look briefly at just what was happening to medicine near the end of the Renaissance. This was the age in which Andreas Vesalius, and many of his contemporaries, discovered that much of the Galenic anatomy and physiology that had been taken for granted by physicians in the Middle Ages was incorrect,

Journal of Social History 17 (Winter 1983), 271–84.

sometimes embarrassingly so. These discoveries were part of a wider movement in which the relation of the medical fact to medical theory was being dramatically altered. In the Middle Ages medical facts, while they may have been used to overthrow specific diagnoses, always confirmed medical theory in general. In a manner similar to that described for the Azande poison oracle by the anthropologist E. E. Evans-Pritchard, circularity and secondary elaboration prevented potentially anomalous facts from threatening the integrity of the medical system as a whole.[4] An incorrect diagnosis or a therapeutical failure was almost never thought to indicate that the theories on which they were based were wrong. This theoretical inertia was perpetuated by the use of diagnostic techniques like astrology and uroscopy that helped doctors to avoid the morass of particular symptoms that might have easily overwhelmed the radically simplified Galenism which had survived the pruning of a thousand years of epitomizers.

Sometime near the end of the fifteenth century, however, the closed and self-contained medical system of the Middle Ages was short-circuited. We see for the first time since classical antiquity the clear emergence of medical facts which were thought not to support standard Galenism. This emergence has been attributed to many factors including the revival of Neoplatonism, the explosion of medical texts after the invention of printing, the increasing organization of the medical profession and the challenge of new diseases imported from Asia and from the New World. All of these factors created a climate in which not only were many well established facts seen for the first time as posing a problem for Greco-Roman medical theory, but some physicians actually sought new facts which might be used to confirm or refute their own particular medical ideas. An inevitable by-product of this new, more "scientific" attitude was the slow disintegration of the medical view of the Middle Ages. Medieval Galenism grew increasingly cumbersome as one theorist after another added to and elaborated its simple hypotheses in order to be able to take into account an increasingly diverse medical environment. Eventually, wholly new medical theories were advanced which openly opposed those of the old system.[5]

One of the most important but least studied concomitants of this process of decay was the disintegration of the simple nosological categories that had governed medicine in the Middle Ages. The medieval doctor had based his diagnoses on a few relatively simple indicators, not all of which were symptoms according to our modern understanding of this term. So simple, in fact, was his job that the average "physician could make rapid calculations and decide within a matter of seconds what was ailing the patient, what the treatment should be and what success or failure was likely to ensue."[6] But as physicians began to pay increasing attention to the patient and to his unique pathological state, and less to the color of his urine or to the position of the stars at the first onset of his illness, medieval nosological categories proved increasingly inadequate. As an ever larger number and type of symptoms were noted by physicians, and taken into account in their diagnoses, Galenic theory was parsed ever more elaborately to provide the theoretical wherewithal to group these symptoms into cogent and intelligible disease classes. The humors were subdivided and the qualities broken down into various degrees.[7] Some gave up humoral medicine altogether and even the very attempt to establish disease categories. Paracelsus, for instance, occasionally wrote as if each ailment was a wholly individual entity which did not conform to any generic criteria whatsoever, and which could only be known and diagnosed directly through an intuitive process peculiar to the born physician.[8] But most physicians sought some kind of via media which allowed them to remain within the Galenic tradition yet which also allowed a certain cognitive freedom to group and regroup symptoms in order to create a new disease category as the occasion demanded. The key figure in this movement was Jean Fernel, whose reintroduction of Aristotelian epistemology into medicine allowed physicians to discuss symptoms and of the supposed underlying humoral pathology.[9]

Yet the increasing attention that the medical profession was paying to specific pathological states, linked with the inability of medical theory to expand or change fast enough to provide adequate explanations for all of the new facts that were emerging, meant that the individual physician would certainly encounter many ailments whose symptomatology was so unusual or so irregular that he could not easily fit them into a known disease category and, consequently, for which he could not offer an intelligible remedy. What was he to do and how was he to proceed in such a situation? How was he to explain such an ailment? Fernel argued, and most physicians for the next century followed him in this as in so many other things, that such diseases had an unnatural or supernatural cause, and were probably the result of the intervention of the Devil. The physician, whose theories were wholly concerned with the natural, need not, could not and must not pursue the etiological status of his patients' illnesses beyond the natural and physical realm. It might not even be proper for a physician to treat such devilishly-inspired illnesses. His best course of action was to inform the secular and religious authorities. It was very likely that only they could provide any real relief. [10]

Medieval medicine had not provided an impenetrable barrier between this world and the next. People did die, diseases and accidents oftentimes did prove fatal. But at least medicine provided a relatively simple and mostly consistent explanation of death and suffering. For most illnesses it had a reason, for most diseases it offered a remedy. The failure of the remedy was not attributed to medical theory, but to the weaknesses of individual physicians or to the necessary dictates of God's plan for the world or for the individual. But in Europe after 1500 the medieval medical view began to come apart. Gaps began to appear in what one anthropologist has called the "mapped area of security" that kept "chaos at bay."[11] For some, these gaps were seen as anomalies, as a chance to destroy the old sytem and replace it with a new one. [12] Such was the vision of Paracelsus, Vesalius and William Harvey. But for many, probably the vast majority, these gaps were frightening windows on a primordial chaos beyond. They were not a stimulus to new creative activity, but a terrifying reminder of just how limited was man's control over his physical environment. They were also a clear indication to the afflicted that if their illnesses were strange or irregular they could expect little or no help from the medical establishment. Certain illnesses could expose them to the vagaries of an unstructured and thus uncontrollable world. The result of this disintegration of what was thought to be society's defenses against disease and dying probably greatly increased the load of fear that European man carried with him into the early modern world.

At the same time that medicine seemed to be losing its control over a category of irregular diseases, it was actually extending its reach in other directions. Many diseases in the Middle Ages whose symptomatology was regular, but which had been traditionally associated with demons and sorcery, as for instance impotence, the falling sickness and the nightmare, were brought increasingly within the natural realm. It is not entirely clear from medieval texts if these diseases had been widely considered by physicians to be of demonic origin or whether this was only the view of a few. Perhaps physicians were merely showing some small deference to popular beliefs. Certainly, most of the classical medical texts that survived and were still being used did not support such an etiology. What is more, even when the Devil was suspected, the physician did not balk at suggesting a natural remedy, which he fully expected to be effective.[13] In this the medieval doctor's attitude towards the demonic in disease differed radically from his early modern counterpart. Sixteenth- and seventeenth-century doctors, while they were often willing to treat strange and irregular illnesses symptom by symptom, were not willing, nor really able to treat the disease as a whole. Moreover, most do not appear to have been confident that any medical treatment whatsoever could be effective. In fact, as the English physician John Cotta argued, one of the chief indications of a demonic ailment was

> when natural remedies or means according unto art and due discretion applied, do extraordinarily or miraculously either lose their manifest inevitable nature, use, and operation, or else produce effects and consequences, against or above their nature.[14]

It would seem then that medical theory in the early modern period was changing in such a way as to at least suggest the possibility of a new type of demonic illness. But did this change substantially influence the evidentiary basis of the witchcraft prosecutions? Many historians would say no. After all, it would seem that there was no mishap or illness so ordinary or inconsequential that someone somewhere did not suspect that it might be caused by a witch. If a mare died, if beer went stale, if a person tripped on a fence, or even if cream refused to turn to butter, people might suspect witchcraft. We find examples of such suspicions in the Middle Ages, in the early modern period, and we still find them in Western Europe today.[15] But suspicions of this sort did not usually lead to an accusation in a court of law and rarely, by themselves, to a conviction and execution. Normally, it was an illness or a death that led to a charge of witchcraft that was generally supported and might provide the basis for a prosecution.[16] This is not to say that any illness or death was liable to generate an actionable case. Unlike the classic Azande situation described by

Evans-Pritchard, most illnesses and deaths in early modern Europe could be explained in natural terms. Pandemic and epidemic diseases, as well as the regular infirmities of old age and accidents, were rarely laid to witches in indictments. [17] But illnesses that were strange and irregular, or which reacted in unusual ways to standard modes of treatment, often resulted in witchcraft trials. A critic of the hunts, John Gaule, pointedly remarked of witch hunters that "every disease whereof they neither understand the cause, nor are acquainted with the symptoms must be suspected for witchcraft." [18] I would like to suggest that it was this stereotypical witch disease, and not a witch figure, as has often been supposed, that stimulated the hunt for witches. European civilization was not really trying to uproot a certain type of human being, but was instead looking for the "spreaders" of a certain type of illness.

When speaking of European civilization I do not mean to imply that attitudes towards witches were in every place and at every social and economic level the same. It is quite obvious that this was not the case. Clearly, a great divide separated those who were literate, and thus who participated fully in the cultural advance of which the medical revolution was only a small part, and those who were not. Yet too much can be made of this great division, especially in the case of medicine. For recent research has indicated that, in fact, the average European, that is the peasant, was more fully in touch with changes in learned medicine than has heretofore been assumed. Those with at least a partial knowledge of the great tradition in medicine were very common indeed. University-trained physicians were forever complaining of the competition that such "empirics" offered.

So many and so infinitely do the numbers of barbarous and unlearned councilors of health at this time overspread all corners of this kingdom, that (they) do not only everywhere cover and eclipse the sunshine of all true learning and understanding but generally darken and extinguish the very light of common sense and reason. [19]

It must be remembered that the half century before 1600 was in Northern Europe a period of explosive gains in literacy, and anyone who had the ability to read one of the many popular diagnostic and health care manuals could practice medicine. [20] Even more could be learned about changes in medical theory by those who had, over the years, accumulated enough stray knowledge to convince those on the lower social rungs that they were medically competent. The practice of medicine by such individuals was widespread. Perhaps just as common was the practice of medicine by the clergy. A fairly large proportion of European parishes were ministered to by a man who had at least limited university experience. And as part of this experience he was very likely to have read a little Hippocrates or Galen. Many priests had read much more. Michael MacDonald has recently analyzed the medical career of the rural Northamptonshire cleric and Oxford MA, Richard Napier, whose medical records have miraculously survived intact. Napier treated almost 60,000 patients in a 37 year period, most of these being of humble origin.[21] And it is clear that he did occasionally diagnose a disease as having been caused by a witch.[22] Such diagnoses were probably very common among those who had been influenced by the high tradition in medicine, but who were not sufficiently a part of that tradition to have absorbed its naturalistic ethos to the full.[23]

It cannot be denied, however, that while the peasantry was influenced by changes in the high medical tradition, this influence was limited in its extent and certainly was not as important at this social level as in those above it. Ancient, preliterate ideas continued to dominate medical thought among the peasantry, the special knowledge of "old women, Egyptians (gypsies), and such-like persons" to which Paracelsus and his disciples were always referring.[24] Keith Thomas has caught the roughest outlines of this medical system in his *Religion and the Decline of Magic*. Diseases and accidents of the widest variety were attributed to the machinations of fairies, house cobolds, stable goblins, hobhurts, dwarfs, trolls, hillmen, pixey-leds and will-o-the-wisps. They were also often attributed to sorcerers and witches.[25] The mix of such diagnoses varied from country to country, region to region, and even from village to village. They also probably varied over time.

To this mixture was added in the sixteenth and seventeenth centuries the specific witch-disease complex that grew out of the medical revolution previously discussed. The peasantry of the early modern epoch probably generated many accusations based on this new complex, but peasants also continued to accuse one another of causing various diseases and accidents that were rooted in older medical paradigms. These older paradigms, however, while they might have provided a convincing basis for an accusation in a particular village, would have seemed less compelling to a literate member of the local gentry and appeared positively absurd to a judge who might very well have come from hundreds of miles away. To achieve any standing in a court of law the charge would not only have had to have found support in the local cosmology of the accuser, but also in the great medical tradition with which the "judicial classes" were closely in touch. That is, it would have had to make sense in terms of the latest and best medical opinion, that supported and taught by the universities and propagated in the literature of that period. Sometimes the peasantry was sufficiently conversant with the contemporary movement of medical ideas to "tailor" the charge to fit the intellectual requirements of the court. Other times, I suspect, charges based on local medical paradigms were sufficiently similar to that of the high medical tradition to pass easily from one intellectual foundation to the other. But it did usually have to make this passage. It did generally have to find support in the high tradition. As has been shown for England by Thomas and for France by Jean Delumeau, elite culture in the early modern period was pulling away from that of the village and, consequently, those who manned the European judicial systems in this age were more likely than earlier to hold mere peasant beliefs in contempt.[26] Thus the seeming paradox, that most of the demonologists, while they argued that witches were real and should be punished, also argued that many peasant beliefs, including many concerning witches, were delusions and should be stamped out.[27]

As might be expected, the craze did not proceed much beyond the boundaries of Latin-reading culture. Orthodoxy was little affected and the Moslem countries not at all.[28] The scientific and medical revolutions were confined almost exclusively to the peoples of Western and Central Europe, and so was witch hunting. Yet not all of the areas of the Latin West were equally affected. In some places the craze came later than in others, and in some places it did not come at all. How might this be explained? It is probably first worth noting that the craze, in a general sort of way, tended to spread from the cultural centers to the periphery, from the densely settled lowlands to the more sparsely inhabited highland regions, from the near urban to the rural world. It thus would appear to have followed the probable lines of diffusion of new medical ideas and of a burgeoning medical profession. In England, for instance, the craze was very strong in the counties immediately surrounding London in the sixteenth century. In the seventeenth century the weight of witch hunting shifted towards the northern and western portions of the country.[29] Surviving evidence would suggest that the new medical ideas spread in a similar manner.[30] Yet it must be pointed out that while cities and their cultures seem to have been the intellectual epicenter of the craze, they were not its social fount. The great metropolises do not seem to have supported a social structure conducive to the generation of witchcraft accusations. London provided the judges that administered the craze in the surrounding counties, but the city itself was only marginally affected. And, while the citizens of the city of Geneva manned the legal apparatus that directed the hunts in the Genevan Republic, a proportionately greater number of accusations came from nearby rural parishes.[31]

Some areas were not only less affected than others, they were hardly affected at all. Spain and Portugal, Central and Southern Italy, and the Dutch Republic are outstanding examples, although other areas were also more or less immune. In some places this immunity can be attributed to the idiosyncrasy of the ruling prince. Duke William of Cleves not only protected the great sixteenth century opponent of the craze, Johann Weyer, he also long prevented the hunting of witches within his realm.[32] But personal idiosyncrasy cannot be used to explain the lack of witch hunting in most cases. More general explanations should be offered.

It seems likely that the reason the witch craze never really caught on in Spain was the continued control of the whole domain of witchcraft and sorcery in that country, as also in Portugal and Central and Southern Italy, by the Catholic Church. Gustav Henningsen has shown us how suspicious the Spanish Inquisition was of the witch craze when it spread into the Basque regions of Northern Spain from France. The Inquisition did not wish to be diverted from its main goal, the extirpation of heresy.[33] Moreover, the conservatism of the Inquisitorial courts involved in the Basque witch scare made it very difficult to convict anyone of having caused the new witch disease, or any other sorcery-related crime. For these courts insisted not merely on the existence of the witch disease, but also substantial physical proof that the accused person was actually a sorcerer or a sorceress. The Inquisition wanted real ointments and poisons, real books of spells, and hard evidence of a sabbat.[34] The more forward looking courts to the north were not nearly so rigorous in their demands. In fact, theories were developed which made the existence of such hard evidence more or less superfluous.

Witch hunting might also fail where its espousal became a partisan issue. When James VI of Scotland acceded to the English throne on the death of Elizabeth I, few doubted that this author of a demonology and notorious scourge of witches in his homeland would intensify the hunts in his new kingdom. But in England witch hunting had become a partisan religious issue, with insurgent Puritan interests using it to further highlight the shortcomings of the Anglican establishment. James, who supported the efforts of his Anglican bishops to impose a measure of religious uniformity, greatly reduced witch hunting in England by personally exposing as frauds several demoniacs being used in witch-finding campaigns. As in Spain, witch hunting in England was curtailed because it indirectly threatened the attainment of a more fundamental goal.[35]

Certainly the conflicts that developed between witch hunting and other social, economic and political pursuits were important in bringing the former into disrepute among those in power, and thus to end. Yet there was probably a more fundamental reason why some areas were spared the horrors of hunting while others, often quite close by, were not. If it is true that the judicial and literate classes acted as "gatekeepers" in the craze, letting some peasant accusations concerning witches into court, but keeping many others out, then it very well might be that certain village, regional or even national cosmologies inherited from previous centuries were less liable to generate acceptable accusations than others. Alan MacFarlane has discovered that about one out of four villages in the county of Essex produced a witchcraft accusation that was eventually converted into an official indictment. It seems unlikely that in the other three-quarters, people were unconcerned with the problem of witchcraft or of some other related phenomenon.[36] It might very well be, however, that the structure of their suspicions and accusations was such that they could not easily pass from the medical cosmology of the village to that of the great tradition. They simply were not compatible with the new modes of thinking of the literate classes and thus were probably dismissed as vulgar peasant superstitions. This might explain why the craze never passed to Wales, to Ireland, or to the Highlands of Scotland, despite the fact that old-style witch beliefs were strong there not only in the sixteenth and seventeenth centuries, but even today. The English and Lowland Scottish judges who carried the high tradition of European culture into these regions could probably find little similarity between what they believed to be the wild superstitions of the savage races whose problems they had been sent to adjudicate and the extraordinarily complex and sophisticated problem of the existence of a class of irregular diseases.[37]

It might be worthwhile to look at how such a hunt for the witch disease might plausibly proceed. Demonologists argued that almost anyone was potentially a witch.[38] A peculiar illness might be the work of almost anyone in the village. However, it has been well demonstrated that only a small class of people were normally openly accused. If we reject the idea that the hunts were directed by a witch mythology inherited from the Middle Ages, then we must explain this special susceptibility by suggesting that while suspicion might potentially fall on anyone, it would not fall with the same degree of safety. The rich, the powerful, the well-connected and those well situated within a large group of kin, could and probably would retaliate if they were accused of witchcraft. Such accusations would have been pushed only in unusual circumstances. But against those who were more or less incapable of retaliation, the old, the poor and especially women, and those who had already alienated the community by their lewd, immoral or quarrelsome behavior, accusations could be brought with relative impunity.[39] Over the years individuals in these categories would tend to collect such accusations until "a mass of latent or potential testimony (became) kinetic" and formal proceedings were instituted.[40] In this model of the craze the stereotype of the witch did not precede the hunts, but was the result of the hunts themselves. Put another way, it was the witch craze that produced the witch and not, as has been traditionally argued, the figure of the witch that stimulated hunting.

The acceptance of my model of the witch craze has certain conceptual advantages, a few of which might be worth briefly examining. It eliminates the need for working up a long demonological pedigree for the hunts. No longer is it necessary to explain why there was no edition of the *Malleus Maleficarum* between 1520 and 1574, the period in which it is clear from extant trial records that the craze took root.[41] Neither is it necessary to explain why the English witchcraft statute of 1563 was preceded neither by an English demonology nor a pamphlet literature that, according to some older theories, should have existed in order to transmit the theological conceptions of the fifteenth-century demonologists to the peasantry.[42] This paucity of witchcraft literature is highly suggestive, as is also the fact that the statute itself was almost completely unconcerned with the theological implications of the existence of witches.[43] More generally, it is no longer necessary to explain why modern researchers have found only occasional references to the problem of witchcraft in the theological works of the mid-sixteenth century, the period when the first statutes designed specifically against the crime of witchcraft were being promulgated.[44] Few important works on this crime were published until well after the craze had gotten under way.[45]

Focusing on the witch disease and relegating the witch stereotype to a secondary and derivative position also helps to explain why so few "sorcerers," "wizards" and folkhealers were dragged into the hunts, despite their close connection with the witch figure of the Middle Ages.[46] All magic had traditionally been considered heretical by the Church, even the simple magic of the village folkhealer. The vast magical appartus of the Renaissance magus was considered by religious authorities almost everywhere to be especially evil and deserving of condemnation. Yet, even at the height of the craze, neither the village wizard nor the magus was much bothered.[47] This has always presented something of a problem for those holding the traditional view of the hunts. But when we focus on the type of *maleficia* that the witch was generally supposed to have caused we can see why the wizard and the magus were relatively safe. For, although the sorcerer was believed to have some connection with supernatural powers or beings, for the most part his "science" was seen as being naturally grounded and was thought to produce natural results. "It operates through occult properties and qualities, but it is natural because the forces through which it achieves its effects are objectively present in nature."[48] The type of disease that a sorcerer might produce would look more like a natural disease, or poisoning, than anything a witch was capable of. In fact, sorcerers were often accused of providing poisons for the use of their clients.[49] A witch, on the other hand, produced a disease or ailment which by its very nature was thought not to be explicable by ordinary means. It was strange and irregular, and was generally untreatable by the usual methods. It was not considered necessary when prosecuting a witch to introduce into evidence the poisons or other physical means by which she might have worked.[50] Such evidence was thought to be superfluous in the witch's case. For, even if the witch did possess some kind of mysterious ointment or potion, it was generally argued that its efficacy as a poison was not related to any intrinsic property that it might possess, but was the result of the direct intervention of the Devil on the witch's behalf.[51] It seems to have been believed that if the witch was actually using real, physically based poisons the illness which she was accused of causing would have had a more regular character and would have been thought of as having been naturally caused.

Interestingly enough, although the unusual symptomatology of the typical witch disease tended to protect those like sorcerers, wizards, magicians and folkhealers (as also perhaps physicians,[52] Gypsies and Jews,[53]) who were thought to act by natural or semi-natural means, this particular structure of symptoms probably increased suspicion of those who were not normally associated with the use of herbs and simples. It seems to have been thought that those who had access to things of this sort would have been less tempted to act by purely supernatural means. On the other hand, those who did not have such access, it was believed, would have been especially tempted to have relied on the much less demanding discipline of witchcraft because it was thought that the witch only had to will harm for it to be done, no complicated devices or herbs being necessary. This was true especially of the poor, who did not have the money for the typical paraphernalia of the sorcerer, and, to a lesser extent, women, who were thought to be less intelligent than men and certainly were less well educated.

Although a number of scholars have written on the medical aspects of the witch craze and of the role of physicians in particular witchcraft cases, no one to my knowledge has suggested that the rise of the craze could be traced to the revolution in medical thinking that marched beside it so closely. In fact, the tendency of scholarship has been in quite the opposite direction. Most of those who have dealt with this topic have either openly asserted or silently assumed that where the physician could safely insist on adherence to academic medicine witch hunting was unlikely to prosper.[54] I have attempted to show that not only did the medical revolution not bring witch hunting to a halt, it might very well have provided both its intellectual form and its emotional impetus. I have also tried to show that if one follows the social and cultural implications of this view to their natural conclusions a number of heretofore difficult problems in the historiography of the craze seem to resolve themselves. But much work is still yet to be done; the dynamics of theoretical breakdown need to be more fully studied, the role of physicians in specific trials must be more closely examined, and the structure of "demonic" medicine during the craze's decline is also probably worth a closer look.[55] I, myself, have been particularly interested in the implications that my ideas have for the place of hysterical possession in promoting witchcraft accusations and for the nature of the evidence that was deemed acceptable as proof against a witch. These suggestions do not begin to exhaust the possibilities for further research. But they do indicate, I believe, that a potentially fruitful new line of inquiry has been opened.

Notes

1. Joseph Hansen, *Zauberwahn, Inquisition und Hexenprozesse im Mittelalter, und die Entstehung der grossen Hexenverfulgung* (Munich, 1900), pp. 4–9; Henry Charles Lea, "The Witch Persecution in Transalpine Europe," in *Minor Historical Writings: and Other Essays*, ed. Arthur C. Howland (Philadelphia, 1942), p. 7; *Materials Towards a History of Witchcraft*, ed. Arthur C. Howland, 3 vols. (Philadelphia, 1939), passim. For modern writers who continue to support this thesis explicitly see Rossell Hope Robbins. "The Heresy of Witchcraft," *South Atlantic Quarterly* 65, no. 4 (autumn, 1966): 532–43; *The Encyclopedia of Witchcraft and Demonology* (New York, 1959), passim; Jeffrey Burton Russell, "Medieval Witchcraft and Medieval Heresy," in *On the Margin of the Visible: Sociology, the Esoteric, and the Occult*, ed. Edward A. Tiryakian (New York, 1974), pp. 179–89; *Witchcraft in the Middle Ages* (Ithaca, N.Y., 1972), ch. 9; H. R. Trevor-Roper, "Witches and Witchcraft: An Historical Essay (I and III)," *Encounter* 28 (1967): (May) pp. 3–25, (June) pp. 13–34.

2. Keith Thomas, *Religion and the Decline of Magic* (New York, 1971), pp. 444–45; Alfred Soman, "The Parlement of Paris and the Great Witch Hunt (1565–1640)," *Sixteenth Century Journal* 9, no. 2 (summer 1978): 43; Edward Peters, *The Magician, the Witch and the Law* (Philadelphia, 1978).

3. Research over the last decade or so has shown how witchcraft accusations could be used to attack the deserving poor, the economically progressive, political rivals, women folkhealers, the aged and, of course religious and social heretics. The most important contributions to this line of inquiry are: Alan D. J. MacFarlane,

Witchcraft in Tudor and Stuart England: A Regional and Comparative Study (New York, 1970) (deserving poor); Thomas, *Religion and the Decline of Magic* (deserving poor); H. C. Erik Midelfort, *Witch Hunting in Southwestern Germany 1562–1684: The Social and Intellectual Foundations* (Stanford, Calif., 1972) (women); Paul Boyer and Stephen Nissenbaum, *Salem Possessed: The Social Origins of Witchcraft* (Cambridge, Mass., 1974) (economically progressive and political rivals); E. William Monter, *Witchcraft in France and Switzerland: The Borderlands during the Reformation* (Ithaca, NY, 1976) (women); Robert Muchembled, *Prophètes et Sorciers dans les Pays-Bas, XVIe-XVIIIe siècle* (Paris, 1978) (religious and social heretics); Christina Larner, *Enemies of God: The Witch-Hunt in Scotland* (Baltimore, 1981) (political rivals and women); John Putnam Demos, *Entertaining Satan: Witchcraft and the Culture of Early New England* (New York, 1982) (women and deserving poor).

4. *Witchcraft, Oracles, and Magic Among the Azande* (Oxford, 1937), ch. 9. See also Michael Polanyi's discussion of Evans-Pritchard's ideas in *Personal Knowledge* (Chicago, 1958), pp. 286–94.

5. On these points see Richard Harrison-Shyrock, *The Development of Modern Medicine: An Interpretation of the Social and Scientific Factors* (1936; rpt. Madison, Wis., 1974), pp. 5–8; Lester King, *The Growth of Medical Thought* (1963; rpt. Chicago, 1973), pp. 139–41.

6. Charles H. Talbot, *Medicine in Medieval England* (London, 1967), p. 126. See also Ernest William Talbert, "The Notebook of a Fifteenth-Century Practicing Physician," (Texas) *Studies in English* (22) no. 4226 (8 July 1942): 27–29; Lynn White, "Medical Astrologers and Late Medieval Technology," *Viator* 6 (1975): 295–97.

7. Charles Greene Cumston, *An Introduction to the History of Medicine: From the Time of the Pharoahs to the End of the XVIIIth Century* (New York, 1927), pp. 248, 314–15; Allen G. Debus, *The English Paracelsians* (New York, 1966), p. 73; Peter H. Niebyl, "Sennert, Van Helmont, and Medical Ontology," *Bulletin of the History of Medicine* 45, no. 2 (Mar.-Apr. 1971); 115–37.

8. Walter Pagel. *Paracelsus: An Introduction to Philosophical Medicine in the Era of the Renaissance* (Basel, 1958), pp. 58, 61.

9. *De abditis rerum causis*, (Paris, 1548), pp. 291–93; *Medicina* (Venice, 1555), fol. 6v–7r, 95r–v.

10. *De abditis rerum causis*, bk. 2, ch. 16. Also see Ambroise Paré, *On Monsters and Marvels*, trans. Janis L. Pallister (Chicago, 1982 [1st Fr. ed. 1573]), pp. 97–104; Felix Plater, *Observationum in hominis affectibus plerisque, corpori et animo* (Basel, 1614), p. 20; Daniel Sennert, *Nine Books of Physick and Chirurgery . . . The First five being his Institutions of the Whole Body of Physick*, trans. N.D.B.P. (London, 1658 [1st Lat. ed. 1628]), bk, 5; Friedrich Hoffman, *De diaboli potentia in corpora* in *Opera Omnia*, 6 vols. (Geneva, 1741) 5, sec. 24, 26.

11. Victor Turner, "Metaphors of Anti-Structure in Religious Culture," in *Dramas, Fields, and Metaphors: Symbolic Action in Human Society* (Ithaca, N.Y., 1974), p. 297.

12. Thomas S. Kuhn, *The Structure of Scientific Revolutions* (Chicago, 1962), ch. 6; Larry Lauden, *Progress and Its Problems: Towards a Theory of Scientific Growth* (Berkeley, 1977), pp. 26–31.

13. Wilfrid Bonser, *The Medical Background of Anglo-Saxon England: A Study in History, Psychology, and Folklore* (London, 1963), ch. 16; Felix Marti-Ibanez, ed., "Impo-

tence as a Result of Witchcraft," in *Henry E. Sigerist on the History of Medicine* (New York, 1960), pp. 146–52; Oskar Diethelm, "The Medical Teaching of Demonology in the 17th and 18th Centuries," *Journal of the History of the Behavioral Sciences* 6, no. 1 (Jan. 1970): 11; Jane Crawford, "Evidence for Witchcraft in Anglo-Saxon England," *Medium Aevum* 32, no. 2 (1963): 99–116.

14. *A Trial of Witch-craft* (London, 1616), p. 70. See also Levinus Lemnius, *The Secret Miracles of Nature* (London, 1658 [1st Lat. ed. 1559]), bk. 4.

15. On the persistence of these superstitions into the twentieth century see Jeanne Favret-Saada, *Deadly Words: Witchcraft in the Bocage*, trans. Catherine Cullen (Cambridge, Eng., 1980); Hans Sebald, *Witchcraft: The Heritage of Heresy* (New York, 1978).

16. MacFarlane has highlighted the importance of illness and death in official indictments for witchcraft in England by comparing charges which led to indictments with charges that were evidenced in the pamphlet literature on the same trials. Illness and death were more heavily represented in the indictments than in the pamphlets, all but excluding other charges in the former. *Witchcraft in England*, p. 153.

17. *Ibid.*, pp. 179–80; Midelfort, *Witch Hunting in Southwestern Germany*, p. 122; Thomas, *Religion and the Decline of Magic*, pp. 559, 583. The *engraisseurs*, or plague-spreaders, discussed by Monter, *Witchcraft in France and Switzerland*, pp. 44–45, 47–49, 52, 65, 94–95, 115–18, 121–27, seem to me to have been suspected of engaging in activities more closely allied to those once attributed to lepers, and sometimes Jews and heretics, than to anything closely resembling the typical crimes associated with witchcraft in the sixteenth and seventeenth centuries. *Witchcraft, Oracles, and Magic Among the Azande*, passim.

18. *Select Cases of Conscience Touching Witches and Witchcrafts* (London, 1646), p. 85.

19. John Cotta, *A Short Discoverie of the Unobserved Dangers of Severall sorts of ignorant and unconsiderate Practisers of Physicke* (London, 1612), sig. A3f. See also John Halle, *An Historical Expostulation: Against the Beastlye Abusers, Both of Chyrurgerie and Physyke in Oure Tyme* (1565; rpt. London, 1844); L. R. C. Agnew, "Quackery," in *Medicine in Seventeenth Century England*, ed. Allen G. Debus (Berkeley, Calif., 1974), pp. 314–15.

20. On the literacy explosion see Lawrence Stone, "The Educational Revolution in England 1560–1640," *Past & Present*, no. 28 (July 1964): 41–80; David Cressy, "Levels of Illiteracy in England, 1530–1730," *The Historical Journal* 20, no. 1 (Mar. 1977): 1–23. Popular diagnostic manuals were written by physicians who either also wrote demonologies or are known to have diagnosed witchcraft in a particular case: William Drage, *Physical Experiments: Being a Plain Description of the Causes, Signes, and Cures of Most Diseases Incident to Man. To Which Is Added a Discourse of Diseases Proceeding from Witchcraft* (London, 1668). The Cambridge physician Philip Barrough, author of *Method of Physicke, Containing the Causes, Signs, and Cures of Inward Diseases in Man's Body from Head to Foot* (London, 1583), is known to have suggested witchcraft as a possible diagnosis in the famous case of the Throckmorton children in Huntingdonshire, England. *The Most Strange and Admirable Discoverie of the Three Witches of Warboys* (London, 1593), sig. A3.

21. *Mystical Bedlam: Madness, Anxiety, and Healing in Seventeenth-Century England* (Cambridge, Eng., 1981), pp. 26, 30.

22. Of approximately 2000 patients that Napier saw for psychological distur-

bances, nine were diagnosed as bewitched and 18 as possessed or haunted. MacDonald quite rightly argues that Napier was not over-credulous in this respect. *Ibid.*, p. 211. See also pp. 32, 107–10, 155, 174–5, 202, 205, 207–10, 250–1.

23. John Cotta explains this phenomenon by arguing that "it is manifest an͵ apparent, that the mixture and implication of diverse and differing diseases in the same subject, may and do oft bring forth a wild and confused concourse of accidents seeming therefore of monstrous and wondered shapes, and therefore in their deceiving appearance coming near unto the similitude of bewitching. But because every eye is not able in so various a chaos to analyze and reduce them unto their several heads, and proper diseases, (so intricately confounded one within another) it is not therefore sufficient for reputing them as things without causes in nature." *Short Discoverie*, pp. 58–59.

24. Paracelsus, *Of the Supreme Mysteries of Nature*, trans. R. Turner (London, 1656).

25. Thomas, *Religion and the Decline of Magic*, ch. 7, 8. George Lyman Kittredge, *Witchcraft in Old and New England* (Cambridge, Mass., 1929), p. 119.

26. Thomas, *Religion and the Decline of Magic*, ch. 22; Jean Delumeau, *Le Catholicisme entre Luther et Voltaire* (Paris, 1971); Peter Burke, *Popular Culture in Early Modern Europe* (New York, 1978), pp. 270–81.

27. William Perkins not only wrote to condemn witches, but all "such superstitious persons . . . as use charms and Inchantments." *A Discourse of the Damned Art of Witchcraft So farre forth as it is Revealed in the Scripture and Manifest by True Experience* (Cambridge, Eng., 1608), pp. 170–1.

28. Russell Zguta has recently argued that the craze reached Muscovy in the seventeenth century. Yet all of the cases that he adduces to prove his argument suggest traditional sorcery rather than the special type of witchcraft associated with the craze. "Witchcraft Trials in Seventeenth-Century Russia," *American Historical Review* 82, no. 5 (Dec. 1977): 1187–1207.

29. Thomas, *Religion and the Decline of Magic*, pp. 451–52.

30. *Ibid.*, p. 10; J. H. Raach, *A Directory of English Country Physicians 1603–1643* (London, 1962); R. M. S. McConaghey, *The History of Rural Medical Practice in the Evolution of Medical Practice in Britain*, ed. F. N. L. Poynter (London, 1961), pp. 117–44.

31. E. William Monter, "Witchcraft in Geneva, 1537–1662," *Journal of Modern History* 43, no. 2 (June 1971).

32. J. J. Cobben, *Jan Weir, Devils, Witches and Magic*, trans. Sal A. Prins (Philadelphia, 1976), pp. 13–18.

33. *The Witches' Advocate: Basque Witchcraft and the Spanish Inquisition 1609–1614* (Reno, Nev., 1980), passim.

34. *Ibid.*, pp. 44, 58, 177–80, 295–98, 315–17, 347–55.

35. Christina Larner, "James VI and I and Witchcraft," in *The Reign of James VI and I*, ed. A. G. R. Smith (London, 1973), pp. 74–90.

36. *Witchcraft in England*, p. 29.

37. Thomas, *Religion and the Decline of Magic*, pp. 39, 609; Christina Larner, *Enemies of God*, pp. 80–82.

38. Nicolas Remy, *Demonolatry*, trans. E. A. Ashwin, ed. Montague Summers (London, 1930 [1st Lat. ed. 1595]), p. 56.

39. The quarrelsomeness and general immorality of witch suspects has been widely commented on. See Thomas, *Religion and the Decline of Magic*, p. 530; MacFarlane, *Witchcraft in England*, pp. 158–60; Monter, *Witchcraft in France and Switzerland*, pp. 136–37; Demos, *Entertaining Satan*, pp. 54–56.

40. Kittredge, *Witchcraft in Old and New England*, p. 110.

41. Montague Summers, "A Note Upon the Bibliography of the *Malleus Maleficarum*," in *The Malleus Maleficarum*, ed. and trans. Montague Summers (New York, 1971), p. xii.

42. Even the idea that Marian Exiles brought the craze back with them from the Continent and propagated it through their sermons and letters has been destroyed. Kittredge, *Witchcraft in Old and New England*, pp. 262–4.

43. Thomas, *Religion and the Decline of Magic*, p. 142.

44. Martin Luther mentions it only a few times in passing. Lea, *Material*, pp. 417–23. Jean Calvin's contribution was similarly negligible. Monter, "Witchcraft in Geneva," p. 180.

45. Except for a few isolated exceptions, most of the great demonologies were published during the year 1580 and after, a generation followed the beginning of the craze. Monter, *Witchcraft in France and Switzerland*, pp. 34–5. It is worth noticing that in two areas, the Germanies and England, the great native critiques of the European witch craze actually preceded by some years the vast majority of the indigenous demonologies. Reginald Scot, *The Discoverie of Witchcraft* (London, 1584); Johann Weyer, *De praestigiis daemonum et incantationibus ac veneficiis* (Basel, 1563). See also Leland L. Estes, "Reginald Scot and his *Discoverie of Witchcraft*. Religion and Science in the Opposition to the European Witch Craze," *Church History* (forthcoming Dec. 1983).

46. Monter, *Witchcraft in France and Switzerland*, p. 171; Thomas, *Religion and the Decline of Magic*, pp. 245–46. Attempts by the ducal courts of Lorraine to prosecute folkhealers as witches failed. Etienne Delcambre, *Les devins-guérisseurs dans la Lorraine ducale: Leur activité et leurs méthodes*. vol. 3 of *La concept de la sorcellerie dans le duché de Lorraine au XVIe siècle*, 3 vols. (Nancy, 1948–51), p. 217. See also Richard Heberling, "Zauberie- und Hexenprozesse in Schleswig-Holstein-Lauenburg," *Zeitschrift de Gesellschaft für Schleswig-Holsteinische Geschichte* 45 (1915): 116–247.

47. H. C. Erik Midelfort, "Were There Really Witches?" in *Transition and Revolution: Problems and Issues of European Renaissance and Reformation History*, ed. Robert M. Kingdom (Minneapolis, 1974), pp. 194–98.

48. Wayne Shumaker, *The Occult Sciences in the Renaissance: A Study in Intellectual Patterns* (Berkeley, Calif. 1972), p. 108. See also James VI and I, *Daemonologie*, ed. G. B. Harrison (London, 1922 [1st ed. 1597]), p. 15.

49. The sorceress of southern Spain and Italy, of ill-repute and a dispenser of natural poisons, was all but immune from witch hunting. Julio Caro Baroja, *The World of the Witches*, trans. O. N. V. Glendinning (Chicago, 1965 [1st Sp. ed. 1961]), pp. 100–102. She was, however, harassed by the church and was occasionally prosecuted for the use of real poisons. Such figures were also lightly handled in Northern Europe. They were often prosecuted in the church courts, but rarely executed for their crimes. See Philip Tyler, "The Church Courts at York and Witchcraft Prosecutions, 1597–1640," *Northern History* 4 (1969): 84–110.

50. It was uncommon in Northern Europe for a witch's paraphernalia to be introduced in court against her. For sorcery, however, concrete evidence of this kind was usually required, and "this healthy skepticism perhaps explains why the prosecution against magicians never degenerated into mania." Gene A. Brucker, "Sorcery in Early Renaissance Florence," *Studies in the Renaissance* 10 (1963): p. 22.

51. Henri Boguet, *An Examen of Witches Drawn from Various Trials*, trans. E. Allen Ashwin, ed. Montague Summers (London, 1929), pp. xliv. 67; Thomas Erastus, *Histoires, disputes et discours des illusions et impostures des diables . . . Deux dialogues par Thomas Erastus, Touchant le pouvoir des sorciers* (Paris, 1885), pp. 404, 417; Johann Godelmann, *Tractatus de magis, veneficis et lamiis, deque his recte cognoscendis et puniendis* (Frankfurt, 1591), pp. 65–66; Henry Holland, *A Treatise Against Witchcraft* (Cambridge, Eng., 1590), sig. F2f.

52. The extraordinary immunity of physicians has been little remarked on. I am unaware of a single, university-trained medical man executed as a witch. Larner, although she has discovered victims of the craze in almost every other occupational and social category, including 16 from the nobility, has not found a physician, a surgeon or an apothecary executed as a witch in Scotland. *Enemies of God*, p. 89. Members of officially established medical groups in England were similarly invulnerable. This invulnerability is probably not unrelated to the role of the physician in establishing the criteria of what was to be accepted as a witch disease. See also Midelfort, *Witch Hunting in Southwestern Germany*, p. 181.

53. It has long been argued that since witchcraft was a Christian heresy Jews and Gypsies could not be witches. Robbins, *Encyclopedia*, p. 550. But it is much more likely that this seeming invulnerability derived from their reputation for charming and "natural" magic. Jews especially had a reputation for arcane learning, cabala for instance, that would have led people to group them with sorcerers and wizards rather than with witches. Midelfort, *Witch Hunting in Southwestern Germany*, p. 189. Thomas, *Religion and the Decline of Magic*, pp. 295, 560; Joshua Trachtenberg, *The Devil and the Jews: The Medieval Conception of the Jew and Its Relation to Modern Anti-Semitism* (New Haven, 1943), p. 67.

54. See Gregory Zilboorg, *The Medical Man and the Witch During the Renaissance* (Baltimore, 1935), passim; Joost A. M. Meerloo, "Four Hundred Years of 'Witchcraft', 'Projection' and 'Delusion'," *American Journal of Psychiatry* 120, no. 1 (July 1963): 83–6; S. Mouchly Small, "Concept of Hysteria: History and Re-Evaluation," *New York State Journal of Medicine* 69 (1 July 1969): 1867; Denis Leigh, "Recurrent Themes in the History of Psychiatry," *Medical History* 1, no. 3 (July 1957): 237–40; Harry Friedenwald, "Andres a Laguna. A Pioneer in his Views on Witchcraft," *Bulletin of the History of Medicine* 7, no. 8 (1939): 1043; Jack L. Evans, "Witchcraft, Demonology and Renaissance Psychiatry," *Medical Journal of Australia* 53, no. 23 (2 July 1966): 34–39; George E. Ehrligh, "Johann Weyer and the Witches," *New England Journal of Medicine* 263, no. 5 (4 Aug. 1960): 245–6; George Mora, "On the 400th Anniversary of Johann Weyer's 'De praestigiis daemonum'—Its Significance for Today's Psychiatry." *American Journal of Psychiatry* 120. no. 5 (Nov. 1963): 417–28; George Sarton, *Six Wings: Men of Science in The Renaissance* (Bloomington, Ind. 1957), p. 214; George Lincoln Burr, *New England's Place in the History of Witchcraft* (Freeport, N.Y., 1979 [1st ed. 1911]), p. 30; W. E. H. Lecky, *History of the Rise and Influence of the Spirit of Rationalism in Europe*, 3rd ed. (London, 1866) i,

pp. 67, 91, 94–95, 98; Monter, "Witchcraft in Geneva," p. 200; Monter, "Law, Medicine, and the Acceptance of Witchcraft," in *European Witchcraft*, ed. E. William Monter (New York, 1969), pp. 66–67; Sona Rosa Burstein, "Demonology and Medicine in the Sixteenth and Seventeenth Centuries." *Folk-lore* 67, no. 1 (31 Mar. 1956): 32–33.

55. Some recent scholars have realized that medicine and the medical profession were not quite the force for enlightenment that earlier historians had so easily supposed. See especially Garfield Tourney, "The Physician and Witchcraft in Restoration England," *Medical History* 16, no. 2 (Apr. 1972): 143–55; Nicholas P. Spanos, "Witchcraft in Histories of Psychiatry: A Critical Analysis and an Alternative Conceptualization." *Psychological Bulletin* 85, no. 2 (1978): 417–39; Thomas J. Schoeneman, "The Role of Mental Illness in the European Witch Hunts of the Sixteenth and Seventeenth Centuries: An Assessment," *Journal of the History of the Behavioral Sciences* 13, no. 4 (Oct. 1977): 337–51; Robert Minder, "Der Hexenglaube bei den Iatrochemikern des 17. Jahrhundrets," (Ph.D. diss., Zurich, 1963); Lester S. King, "Friedrich Hoffman and some Medical Aspects of Witchcraft," *Clio Media* 9, no. 4 (1974): 299–309; Diethelm, "The Medical Teaching of Demonology," pp. 3–15.

SECTION V

Myths and Legends

Introduction

𝔉rom reading the myths and legends in this section of the *Reader*, it will become apparent that the werewolf myth (and the narratives that sprang from it and propagated it) defies simplistic analysis and classification. The study of myth is a complex one: it involves not only theories of myth but includes the moral, the metaphysical, the symbolic, the religious, the unconscious, and even the forms of narrative art.

On the moral level, the werewolf myth is a realistic assessment of the range of choices available to human beings. Humans who become werewolves in the myths and legends, or who cause others to become werewolves, are involved in moral metamorphosis: a process that recognizes the exhilaration that comes with engaging in degrading lycanthropic acts but also reveals the degradation that comes to those who deliberately choose to exhibit bestiality. The werewolf myth, then, is a profound insight into human life. Lycaon, for example, whose bestiality and cannibalism outraged Jupiter, was justifiably transformed into a wolf. (The linguistic repercussions may perhaps be apparent in the word *lycanthropy* and its relationship to Lycaon.) By the time the werewolf myth reached John Milton's *Comus* (1634), there was an easy acceptance of the moral fact that those whose sexual appetites include attacks on and intended rape of a helpless young virgin "howl / Like stabled wolves." Regarded as a moral myth, the presence in the human spirit of werewolves can direct the culture, the society, the individual human being to sources of healing. If it does so, it is a myth not of despair but of hope.

On the metaphysical level, the ancient, medieval, and Renaissance manifestations of the werewolf myth can be understood in the light of Marsilio Ficino's *Platonic Theology* and Pietro Pomponazzi's *On the Immortality of the Soul.* Establishing man as the "knot and bond of the universe," Ficino sees that the spirit of a human being attempts to transcend material forms but that the body "knows the corporeal things towards which it declines by nature." To become a werewolf, then, is to deny the spiritual and to descend into the material. Man, however, must rule the animals, must not be ruled by them:

> Man not only makes use of the elements, but also adorns them, a thing which no animal ever does. . . . Man is really the vicar of God. . . . Not only does he make use of the animals, he also rules them. . . . Who has ever seen any human beings kept under the control of animals. . . . Certainly he is the god of the animals, for he makes use of them all, rules them all, and instructs many of them. . . . Whatever assumes the form of something else in such a way that it makes a single thing out of itself and that form, almost becomes the very thing whose form it assumes . . . our soul by means of the intellect and will as by those twin Platonic wings flies toward God, since by means of them it flies toward all things. [2]

Pomponazzi's expansion of this theme throws light on the metaphysics of the werewolf myth:

> Therefore the human soul also has some of the properties of the intelligences and some of the properties of all material things. Hence it is that, when it performs functions through which it agrees with the intelligences, it is said to be divine and to be changed into Gods; but when it performs functions of the beasts, it is said to be changed into a beast; for by reason of its malice it is called a serpent or a fox, by reason of its cruelty a tiger, and so on. For there is nothing in the world that by reason of some property cannot agree with man himself; wherefore not undeservedly is man called the microcosm or the little world. Therefore some have said that man is a great marvel, since he is the whole world and convertible into every nature, since power has been given him to assume whatever property he may prefer. Therefore the ancients were telling wise myths when they said that some men had been made Gods, some lions, some wolves . . . since some men

have followed the intellect, some the senses, and some the powers of the vegetative soul, and so on. Therefore all those who place bodily pleasures before moral or intellectual virtues make man a beast rather than a God. . . . [3]

Obviously, the metaphysics of the myth has moral implications: metaphysics cannot be divorced from the moral universe in which a human being lives and is endowed with god-like qualities. The human soul that sinks in the werewolf myth to the level of a beast has made its own metaphysical transformation.

Myth is symbolic. The moral and the metaphysical do not stand apart from the form of the myth but are embodied in it; and, whether the myth is a symbol of the religious or the unconscious (or both), myth, by its very nature is truer than history. As a long line of thinkers from Aristotle to Sir Philip Sidney have observed, history is tied "to the particular truth of things, and not to the general reason of things" (Sidney, *The Defence of Poesie*). Because myth transcends historical events, it can give penetrating insights into all human life, not just into a particular life at a particular moment in history. Its symbols make this possible. As W. H. Auden insists, myth gives "symbolic images of the life of the psyche." The werewolf myth, like other myths,

can travel from one country to another, one culture to another culture, whenever what it has to say holds good for human nature in both, despite their differences. Insofar as the myth is valid, the events of the story and its basic images will appeal irrespective of the artistic value of their narration; a genuine myth, like the Chaplin clown, can always be recognized by the fact that its appeal cuts across all differences between highbrow and lowbrow tastes. Further, no one conscious analysis can exhaust its meaning. There is no harm, however, if this is realized, in trying to give one. [4]

Even though the werewolf myth has profound implications for human life which can elude critical analysis, there is no harm in attempting a conscious analysis of it, as Auden suggests. As the myths in this section of the *Reader* show, however, the werewolf myth defies attempts to give it a single meaning.

The question of the origin of myths is a tangled, controversial one: Did the narratives spawn the symbols, or did the symbols generate the narratives? Whatever the origin, one thing is clear: the werewolf myth speaks powerfully of matters touching the heart of human existence.

The myths and legends in this section of the *Reader* cut across chronological lines. There are two from the ancient classical world, two from the medieval European world, and two from the modern world—the two modern legends, however (Field's and Stenbock's), have their origins in Norse and Celtic mythology. All six of the stories are highly structured narratives whose surface is deceptively simple. Beneath the narrative surface lurk moral, metaphysical, religious, and psychological meanings. And in the center is the myth of lycanthropic transformation. No matter what the reader's response is to the individual narratives, all six will have the same strangely disquieting effect.

Notes

1. For a study of myth, see G. S. Kirk, *Myth* (Berkeley: University of California Press, 1970).

2. Marsilio Ficino, *Platonic Theology*, translated by Josephine L. Burroughs, *Journal of the History of Ideas* V (April 1944), 227–42 passim.

3. Pietro Pomponazzi, *On the Immortality of the Soul*, translated by Josephine L. Burroughs, *Journal of the History of Ideas* V (April 1944), 227–42 passim.

4. W. H. Auden, *Forewords and Afterwords* (New York: Vintage, 1974), 203.

20.

Lycaon and Jupiter

OVID

So the gods took their seats in the marble council chamber, and their lord sat, throned high above them, leaning on his ivory sceptre. Three times, four times, he shook those awe-inspiring locks and with them moved the earth, the sea, the stars. Then he opened his lips, and spoke these indignant words: "Never was I more anxious concerning the sovereignty of the universe, no, not even at that time when each of the snaky-footed giants was preparing to throw his hundred arms round the sky and take it captive. For then the attack was made by one small group of enemies and, although there were fierce ones, still the trouble originated from one source. Now the entire human race must be destroyed, throughout all the lands which Nereus surrounds with his roaring waters. I swear by the rivers of the under-world that flow through the Stygian grove beneath the earth: all other remedies have already been tried. This cancer is incurable, and must be cut out by the knife, in case the healthy parts become infected. We have the demigods to care for, the spirits of the countryside, nymphs and fauns, satyrs and silvani, who roam the hills. Since we have not, as yet, considered them worthy of the honour of a place in heaven, let us at least ensure that they can live on the earth which we have given them. For can you believe, you gods, that they will go unmolested when Lycaon, a man notorious for his savagery, has laid plots against me, the lord and master of the thunderbolt, aye, and your king and master too?"

All the gods muttered uneasily, and eagerly demanded the punishment of the man who had dared to do such a deed. Their dismay was such as was felt by the human race, when a wicked band of fanatics tried to extinguish the Roman name by shedding Caesar's blood: all men were seized by panic fear of instant destruction, and the whole world shuddered. Just as the loyal devotion of your subjects pleases you, Augustus, so did that of the gods please Jupiter. He checked their

The Metamorphoses of Ovid. Translated by Mary M. Innes (Harmondsworth: Penguin, 1955), 36–38.

murmurs with a word, and as he raised his hand, all fell silent. When the uproar had subsided, hushed by the authority of the king of heaven, Jupiter again broke the silence with these words: "As far as he is concerned, he has paid the penalty. Have no fear on that score. But I shall tell you what his crime was, and what his punishment.

"Scandalous rumours concerning the state of the times had reached my ears. Hoping to find them false, I descended from the heights of Olympus, and walked the earth, a god in human form. It would take long to tell what wickedness I found on every side. Even the scandalous rumours were less than the truth. I had crossed over the ridge of Maenalus, a place bristling with the lairs of wild beasts, over Cyllene, and through the pinewoods of chill Lycaeus. From there, when the last shades of twilight were heralding the night, I entered the inhospitable home of the Arcadian tyrant. I revealed myself as a god, and the people began to do me homage. Lycaon, however, first laughed at their pious prayers, and then exclaimed: 'I shall find out, by an infallible test, whether he be god or mortal: there will be no doubt about the truth.' His plan was to take me unawares, as I lay sound asleep at night, and kill me. This was the test of truth on which he was resolved. Not content with that, he took a hostage sent him by the Molossian people, slit the man's throat with his sharp blade, and cooked his limbs, still warm with life, boiling some and roasting others over the fire. Then he set this banquet on the table. No sooner had he done so, than I with my avenging flames brought the house crashing down upon its household gods, gods worthy of such a master. Lycaon fled, terrified, until he reached the safety of the silent countryside. There he uttered howling noises, and his attempts to speak were all in vain. His clothes changed into bristling hairs, his arms to legs, and he became a wolf. His own savage nature showed in his rabid jaws, and he now directed against the flocks his innate lust for killing. He had a mania, even yet, for shedding blood. But, though he was a wolf, he retained some traces of his original shape. The greyness of his hair was the same, his face showed the same violence, his eyes gleamed as before, and he presented the same picture of ferocity.

"One house has fallen, but far more than one have deserved to perish. To the ends of the earth, the dread Fury holds sway. You would think men had sworn allegiance to crime! They shall all be punished, forthwith, as they deserve. Such is my resolve."

Lycaon transformed by Jupiter into a werewolf. From Ovid, *Meta-morphoses* (London, ·1717), Lud. Du Guernier, Sculp. Courtesy of The Newberry Library, Chicago.

Some of the gods, shouted their approval of Jove's words, and sought to increase his indignation: others played the part of silent supporters. Yet all were grieved at the thought of the destruction of the human race, and wondered what the earth would be like, in future, when it had been cleared of mortal inhabitants. They inquired who would bring offerings of incense to their altars, whether Jove meant to abandon the world to the plundering of wild beasts. In answer to their questions, the king of the gods assured them that they need not be anxious, for he himself would attend to everything. He promised them a new stock of men, unlike the former ones, a race of miraculous origin.

21

The Satyricon of Petronius

T. PETRONIUS ARBITER

After this, when all of us had wished him Health and Happiness, Trimalchio, turning to Niceros, "You were wont," said he, "to be a good Companion, but what's the matter we get not a word from ye now? Let me entreat ye, as you would see me Happy, do not break an old Custom."

Niceros, pleased with the frankness of his Friend: "Let me never thrive," said he, "if I am not ready to caper out of my Skin, to see you in so good a Humour; therefore what I say shall be all Mirth; tho' I am afraid those Grave Fopps may laugh: but let them look to 't, I'll go on nevertheless; for what am I the worse for any one Swearing? I had rather they laugh at what I say, than at my self."

Thus when he spake— —he began this Tale: —

"While I was yet a Servant we liv'd in a narrow Lane, now the House of Gavilla: There, as the Gods would have it, I fell in Love with Tarentius's Wife; he kept an Eating-house. Ye all knew Melissa Tarentina, a pretty little Punching-block, and withal Beautiful; but (so help me Hercules) I minded her not so much for the matter of the point of that, as that she was good-humour'd; if I asked her any thing, she never deny'd me; and what Money I had, I trusted her with it; nor did she ever fail me when I'd occasion. It so happened, that a she-companion of hers had dy'd in the Country, and she was gone thither; how to come at her I could not tell; but a Friend is seen at a dead lift; it also happened my Master was gone to Capua to dispatch somewhat or other: I laid hold of the opportunity, and persuaded mine Host to take an Evenings Walk of four or five Miles out of Town, for he was a stout Fellow, and as bold as a Devil: The Moon shone as bright as Day, and about Cockcrowing we fell in with a Burying-place, and certain Monuments of the Dead: my Man loitered behind me a star-gazing, and I sitting expecting him, fell a Singing and numbering them; when looking round me, what should I see but mine Host stript stark-naked, and

Translated by William Burnaby, 1694. Edited and illustrated by Norman Lindsay (London, 1910), 107–11.

The host transformed into a werewolf. From T. Petronius Arbiter, *The Satyricon*. Illus. Norman Lindsay (London, 1910). Courtesy of University of Chicago Library, Department of Special Collections.

his Cloaths lying by the High-way-side. The sight struck me every where, and I stood as if I had been dead; but he Piss'd round his Cloaths, and of a sudden was turned to a Wolf: Don't think I jest; I value no Man's Estate at that rate, as to tell a Lye. But as I was saying, after he was turned to a Wolf, he set up a Howl, and fled to the Woods. At first I knew not where I was, till going to take up his Cloaths, I found them also turn'd to Stone. Another Man would have dy'd for fear, but I drew my Sword, and slaying all the Ghosts that came in my way, lighted at last on the place where my Mistress was: I entred the first Door; my eyes were sunk in my Head, the Sweat ran off me by more streams than one, and I was just breathing my last, without thought of recovery; when my Melissa coming to me, began to wonder why I'd be walking so late; and 'if,' said she, 'you had come a little sooner, you might have done us a kindness; for a Wolf came into the Farm, and has made Butchers work enough among the Cattle; but tho' he got off, he has no reason to laugh, for a Servant of ours ran him through the Neck with a Pitch-fork.' As soon as I had heard her, I could not hold open my Eyes any longer, and ran home by Daylight, like a Vintner whose House had been robb'd: But coming by the place where the Cloaths were turned to Stone, I saw nothing but a Puddle of Blood; and when I got home, found mine Host lying a-bed like an Oxe in his Stall, and a Chirurgeon dressing his Neck. I understood afterwards he was a Fellow that could change his Skin; but from that day forward, could never eat a bit of Bread with him, no if you'd have kill'd me. Let them that don't believe me, examine the truth of it; may your good Angels plague me as I tell ye a Lye."

22.

Arthur and Gorlagon[1]

Translated by FRANK A. MILNE, with notes by ALFRED NUTT

$\mathfrak{A}$t the City of the Legions King Arthur was keeping the renowned festival of Pentecost, to which he invited the great men and nobles of the whole of his kingdom, and when the solemn rites had been duly performed he bade them to a banquet, furnished with everything thereto pertaining. And as they were joyfully partaking of the feast of rich abundance, Arthur, in his excessive joy, threw his arms around the Queen, who was sitting beside him, and embracing her, kissed her very affectionately in the sight of all. But she was dumbfounded at his conduct, and blushing deeply, looked up at him and asked why he had kissed her thus at such an unusual place and hour.

Arthur: Because amidst all my riches I have nothing so pleasing and amidst all my delights nothing so sweet, as thou art.

The Queen: Well, if, as you say, you love me so much, you evidently think that you know my heart and my affection.

Arthur: I doubt not that your heart is well disposed towards me, and I certainly think that your affection is absolutely known to me.

The Queen: You are undoubtedly mistaken, Arthur, for you acknowledge that you have never yet fathomed either the nature or the heart of a woman.

Arthur: I call heaven to witness that if up to now they have lain hid from me, I will exert myself, and sparing no pains, I will never taste food until by good hap I fathom them.

So when the banquet was ended Arthur called to him Caius, his sewer, and said, "Caius, do you and Walwain my nephew mount your horses and accompany me on the business to which I am hastening. But

Folk-Lore 15 (1904): 40–67.

let the rest remain and entertain my guests in my stead until I return."
Caius and Walwain at once mounted their horses as they were bidden,
and hastened with Arthur to a certain king famed for his wisdom,
named Gargol, who reigned over the neighbouring country; and on
the third day they reached a certain valley, quite worn out, for since
leaving home they had not tasted food nor slept, but had ever ridden
on uninterruptedly night and day. Now immediately on the further side
of that valley there was a lofty mountain, surrounded by a pleasant
wood, in whose recesses was visible a very strong fortress built of
polished stone. And Arthur, when he saw it at a distance, commanded
Caius to hasten on before him with all speed, and bring back word to
him to whom the town belonged. So Caius, urging on his steed,
hastened forward and entered the fortress, and on his return met
Arthur just as he was entering the out trench, and told him that town
belonged to King Gargol, to whom they were making their way. Now
it so happened that King Gargol had just sat down at table to dine; and
Arthur, entering his presence on horseback, courteously saluted him
and those who were feasting with him. And King Gargol said to him,
"Who art thou? and from whence? And wherefore hast thou entered
into our presence with such haste?"

Arthur: "I am Arthur," he replied, "the King of Britain: and I wish to
learn from you what are the heart, the nature, and the ways of women,
for I have very often heard that you are well skilled in matters of this
kind."

Gargol: Yours is a weighty question, Arthur, and there are very few
who know how to answer it. But take my advice now, dismount and eat
with me, and rest to-day, for I see that you are overwrought with your
toilsome journey; and to-morrow I will tell you what I know of the
matter.

Arthur denied that he was overwrought, pledging himself withal
that he would never eat until he had learnt what he was in search of. At
last, however, pressed by the King and by the company who were
feasting with him, he assented, and, having dismounted, he sat at table
on the seat which had been placed for him opposite the King. But as
soon as it was dawn, Arthur, remembering the promise which had been

made to him, went to King Gargol and said, "O my dear King, make known to me, I beg, that which you promised yesterday you would tell me to-day."

Gargol: You are displaying your folly, Arthur. Until now I thought you were a wise man: as to the heart, the nature, and the ways of woman, no one ever had a conception of what they are, and I do not know that I can give you any information on the subject. But I have a brother, King Torleil by name, whose kingdom borders on my own. He is older and wiser than I am: and indeed, if there is any one skilled in this matter, about which you are so anxious to know, I do not think it has escaped him. Seek him out, and desire him on my account to tell you what he knows of it.

So having bidden Gargol farewell, Arthur departed, and instantly continuing his journey arrived after a four days' march at King Torleil's, and as it chanced found the King at dinner. And when the King had exchanged greetings with him and asked him who he was, Arthur replied that he was King of Britain, and had been sent to the King by his brother King Gargol, in order that the King might explain to him a matter, his ignorance of which had obliged him to approach the royal presence.

Torleil: What is it?

Arthur: I have applied my mind to investigate the heart, the nature, and the ways of women, and have been unable to find anyone to tell me what they are. Do you therefore, to whom I have been sent, instruct me in these matters, and if they are known to you, do not keep them back from me.

Torleil: Yours is a weighty question, Arthur, and there are few who know how to answer it.. Wherefore, as this is not the time to discuss such matters, dismount and eat, and rest to-day, and to-morrow I will tell you what I know about them.

Arthur replied, "I shall be able to eat enough by-and-by. By my faith, I will never eat until I have learned that which I am in search of."

Pressed, however, by the King and by those who were sitting at table with him, he at length reluctantly consented to dismount, and sat down at the table opposite the King. But in the morning he came to King Torleil and began to ask him to tell what he had promised. Torleil confessed that he knew absolutely nothing about the matter, and directed Arthur to his third brother, King Gorlagon, who was older than himself, telling him that he had no doubt that Gorlagon was mighty in the knowledge of the things he was inquiring into, if indeed it was certain that anyone had any knowledge of them. So Arthur hastened without delay to his destined goal, and after two days reached the city where King Gorlagon dwelt, and, as it chanced, found him at dinner, as he had found the others.

After greetings had been exchanged Arthur made known who he was and why he had come, and as he kept on asking for information on the matters about which he had come, King Gorlagon answered, "Yours is a weighty question. Dismount and eat: and to-morrow I will tell you what you wish to know."

But Arthur said he would by no means do that, and when again requested to dismount, he swore by an oath that he would yield to no entreaties until he had learned what he was in search of. So when King Gorlagon saw that he could not by any means prevail upon him to dismount, he said, "Arthur, since you persist in your resolve to take no food until you know what you ask of me, although the labour of telling you the tale be great, and there is little use in telling it, yet I will relate to you what happened to a certain king, and thereby you will be able to test the heart, the nature, and the ways of women. Yet, Arthur, I beg you, dismount and eat, for yours is a weighty question and few there are who know how to answer it, and when I have told you my tale you will be but little the wiser.

Arthur: Tell on as you have proposed, and speak no more of my eating.

Gorlagon: Well, let your companions dismount and eat.

Arthur: Very well, let them do so.

So when they had seated themselves at table, King Gorlagon said, "Arthur, since you are so eager to hear this business, give ear, and keep in mind what I am about to tell you."

Gorlagon: There was a king well known to me, noble, accomplished, rich, and far-famed for justice and for truth. He had provided for himself a delightful garden which had no equal, and in it he had caused to be sown and planted all kinds of trees and fruits, and spices of different sorts: and among the other shrubs which grew in the garden there was a beautiful slender sapling of exactly the same height as the King himself, which broke forth from the ground and began to grow on the same night and at the same hour as the King was born. Now concerning this sapling, it had been decreed by fate that whoever should cut it down, and striking his head with the slenderer part of it, should say, "Be a wolf and have the understanding of a wolf," he would at once become a wolf, and have the understanding of a wolf. And for this reason the King watched the sapling with great care and with great diligence, for he had no doubt that his safety depended upon it. So he surrounded the garden with a strong and steep wall, and allowed no one but the guardian, who was a trusted friend of his own, to be admitted into it; and it was his custom to visit that sapling three or four times a day, and to partake of no food until he had visited it, even though he should fast until the evening. So it was that he alone understood this matter thoroughly.

Now this king had a very beautiful wife, but though fair to look upon she did not prove chaste, and her beauty was the cause of her undoing. For she loved a youth, the son of a certain pagan king; and preferring his love to that of her lord, she had taken great pains to involve her husband in some danger so that the youth might be able lawfully to enjoy the embraces for which he longed. And observing that the King entered the garden so many times a day, and desiring to know the reason, she often purposed to question him on the subject, but never dared to do so. But at last one day, when the King had returned from hunting later than usual, and according to his wont had entered the plantation alone, the Queen, in her thirst for information, and unable to endure that the thing should be concealed from her any longer (as it is customary for a woman to wish to know everything), when her husband had returned and was seated at table, asked him with a treacherous smile why he went to the garden so many times a day, and had been there even then late in the evening before taking food. The King answered that that was a matter which did not concern her, and that he was under no obligation to divulge it to her; whereupon she became furious, and improperly suspecting that he was in the habit of consorting with an adulteress in the garden, cried out, "I call all the gods of heaven to witness that I will never eat with you henceforth until you tell me the reason." And rising suddenly from the table she went to her bedchamber, cunningly feigning sickness, and lay in bed for three days without taking any food.

On the third day, the King, perceiving her obstinacy and fearing that her life might be endangered in consequence, began to beg and exhort her with gentle words to rise and eat, telling her that the thing she wished to know was a secret which he would never dare to tell anyone. To which she replied, "You ought to have no secrets from your wife, and you must know for certain that I would rather die than live, so long as I feel that I am so little loved by you," and he could not by any means persuade her to take refreshment. Then the King, in too changeable and irresolute a mood and too devoted in his affection for his wife, explained to her how the matter stood, having first exacted an oath from her that she would never betray the secret to anyone, and would keep the sapling as sacred as her own life.

The Queen, however, having got from him that which she had so dearly wished and prayed for, began to promise him greater devotion and love, although she had already conceived in her mind a device by which she might bring about the crime she had been so long deliberating. So on the following day, when the King had gone to the woods to hunt, she seized an axe, and secretly entering the garden, cut down the sapling to the ground, and carried it away with her. When, however, she found that the King was returning, she concealed the sapling under her sleeve, which hung down long and loose, and went to the threshold of the door to meet him, and throwing her arms around him she embraced him as though she would have kissed him, and then suddenly thrust the sapling out from her sleeve and struck him on the head with it once and again, crying, "Be a wolf, be a wolf," meaning to add "and have the understanding of a wolf," but she added instead the words "have the understanding of a man." Nor was there any delay, but it came about as she had said; and he fled quickly to the woods with the hounds she set on him in pursuit, but his human understanding remained unimpaired. Arthur, see, you have now learned in part the heart, the nature, and the ways of woman. Dismount now and eat, and afterwards I will relate at greater length what remains. For yours is a weighty question, and there are few who know how to answer it, and when I have told you all you will be but little the wiser.

Arthur: The matter goes very well and pleases me much. Follow up, follow up what you have begun.

Gorlagon: You are pleased then to hear what follows. Be attentive and I will proceed. Then the Queen, having put to flight her lawful husband, at once summoned the young man of whom I have spoken, and having handed over to him the reins of government became his wife. But the wolf, after roaming for a space of two years in the recesses of the woods to which he had fled, allied himself with a wild she-wolf, and begot two cubs by her. And remembering the wrong done him by his wife (as he was still possessed of his human understanding), he anxiously considered if he could in any way take his revenge upon her. Now near that wood there was a fortress at which the Queen was very often wont to sojourn with the King. And so this human wolf, looking out for his opportunity, took his she-wolf with her cubs one evening, and rushed unexpectedly into the town, and finding the two little boys of whom the aforesaid youth had become the father by his wife, playing by chance under the tower without anyone to guard them, he attacked and slew them, tearing them cruelly limb from limb. When the bystanders saw too late what had happened they pursued the wolves with shouts. The wolves, when what they had done was made known, fled swiftly away and escaped in safety. The Queen, however, overwhelmed with sorrow at the calamity, gave orders to her retainers to keep a careful watch for the return of the wolves. No long time had elapsed when the wolf, thinking that he was not yet satisfied, again visited the town with his companions, and meeting with two noble counts, brothers of the Queen, playing at the very gates of the palace, he attacked them, and tearing out their bowels gave them over to a frightful death. Hearing the noise, the servants assembled, and shutting the doors caught the cubs and hanged them. But the wolf, more cunning than the rest, slipped out of the hands of those who were holding him and escaped unhurt.

Arthur, dismount and eat, for yours is a weighty question and there are few who know how to answer it. And when I have told you all, you will be but little the wiser.

The wolf, overwhelmed with very great grief for the loss of his cubs and maddened by the greatness of his sorrow, made nightly forays against the flocks and herds of that province, and attacked them with such great slaughter that all the inhabitants, placing in ambush a large pack of hounds, met together to hunt and catch him; and the wolf, unable to endure these daily vexations, made for a neighbouring country and there began to carry on his usual ravages. However, he was at once chased from thence by the inhabitants, and compelled to go to a third country: and now he began to vent his rage with implacable fury, not only against the beasts but also against human beings. Now it chanced that a king was reigning over that country, young in years, of a mild disposition, and far-famed for his wisdom and industry: and when the countless destruction both of men and beasts wrought by the wolf was reported to him, he appointed a day on which he would set about to track and hunt the brute with a strong force of huntsmen and hounds. For so greatly was the wolf held in dread that no one dared to go to rest anywhere around, but everyone kept watch the whole night long against his inroads.

So one night when the wolf had gone to a neighbouring village, greedy for bloodshed, and was standing under the eaves of a certain house listening intently to a conversation that was going on within, it happened that he heard the man nearest him tell how the King had proposed to seek and track him down on the following day, much being added as to the clemency and kindness of the King. When the wolf heard this he returned trembling to the recesses of the woods, deliberating what would be the best course for him to pursue. In the morning the huntsmen and the King's retinue with an immense pack of hounds entered the woods, making the welkin ring with the blast of horns and with shouting; and the King, accompanied by two of his intimate friends, followed at a more moderate pace. The wolf concealed himself near the road where the King was to pass, and when all had gone by and he saw the King approaching (for he judged from his countenance that it was the King) he dropped his head and ran close after him, and encircling the King's right foot with his paws he would have licked him affectionately like a suppliant asking for pardon, with such groanings as he was capable of. Then two noblemen who were guarding the King's person, seeing this enormous wolf (for they had never seen any of so vast a size), cried out, "Master, see here is the wolf we seek! see, here is the wolf we seek! strike him, slay him, do not let the hateful beast attack us!" The wolf, utterly fearless of their cries, followed close after the King, and kept licking him gently. The King was wonderfully moved, and after looking at the wolf for some time and perceiving that there was no fierceness in him, but that he was rather like one who craved for pardon, was much astonished, and commanded that none of his men should dare to inflict any harm on him, declaring that he had detected some signs of human understanding in him; so putting down his right hand to caress the wolf he gently stroked his head and scratched his ears. Then the King seized the wolf and endeavoured to lift him up to him. But the wolf, perceiving that the King was desirous of lifting him up, leapt up, and joyfully sat upon the neck of the charger in front of the King.

The King recalled his followers, and returned home. He had not gone far when lo! a stag of vast size met him in the forest pasture with antlers erect. Then the King said, "I will try if there is any worth or strength in my wolf, and whether he can accustom himself to obey my commands." And crying out he set the wolf upon the stag and thrust him from him with his hand. The wolf, well knowing how to capture this kind of prey, sprang up and pursued the stag, and getting in front of it attacked it, and catching it by the throat laid it dead in sight of the King. Then the King called him back and said, "Of a truth you must be kept alive and not killed, seeing that you know how to show such service to us." And taking the wolf with him he returned home.

Arthur, dismount and eat. For yours is a weighty question, and there are few who know how to answer it; and when I have told you all my tale you will be but little the wiser.

Arthur: If all the gods were to cry from heaven "Arthur, dismount and eat," I would neither dismount nor eat until I have learnt the rest.

Gorlagon: So the wolf remained with the King, and was held in very great affection by him. Whatever the King commanded him he performed, and he never showed any fierceness towards or inflicted any hurt upon any one. He daily stood at table before the King at dinner time with his forepaws erect, eating of his bread and drinking from the same cup. Wherever the King went he accompanied him, so that even at night he would not go to rest anywhere save beside his master's couch.

Now it happened that the King had to go on a long journey outside his kingdom to confer with another king, and to go at once, as it would be impossible for him to return in less than ten days. So he called his Queen, and said, "As I must go on this journey at once, I commend this wolf to your protection, and I command you to keep him in my stead, if he will stay, and to minister to his wants." But the Queen already hated the wolf because of the great sagacity which she had detected in him (and as it so often happens that the wife hates whom the husband loves), and she said, "My lord, I am afraid that when you are gone he will attack me in the night if he lies in his accustomed place and will leave me mangled." The King replied, "Have no fear of that, for I have detected no such symptom in him all the long time he has been with me. However, if you have any doubt of it, I will have a chain made and will have him fastened to my bed-ladder." So the King gave orders that a chain of gold should be made, and when the wolf had been fastened up by it to the steps, he hastened away to the business he had on hand.

Arthur, dismount and eat. For yours is a weighty question, there are few who know how to answer it; and when I have told you all my tale you will be but little the wiser.

Arthur: I have no wish to eat; and I beg you not to invite me to eat any more.

Gorlagon: So the King set out, and the wolf remained with the Queen. But she did not show the care for him which she ought to have done. For he always lay chained up, though the King had commanded that he should be chained up at night only. Now the Queen loved the King's sewer with an unlawful love, and went to visit him whenever the King was absent. So on the eighth day after the King had started, they met in the bedchamber at midday and mounted the bed together, little heeding the presence of the wolf. And when the wolf saw them rushing into each other's impious embraces he blazed forth with fury, his eyes reddening, and the hair on his neck standing up, and he began to make as though he would attack them, but was held back by the chain by which he was fastened. And when he saw they had no intention of desisting from the iniquity on which they had embarked, he gnashed his teeth, and dug up the ground with his paws, and venting his rage over all his body, with awful howls he stretched the chain with such violence that it snapped in two. When loose he rushed with fury upon the sewer and threw him from the bed, and tore him so savagely that he left him half-dead. But to the Queen he did no harm at all, but only gazed upon her with venom in his eye. Hearing the mournful groans of the sewer, the servants tore the door from its hinges and rushed in. When asked the cause of all the tumult, the cunning Queen concocted a lying story, and told the servants that the wolf had devoured her son, and had torn the sewer as they saw while he was attempting to rescue the little one from death, and that he would have treated her in the same way had they not arrived in time to succour her. So the sewer was brought half dead to the guest-chamber. But the Queen fearing that the King might somehow discover the truth of the matter, and considering how she might take her revenge on the wolf, shut up the child, whom she had represented as having been devoured by the wolf, along with his nurse in an underground room far removed from any access; everyone being under the impression that he had in fact been devoured.

Arthur, dismount and eat. For yours is a weighty question, there are few who know how to answer it: and when I have told you all my tale you will be but little the wiser.

Arthur: I pray you, order the table to be removed, as the service of so many dishes interrupts our conversations.

Gorlagon: After these events news was brought to the Queen that the King was returning sooner than had been expected. So the deceitful woman, full of cunning, went forth to meet him with her hair cut close, and cheeks torn, and garments splashed with blood, and when she met him cried, "Alas! Alas! Alas! my lord, wretched that I am, what a loss have I sustained during your absence!" At this the King was dumbfounded, and asked what was the matter, and she replied, "That wretched beast of yours, of yours I say, which I have but too truly suspected all this time, has devoured your son in my lap; and when your sewer was struggling to come to the rescue the beast mangled and almost killed him, and would have treated me in the same way had not the servants broken in; see here the blood of the little one splashed upon my garments is witness of the thing." Hardly had she finished speaking, when lo! the wolf hearing the King approach, sprang forth from the bedchamber, and rushed into the King's embraces as though he well deserved them, jumping about joyfully, and gambolling with greater delight than he had ever done before. At this the King, distracted by contending emotions, was in doubt what he should do, on the one hand reflecting that his wife would not tell him an untruth, on the other that if the wolf had been guilty of so great a crime against him he would undoubtedly not have dared to meet him with such joyful bounds.

So while his mind was driven hither and thither on these matters and he refused food, the wolf sitting close by him touched his foot gently with his paw, and took the border of his cloak into his mouth, and by a movement of the head invited him to follow him. The King, who understood the wolf's customary signals, got up and followed him through the different bedchambers to the underground room where the boy was hidden away. And finding the door bolted the wolf knocked three or four times with his paw, as much as to ask that it might be opened to him. But as there was some delay in searching for the key— for the Queen had hidden it away—the wolf, unable to endure the delay, drew back a little, and spreading out the claws of his four paws he rushed headlong at the door, and driving it in, threw it down upon the middle of the floor broken and shattered. Then running forward he took the infant from its cradle in his shaggy arms, and gently held it up to the King's face for a kiss. The King marvelled and said, "There is something beyond this which is not clear to my comprehension." Then he went out after the wolf, who led the way, and was conducted by him to the dying sewer; and when the wolf saw the sewer, the King could scarcely restrain him from rushing upon him. Then the King sitting down in front of the sewer's couch, questioned him as to the cause of his sickness, and as to the accident which had occasioned his wounds. The only confession, however, he would make was that in rescuing the boy from the wolf, the wolf had attacked him; and he called the Queen to witness to the truth of what he said. The King in answer said, "You are evidently lying: my son lives; he was not dead at all, and now that I have found him and have convicted both you and the Queen of treachery to me, and of forging lying tales, I am afraid that something else may be false also. I know the reason why the wolf, unable to bear his master's disgrace, attacked you savagely, contrary to his wont. Therefore confess to me at once the truth of the matter, else I swear by the Majesty of highest Heaven that I will deliver thee to the flames to burn." Then the wolf making an attack upon him pressed him close, and would have mangled him again had he not been held back by the bystanders.

What need of many words? When the King insisted, sometimes with threats, sometimes with coaxing, the sewer confessed the crime of which he had been guilty, and humbly prayed to be forgiven. But the King, blazing out in an excess of fury, delivered the sewer up to be kept in prison, and immediately summoned the chief men from the whole of his kingdom to meet, and through them he held an investigation into the circumstances of this great crime. Sentence was given. The sewer was flayed alive and hanged. The Queen was torn limb from limb by horses and thrown into balls of flame.

Arthur, dismount and eat. For yours is a mighty question, and there are few who know how to answer it: and when I have told you all my tale you will be but little the wiser.

Arthur: If you are not tired of eating, you need not mind my fasting a little longer.

Gorlagon: After these events the King pondered over the extraordinary sagacity and industry of the wolf with close attention and great persistence, and afterwards discussed the subject more fully with his wise men, asserting that the being who was clearly endued with such great intelligence must have the understanding of a man, "for no beast," he argued, "was ever found to possess such great wisdom, or to show such great devotion to any one as this wolf has shown to me. For he understands perfectly whatever we say to him: he does what he is ordered: he always stands by me, wherever I may be: he rejoices when I rejoice, and when I am in sorrow, he sorrows too. And you must know that one who has avenged with such severity the wrong which has been done me must undoubtedly have been a man of great sagacity and ability, and must have assumed the form of a wolf under some spell or incantation." At these words the wolf, who was standing by the

King, showed great joy, and licking his hands and feet and pressing close to his knees, showed by the expression of his countenance and the gesture of his whole body that the King had spoken the truth.

Then the King said, "See with what gladness he agrees with what I say, and shows by unmistakable signs that I have spoken the truth. There can be no further doubt about the matter, and would that power might be granted me to discover whether by some act or device I might be able to restore him to his former state, even at the cost of my worldly substance; nay, even at the risk of my life." So, after long deliberation, the King at length determined that the wolf should be sent off to go before him, and to take whatever direction he pleased whether by land or by sea. "For perhaps," said he, "if we could reach his country we might get to know what has happened and find some remedy for him."

So the wolf was allowed to go where he would, and they all followed after him. And he at once made for the sea, and impetuously dashed into the waves as though he wished to cross. Now his own country adjoined that region, being, however, separated from it on one side by the sea, though in another direction it was accessible by land, but by a longer route. The King, seeing that he wished to cross over, at once gave orders that the fleet should be launched and that the army should assemble.

Arthur, dismount and eat. For yours is a weighty question: there are few who know how to answer it: and when I have told you all my tale you will be but little the wiser.

Arthur: The wolf being desirous of crossing the sea, is standing on the beach. I am afraid that if he is left alone he will be drowned in his anxiety to get over.

Gorlagon: So the King, having ordered his ship, and duly equipped his army, approached the sea with a great force of soldiers, and on the third day he landed safely at the wolf's country; and when they reached the shore the wolf was the first to leap from the ship, and clearly signified to them by his customary nod and gesture that this was his country. Then the King, taking some of his men with him, hastened secretly to a certain neighbouring city, commanding his army to remain on shipboard until he had looked into the affair and returned to them. However, he had scarcely entered the city when the whole course of events became clear to him. For all the men of that province, both high and low degree, were groaning under the intolerable tyranny of the king who had succeeded the wolf, and were with one voice lamenting their master, who by the craft and subtilty of his wife had been changed into a wolf, remembering what a kind and gentle master he was.

So having discovered what he wanted to know, and having ascertained where the King of that province was then living, the King returned with all speed to his ships, marched out his troops, and attacking his adversary suddenly and unexpectedly, slew or put to flight all his defenders, and captured both him and his Queen and made them subject to his dominion.

Arthur, dismount and eat. For yours is a mighty question: there are few who know how to answer it: and when I have told you all my tale you will be but little the wiser for it.

Arthur: You are like a harper who almost before he has finished playing the music of a song, keeps on repeatedly interposing the concluding passages without anyone singing to his accompaniment.

Gorlagon: So the King, relying on his victory, assembled a council of the chief men of the kingdom, and setting the Queen in the sight of them all, said, "O most perfidious and wicked woman, what madness induced you to plot such great treachery against your lord! But I will not any longer bandy words with one who has been judged unworthy of intercourse with anyone; so answer the question I put to you at once, for I will certainly cause you to die of hunger and thirst and exquisite tortures, unless you show me where the sapling lies hidden with which you transformed your husband into a wolf. Perhaps the human shape which he has lost may thereby be recovered." Whereupon she swore that she did not know where the sampling was, saying that it was well known that it had been broken up and burnt in the fire. However, as she would not confess, the King handed her over to the tormentors, to be daily tortured and daily exhausted with punishments, and allowed her neither food nor drink. So at last, compelled by the severity of her punishment, she produced the sapling and handed it to the King. And the King took it from her, and with glad heart brought the wolf forward into the midst, and striking his head with the thicker part of the sapling, added these words, "Be a man and have the understanding of a man." And no sooner were the words spoken than the effect followed. The wolf became a man as he had been before, though far more beautiful and comely, being now possessed of such grace that one could at once detect that he was a man of great nobility. The King seeing a man of such great beauty metamorphosed from a wolf standing before him, and pitying the wrongs the man had suffered, ran forward with great joy and embraced him, kissing and lamenting him and shedding tears. And as they embraced each other they drew such long protracted sighs and shed so many tears that all the multitude standing around were constrained to weep. The one returned thanks for all the many kindnesses which had been shown him: the other lamented that he had behaved with less consideration than he ought. What more? Extraordinary joy is shown by all, and the King, having received the submission of the principal men, according to ancient custom, retook possession of his sovereignty. Then the adulterer and adulteress were brought into his presence, and he was consulted as to what he judged ought to be done with them. And he condemned the pagan king to death. The Queen he only divorced, but of his inborn clemency spared her life, though she well deserved to lose it. The other King, having been honoured and enriched with costly presents, as was befitting, returned to his own kingdom.

Now, Arthur, you have learned what the heart, the nature, and the ways of women are. Have a care for yourself and see if you are any the wiser for it. Dismount now and eat, for we have both well deserved our meal, I for the tale I have told, and you for listening to it.

Arthur: I will by no means dismount until you have answered the questions I am about to ask you.

Gorlagon: What is that?

Arthur: Who is that woman sitting opposite you of a sad countenance, and holding before her in a dish a human head bespattered with blood, who has wept whenever you have smiled, and who has kissed the bloodstained head whenever you have kissed your wife during the telling of your tale?

Gorlagon: If this thing were known to me alone, Arthur (he replied), I would by no means tell it you; but as it is well known to all who are sitting at table with me, I am not ashamed that you also should be made acquainted with it. That woman who is sitting opposite me, she it was who, as I have just told you, wrought so great a crime against her lord, that is to say against myself. In me you may recognise that wolf who, as you have heard, was transformed first from a man into a wolf, and then from a wolf into a man again. When I became a wolf it is evident that the kingdom to which I first went was that of my middle brother, King Torleil. And the King who took such great pains to care for me you can have no doubt was my youngest brother, King Gargol, to whom you came in the first instance. And the bloodstained head which that woman sitting opposite me embraces in the dish she has in front of her is the head of that youth for love of whom she wrought so great a crime against me. For when I returned to my proper shape again, in sparing her life, I subjected her to this penalty only, namely, that she should always have the head of her paramour before her, and when I kissed the wife I had married in her stead she should imprint kisses on him for whose sake she had committed that crime. And I had the head embalmed to keep it free from putrefaction. For I knew that no punishment could be more grievous to her than a perpetual exhibition of her great wickedness in the sight of all the world. Arthur, dismount now, if you so desire, for now that I have invited you, you will, so far as I am concerned, from henceforth remain where you are.

So Arthur dismounted and ate, and on the following day returned home a nine days' journey, marvelling greatly at what he had heard.

Notes

1. The Latin original has been edited for the first time by Professor G. L. Kittredge, of Harvard, from the late 14th century Bodleian parchment MS. Rawlinson, B 49, in *Studies and Notes in Philology and Literature*, vol. viii., published by Ginn and Co. of Boston.

The foregoing tale, apart from a possible reference by Madden (*Sir Gawayne*, p.

x., note), seems to have escaped the notice of all Arthurian students until Professor G. L. Kittredge of Harvard edited it last year, and made it the subject of what I do not hesitate to pronounce one of the most remarkable and valuable examples of story-ological research known to me. In what follows I do little more than summarise and paraphrase Professor Kittredge's investigation, with the addition of certain views of my own, and I would strongly urge all interested in mediaeval romance and in folktale research not to content themselves with my summary but to refer to and master the original. Professor Kittredge should not be held responsible for any imperfections in my exposition of his masterly argument, the plan of which I have not thought it necessary to retain.

It will at once be apparent to a storyologist of any experience that the task which Arthur has to achieve is one in which success is only possible by the aid, unwillingly given, of a supernatural personage upon whom pressure has to be put, in this case, the refusal to partake of his hospitality; a pressure analogous to that legally recognised in the codes of Brahminic India and early Ireland for the purpose of exacting settlement of debt. As in most tales of this class, the supernatural helper at first succeeds in eluding the request of his mortal applicant. Twice Arthur yields to the invitation to dismount and eat, and it is only on his showing himself firm that, at the third attempt, he meets with success. Professor Kittredge's conjecture that the three kings are in reality one and the same personage must command universal assent. The three names (if we disregard *Torleil* as due to a scribal error) are variant Welsh terms signifying Werwolf, and in fact etymologically allied to the Teutonic term. [Gorlagon is by metathesis for *Gorgalon*, an expanded form of Gorgol = Old Welsh *Guruol* or *Guorguol*, the first syllable of which is cognate to Latin *vir*, Anglo-Saxon *wer*, whilst the second was equated by Professor Rhys with the Germanic *wolf* over twenty years ago]. The story thus follows the familiar conventions of fairydom—the supernatural helper is compelled to give the mortal three chances, and that mortal, stupid or incurious though he be, always pulls off the third one.

But if this is so, our version has obviously suffered modification. The second and third kings cannot be the werwolf's brothers, as is indeed evident from the conduct of the story. The werwolf knows nothing of the third king when he appeals to him for protection, which would be absurd if he were really his brother. The statement really testifies to a confused reminiscence of the essential identity of the three informants. Furthermore, traces of contamination are glaringly evident. There is "superfluity of naughtiness" in the duplication of the adultery theme; and the *Gellert* episode—the false accusation resting upon the wolf of having slain the child—is dragged in clumsily. On the other hand, the form and conduct of the story wear an archaic and genuine *folk* character; the triadic arrangement, the repeated attempts, couched in a set formula, to induce Arthur to desist, find their parallels in the phenomena of popular story-telling generally, but especially in those of Gaelic popular story-telling as it still flourishes, and as it can be proved to have flourished for the last eight hundred years at least. No one familiar with Gaelic story-telling (whether in its Irish or Scotch form) can fail to recognise in *Arthur and Gorlagon* an example of the genre. Thus by the end of the fourteenth century at the latest, a Celtic and characteristically Celtic folktale was put into Latin, probably suffering in this transition from a vernacular to a learned language those modifications which are immediately apparent, as also, possibly, others. The Latin narrator had a Welsh original, as is proved by the forms of the names: this original was almost certainly complete and homogeneous, as is evident from the "folk" character of the incidents and framework.

Let us now turn to the consideration of parallels. The closest is a folktale still widely current in Gaeldom (Professor Kittredge bases his analysis on some ten versions ranging over the entire Gaelic area from Kerry to the Hebrides), the type-example being MORRAHA (Larminie, *West Irish Folk-Tale*, reprinted in Jacobs, *More Celtic Fairy Tales*). Briefly, it runs thus:

> The hero games with a supernatural being, wins twice, loses third time, has task laid upon him to obtain the sword of light and knowledge of the one story about woman. Acting on the advice of his (fairy) wife, hero rides to her father, is there furnished with another horse that brings him to owner of the sword of light, Niall. At a third attempt he secures the sword, and threatening the owner with it, learns, at the persuasion of latter's wife, the story. Niall knew language of animals, and casually learnt thereby the existence of the magic rod; he laughed, had, on his wife's insistence, to explain why, was by her changed first into a raven, then into a horse, fox, wolf. As wolf he is hunted by, but secures protection of, King, guards the latter's child against the attack of a monstrous hand, is accused, but, trusted by King, recovers the child, whose attendant he becomes, and whom he ultimately persuades to strike him with the magic rod and thereby effect his re-transformation to human shape. His wife offers to drown herself, but Niall says if she will keep the secret, he will. Niall afterwards tracks the monster of the land, slays him, recovers the elder children of the King, and directs the hero how to deal with his supernatural adversary, who is the brother of the monster of the land. [In this summary and in the references to MORRAHA in the following pages, use is made of the other variants; no one version preserves all the incidents and traits.]

The framework here, it will be seen, is more elaborate than in *Arthur and Gorlagon* and is of a different nature. The mortal hero is set in motion by an inimical supernatural being, who wishes to be revenged upon his brother's slayer. He fails, in accordance with the convention of fairydom, as his success would be the hero's failure. The same contamination with the Gellert story appears as in *Arthur and Gorlagon*, also with the theme of the Child-Stealing Monster. The triadic arrangement is not so rigidly kept. The werwolf's wife, instead of being an altogether repugnant personage for whom no punishment is too bad, is not borne upon hardly by the story-teller and comes off at the end quite easily. We may surmise from this that *Arthur and Gorlagon* in addition to modification by the Gellert story, has likewise been modified by one of the current mediaeval versions of the familiar Eastern stories of woman's faithlessness and punishment.

Turn we now to the Medieval parallels. Both style themselves "Breton lays"; one, the *Lai de Melion*, is certainly not later than 1250, and may be much earlier; the other, the *Lai de Bisclaveret* of Marie de France, is not later than 1180.

In MELION the hero, hunting in a wood, meets a beautiful woman who has come to him from Ireland, who loves but him alone and has never loved before; this falls in with a vow he had made to have no *amie* who had ever loved another. He marries her; she learns that he possesses a congenital talisman capable of transforming him into a wolf, lures from him the secret, makes use of it, and returns to her father, taking one of her husband's servants with her. The wolf follows, becomes a leader of a band, and ravages the country. The father-in-law organises a hunt, in which all the wolves are killed except the werwolf; the latter ingratiates himself with his wife's father, by whom he is protected against her. He then attaches himself to Arthur, who comes on a visit to Ireland. One day he sees the servant who had accompanied his wife, and attacks him. The bystanders would slay him, but Arthur protects him, and divining a mystery, forces the servant to confess. Melion is re-transformed and comes to England with Arthur, leaving the guilty wife behind him.

This tale, as is evident, stands in close relation to both ARTHUR AND GORLAGON and to MORRAHA, and represents a simpler stage of development. The framework is lacking, as are also any signs of contamination from the *Gellert* and *Attack on the Child* themes. It has, however, obviously been modified to fit it into the Arthurian cycle, Arthur sharing with the werwolf's father-in-law the role of the protector-king. The hero's relation to this personage explains how it is that he finds his wife at the Court, a point which MORRAHA has preserved, but for which it does not account. In the treatment of the wife MELION is nearer to MORRAHA than to ARTHUR AND GORLAGON; although pronounced guilty, she is spared. The most notable feature is that preserved by the opening; the hero is wooed by a maiden who comes from Ireland, and who returns to her own country when she has, as she thinks, got rid of him. The significance of this will be made plain presently.

In the *Lai de Bisclaveret* of Marie de France the story runs thus:

The hero is a born werwolf, compelled to pass three days of every week in his animal shape; the change is effected by putting off his clothes. The wife discovers this, hides the clothes, and marries a lover of hers. The hunt by the King takes place as in other versions; the werwolf wins the King's favour, resides at his court, and whilst there attacks his wife's second husband, and, later, his wife. The mystery is disclosed, the wife is compelled under torture to give up the clothes, the werwolf regains his human form, and the wife is banished with her second husband.

Here then is a simple and straightforward version of one of the themes, the main one, found in the allied stories. It cannot be derived either from MELION or from the common original which may be assumed to lie at the back of ARTHUR AND GORLAGON and MORRAHA. On the other hand it cannot be their sole source. It proves that what may be styled the *Werwolf's Tale* proper once existed apart from the other elements found in MELION, ARTHUR AND GORLAGON, and MORRAHA.

As regards the relationship of the other three versions, MELION cannot have come from the Welsh original of ARTHUR AND GORLAGON, as it lacks the framework, and as it has preserved an opening of which no traces are found in the Welsh tale. For the same reasons it cannot be the direct source of that tale; which again cannot have originated MORRAHA, as the latter has retained decided traces of that presentment of the wife found in MELION. We must assume that ARTHUR AND GORLAGON and MORRAHA go back to a common original, itself akin to MELION, but neither derived from, not the source of, that version. This further source postulated for all three tales may be called X, and its first offshoot is MELION, modified by insertion into the Arthur cycle. There was probably no framework-setting in X, as otherwise the absence of this feature in MELION would be inexplicable. But at some date X was set in a framework and in this stage gave rise to the Welsh original of ARTHUR AND GORLAGON. It continued to live on in the Gaelic-speaking area subject to both elaboration and change, until it assumed that form in which it is still found among the peasantry of Ireland and Scotland. But X itself, as we have seen, cannot have come from Marie's lay; both must go back ultimately to a common source.

In endeavouring to reconstruct X, made up as we have seen of the *Werwolf's Tale* (found separate in BISCLAVERET) plus elements common to the other three versions, MELION is of most value, and after MELION the current folktales which, though recorded so much later than ARTHUR AND GORLAGON, may fairly be assumed to have retained archaic "folk" elements in a more perfect form. We saw above that both are distinguished from ARTHUR AND GORLAGON by the more lenient view taken of the wife's conduct and by the fact that the latter returns to her father's land whither she is followed by the transformed husband. Only MELION, however, has preserved the significant opening incident which, as Professor Kittredge conjectures, proves the wife to be of supernatural kin. He then reconstructs the basis of X as follows: Allured, it may be, by the hero's prowess, the supernatural maiden comes to woo him, as is so frequently the case in Irish mythic romance. But she has left behind her a lover of her kin, who follows her, and after a while persuades her to return to their own land of Faery. Thither the mortal husband follows and—should recover her. Thus, indeed, the story runs in one of the most famous of old Irish mythic romances, the *Wooing of Etain*. Etain is an immortal, wife of Mider; reborn in mortal form she is met at a spring side by Eochaid, King of Ireland, who is seeking a wife, but will not be content save with one, "whom no man of the men of Erin had known before him." They wed; Mider follows her to mortal land, wins her from Eochaid in a threefold gaming (an incident still found, though in different connection, in the current folktale), and carries her back to fairyland, whither Eochaid pursues them, ultimately recovering her.

A story, not necessarily the *Wooing of Etain*, but one constructed on similar lines, was, so Professor Kittredge assumes, amalgamated with the *Werwolf's Tale* in somewhat the same stage of development as we find the latter in BISCLAVERET, and thus originated the postulated version X. The *Werwolf's Tale* itself must have passed through different stages of development corresponding to altered feelings respecting the subject matter. Originally we must assume that the werwolf was a sympathetic personage, firstly because in folk-story-telling the hero is sympathetic by definition, secondly, because in the culture stage to which we may fairly refer the first shaping of the story the half-animal nature would not carry with it an idea of the repugnant or unhallowed. But such an idea undoubtedly did arise, and is reflected in the vast mass of werwolf stories and conceptions. A stage may thus be postulated in which the wife (unsympathetic originally as being opposed to the hero, but not morally culpable), becomes the sympathetic personage. Still later, sympathy would be shifted back by exciting pity for the hero (originally an object of envy as possessor of a highly desirable power), as one subject to a degrading liability, and by attaching moral blame to the faithless wife. The oldest recorded version of Marie's *Bisclaveret* belongs to this stage of development.

The fusion of these two story-types, the one concerned with the love-affairs of a fairy damsel ultimately won and lost by mortal and immortal lover, the other, the *Werwolf's Tale*, dealing with the separation of husband and wife deliberately effected by the latter, offers, it will be seen, no theoretical difficulty. When it took place the Etain type had already in all likelihood suffered considerable change. In the oldest stratum of Irish fairy mistress romances nothing is more notable than the position of the heroine. She woos; she bestows or withdraws her favours with absolute freedom; the mortal lover neither acquires nor claims any rights. But even within the range of Gaelic romance, closely though it clings to ancient convention, slightly as it is affected by non-Gaelic culture, there can be traced a change from this superb, over-moral attitude on the part of the woman to one more consonant with ordinary human conditions. The free self-centered goddess, regally prodigal of her love, jealously guarding her independence, becomes a capricious or faithless woman. Such a process would be facilitated and hastened by the fusion of the two story-types postulated above; what in either was equivocal in the character of the heroine would put on a darker aspect. The process affects the machinery of the tale as well as the attitude of the narrator; it facilitates the change by which, following the lines of another group of tales, the transformation of the werwolf is ascribed to inimicably exercised magic instead of to a congenital attribute; its extreme development is reached in ARTHUR AND GORLAGON, partly remodelled as this is by the clerkly Latin translator upon the lines of the Eastern stories of woman's faithlessness so well represented in the *Seven Sages* cycle. It is noteworthy that the current folktale, whilst exhibiting the altered machinery, which indeed it still further alters and complicates, does not go to anything like the same length in the change of moral attitude. The popular tale retains a blurred but unmistakable kinship of sentiment with the old mythic romance.

I have only given the broad outlines of Professor Kittredge's admirable study; the reader must be referred to the original for the numerous detailed pieces of investigation concerning special story-types and incidents, their action and interaction, the rationale of story-change, which make his work fascinating reading for the storyologist.

23

The Lay of the Were-Wolf

MARIE DE FRANCE

$\mathcal{A}$mongst the tales I tell you once again, I would not forget the Lay of the Were-Wolf. Such beasts as he are known in every land. Bisclavaret he is named in Brittany; whilst the Norman calls him Garwal.

It is a certain thing, and within the knowledge of all, that many a christened man has suffered this change, and ran wild in woods, as a Were-Wolf. The Were-Wolf is a fearsome beast. He lurks within the thick forest, mad and horrible to see. All the evil that he may, he does. He goeth to and fro, about the solitary place, seeking man, in order to devour him. Hearken, now, to the adventure of the Were-Wolf, that I have to tell.

In Brittany there dwelt a baron who was marvellously esteemed of all his fellows. He was a stout knight, and a comely, and a man of office and repute. Right private was he to the mind of his lord, and dear to the counsel of his neighbours. This baron was wedded to a very worthy dame, right fair to see, and sweet of semblance. All his love was set on her, and all her love was given again to him. One only grief had this lady. For three whole days in every week her lord was absent from her side. She knew not where he went, nor on what errand. Neither did any of his house know the business which called him forth.

On a day when this lord was come again to his house, altogether joyous and content, the lady took him to task, right sweetly, in this fashion,

"Husband," said she, "and fair, sweet friend, I have a certain thing to pray of you. Right willingly would I receive this gift, but I fear to anger you in the asking. It is better for me to have an empty hand, than to gain hard words."

When the lord heard this matter, he took the lady in his arms, very tenderly, and kissed her.

French Medieval Romances from the Lays of Marie De France, translated by Eugene Mason (New York: E. P. Dutton, 1911), reprinted 1924, pp. 83–90.

"Wife," he answered, "ask what you will. What would you have, for it is yours already?"

"By my faith," said the lady, "soon shall I be whole. Husband, right long and wearisome are the days that you spend away from your home. I rise from my bed in the morning, sick at heart, I know not why. So fearful am I, lest you do aught to your loss, that I may not find any comfort. Very quickly shall I die for reason of my dread. Tell me now, where you go, and on what business! How may the knowledge of one who loves so closely, bring you to harm?"

"Wife," made answer the lord, "nothing but evil can come if I tell you this secret. For the mercy of God do not require it of me. If you but knew, you would withdraw yourself from my love, and I should be lost indeed."

When the lady heard this, she was persuaded that her baron sought to put her by with jesting words. Therefore she prayed and required him the more urgently, with tender looks and speech, till he was overborne, and told her all the story, hiding naught.

"Wife, I become Bisclavaret. I enter in the forest, and live on prey and roots, within the thickest of the wood."

After she had learned his secret, she prayed and entreated the more as to whether he ran in his raiment, or went spoiled of vesture.

"Wife," said he, "I go naked as a beast."

"Tell me, for hope of grace, what you do with your clothing?"

"Fair wife, that will I never. If I should lose my raiment, or even be marked as I quit my vesture, then a Were-Wolf I must go for all the days of my life. Never again should I become man, save in that hour my clothing were given back to me. For this reason never will I show my lair."

"Husband," replied the lady to him, "I love you better than all the world. The less cause have you for doubting my faith, or hiding any tittle from me. What savour is here of friendship? How have I made forfeit of your love; for what sin do you mistrust my honour? Open now your heart, and tell what is good to be known."

So at the end, outwearied and overborne by her importunity, he could no longer refrain, but told her all.

"Wife," said he, "within this wood, a little from the path, there is a hidden way, and at the end thereof an ancient chapel, where often-times I have bewailed my lot. Near by is a great hollow stone, concealed by a bush, and there is the secret place where I hide my raiment, till I would return to my own home."

On hearing this marvel the lady became sanguine of visage, because of her exceeding fear. She dared no longer to lie at his side, and turned over in her mind, this way and that, how best she could get her from him. Now there was a certain knight of those parts, who, for a great while, had sought and required this lady for her love. This knight had spent long years in her service, but little enough had he got thereby, not even fair words, or a promise. To him the dame wrote a letter, and meeting, made her purpose plain.

"Fair friend," said she, "be happy. That which you have coveted so long a time, I will grant without delay. Never again will I deny your suit. My heart, and all I have to give, are yours, so take me now as love and dame."

Right sweetly the knight thanked her for her grace, and pledged her faith and fealty. When she had confirmed him by an oath, then she told him of his business of her lord—why he went, and what he became, and of his ravening within the wood. So she showed him of the chapel, and of the hollow stone, and of how to spoil the Were-Wolf of his vesture. Thus, by the kiss of his wife, was Bisclavaret betrayed. Often enough had he ravished his prey in desolate places, but from this journey he never returned. His kinsfolk and acquaintance came together to ask of his tidings, when this absence was noised abroad. Many a man, on many a day, searched the woodland, but none might find him, nor learn where Bisclavaret was gone.

The lady was wedded to the knight who had cherished her for so long a space. More than a year had passed since Bisclaveret disappeared. Then it chanced that the King would hunt in the self-same wood where the Were-Wolf lurked. When the hounds were unleashed they ran this way and that, and swiftly came upon his scent. At the view the huntsman winded on his horn, and the whole pack were at his heels. They followed him from morn to eve, till he was torn and bleeding, and was all adread lest they should pull him down. Now the King was very close to the quarry, and when Bisclavaret looked upon his master, he ran to him for pity and for grace. He took the stirrup within his paws, and fawned upon the prince's foot. The King was very fearful at this sight, but presently he called his courtiers to his aid.

"Lords," cried he, "hasten hither, and see this marvellous thing.

Here is a beast who has the sense of man. He abases himself before his foe, and cries for mercy, although he cannot speak. Beat off the hounds, and let no man do him harm. We will hunt no more to-day, but return to our own place, with the wonderful quarry we have taken."

The King turned him about, and rode to his hall, Bisclavaret following at his side. Very near to his master the Were-Wolf went, like any dog, and had no care to seek again the wood. When the King had brought him safely to his own castle, he rejoiced greatly, for the beast was fair and strong, no mightier had any man seen. Much pride had the King in his marvellous beast. He held him so dear, that he bade all those who wished for his love, to cross the Wolf in naught, neither to strike him with a rod, but ever to see that he was richly fed and kennelled warm. This commandment the Court observed willingly. So all the day the Wolf sported with the lords, and at night he lay within the chamber of the King. There was not a man who did not make much of the beast, so frank was he and debonair. None had reason to do him wrong, for ever was he about his master, and for his part did evil to none. Every day were these two companions together, and all perceived that the King loved him as his friend.

Hearken now to that which chanced.

The King held a high Court, and bade his great vassals and barons, and all the lords of his venery to the feast. Never was there a goodlier feast, nor one set forth with sweeter show and pomp. Amongst those who were bidden, came that same knight who had the wife of Bisclavaret for dame. He came to the castle, richly gowned, with a fair company, but little he deemed whom he would find so near. Bisclavaret marked his foe the moment he stood within the hall. He ran towards him, and seized him with his fangs, in the King's very presence, and to the view of all. Doubtless he would have done him much mischief, had not the King called and chidden him, and threatened him with a rod. Once, and twice, again, the Wolf set upon the knight in the very light of day. All men marvelled at his malice, for sweet and serviceable was the beast, and to that hour had shown hatred of none. With one consent the household deemed that this deed was done with full reason, and that the Wolf had suffered at the knight's hand some bitter wrong. Right wary of his foe was the knight until the feast had ended, and all the barons had taken farewell of their lord, and departed, each to his own house. With these, amongst the very first, went that lord whom Bisclavaret so fiercely had assailed. Small was the wonder he was glad to go.

Not long while after this adventure it came to pass that the courteous King would hunt in that forest where Bisclavaret was found. With the prince came his wolf, and a fair company. Now at nightfall the King abode within a certain lodge of that country, and this was known of that dame who before was the wife of Bisclavaret. In the morning the lady clothed her in her most dainty apparel, and hastened to the lodge, since she desired to speak with the King, and to offer him a rich present. When the lady entered in the chamber, neither man nor leash might restrain the fury of the Wolf. He became as a mad dog in his hatred and malice. Breaking from his bonds he sprang at the lady's face, and bit the nose from her visage. From every side men ran to the succour of the dame. They beat off the wolf from his prey, and for a little would have cut him in pieces with their swords. But a certain wise counsellor said to the King,

"Sire, hearken now to me. This beast is always with you, and there is not one of us all who has not known him for long. He goes in and out amongst us, nor has molested any man, neither done wrong or felony to any, save only to this dame, one only time as we have seen. He has done evil to this lady, and to that knight, who is now the husband of the dame. Sire, she was once the wife of that lord who was so close and private to your heart, but who went, and none might find where he had gone. Now, therefore, put the dame in a sure place, and question her straitly, so that she may tell—if perchance she knows thereof—for what reason this Beast holds her in such mortal hate. For many a strange deed has chanced, as well we know, in this marvellous land of Brittany."

The King listened to these words, and deemed the counsel good. He laid hands upon the knight, and put the dame in surety in another place. He caused them to be questioned right straitly, so that their torment was very grievous. At the end, partly because of her distress, and partly by reason of her exceeding fear, the lady's lips were loosed, and she told her tale. She showed them of the betrayal of her lord, and how his raiment was stolen from the hollow stone. Since then she knew not where he went, nor what had befallen him, for he had never come again to his own land. Only, in her heart, well she deemed and was persuaded, that Bisclavaret was he.

Straightway the King demanded the vesture of his baron, whether this were to the wish of the lady, or whether it were against her wish. When the raiment was brought him, he caused it to be spread before Bisclavaret, but the Wolf made as though he had not seen. Then that cunning and crafty counsellor took the King apart, that he might give him a fresh rede.

"Sire," said he, "you do not wisely, nor well, to set this raiment before Bisclavaret, in the sight of all. In shame and much tribulation must he lay aside the beast, and again become man. Carry your wolf within your most secret chamber, and put his vestment therein. Then close the door upon him, and leave him alone for a space. So we shall see presently whether the ravening beast may indeed return to human shape."

The King carried the Wolf to his chamber, and shut the doors upon him fast. He delayed for a brief while, and taking two lords of his fellowship with him, came again to the room. Entering therein, all three, softly together, they found the knight sleeping in the King's bed, like a little child. The King ran swiftly to the bed and taking his friend in his arms, embraced and kissed him fondly, above a hundred times. When man's speech returned once more, he told him of his adventure. Then the King restored to his friend the fief that was stolen from him, and gave such rich gifts, moreover, as I cannot tell. As for the wife who had betrayed Bisclavaret, he bade her avoid his country, and chased her from the realm. So she went forth, she and her second lord together, to seek a more abiding city, and were no more seen.

The adventure that you have heard is no vain fable. Verily and indeed it chanced as I have said. The Lay of the Were-Wolf, truly, was written that it should ever be borne in mind.

24.

The Werewolf

EUGENE FIELD

𝔍n the reign of Egbert the Saxon there dwelt in Britain a maiden named Yseult, who was beloved of all, both for her goodness and for her beauty. But, though many a youth came wooing her, she loved Harold only, and to him she plighted her troth.

Among the other youth of whom Yseult was beloved was Alfred, and he was sore angered that Yseult showed favor to Harold, so that one day Alfred said to Harold: "Is it right that old Siegfried should come from his grave and have Yseult to wife?" Then added he, "Prithee, good sir, why do you turn so white when I speak your grandsire's name?"

Then Harold asked, "What know you of Siegfried that you taunt me? What memory of him should vex me now?"

"We know and we know," retorted Alfred. "There are some tales told us by our grandmas we have not forgot."

So ever after that Alfred's words and Alfred's bitter smile haunted Harold by day and night.

Harold's grandsire, Siegfried the Teuton, had been a man of cruel violence. The legend said that a curse rested upon him, and that at certain times he was possessed of an evil spirit that wreaked its fury on mankind. But Siegfried had been dead full many years, and there was naught to mind the world of him save the legend and a cunning-wrought spear which he had from Brunehilde, the witch. This spear was such a weapon that it never lost its brightness, nor had its point been blunted. It hung in Harold's chamber, and it was the marvel among weapons of that time.

Yseult knew that Alfred loved her, but she did not know of the bitter words which Alfred had spoken to Harold. Her love for Harold was perfect in its trust and gentleness. But Alfred had hit the truth: the curse of old Siegfried was upon Harold—slumbering a century, it had awakened in the blood of the grandson, and Harold knew the curse

In *Second Book of Tales* (New York: Charles Scribner's Sons, 1911), 243–56.

that was upon him, and it was this that seemed to stand between him and Yseult. But love is stronger than all else, and Harold loved.

Harold did not tell Yseult of the curse that was upon him, for he feared that she would not love him if she knew. Whensoever he felt the fire of the curse burning in his veins he would say to her, "To-morrow I hunt the wild boar in the uttermost forest," or, "Next week I go stag-stalking among the distant northern hills." Even so it was that he ever made good excuse for his absence, and Yseult thought no evil things, for she was trustful; ay, though he went many times away and was long gone, Yseult suspected no wrong. So none beheld Harold when the curse was upon him in its violence.

Alfred alone bethought himself of evil things. "'Tis passing strange," quoth he, "that ever and anon this gallant lover should quit our company and betake himself whither none knoweth. In sooth 't will be well to have an eye on old Siegfried's grandson."

Harold knew that Alfred watched him zealously, and he was tormented by a constant fear that Alfred would discover the curse that was on him; but what gave him greater anguish was the fear that mayhap at some moment when he was in Yseult's presence, the curse would seize upon him and cause him to do great evil unto her, whereby she would be destroyed or her love for him would be undone forever. So Harold lived in terror, feeling that his love was hopeless, yet knowing not how to combat it.

Now, it befell in those times that the country round about was ravaged of a werewolf, a creature that was feared by all men howe'er so valorous. This werewolf was by day a man, but by night a wolf given to ravage and to slaughter, and having a charmed life against which no human agency availed aught. Wheresoever he went he attacked and devoured mankind, spreading terror and desolation round about, and the dream-readers said that the earth would not be freed from the werewolf until some man offered himself a voluntary sacrifice to the monster's rage.

Now, although Harold was known far and wide as a mighty huntsman, he had never set forth to hunt the werewolf, and, strange enow, the werewolf never ravaged the domain while Harold was there-in. Whereat Alfred marvelled much, and oftentimes he said: "Our Harold is a wondrous huntsman. Who is like unto him in stalking the timid doe and in crippling the fleeing boar? But how passing well doth he time his absence from the haunts of the werewolf. Such valor beseemeth our young Siegfried."

Which being brought to Harold his heart flamed with anger, but he made no answer, lest he betray the truth he feared.

It happened so about that time that Yseult said to Harold, "Wilt thou go with me tomorrow even to the feast in the sacred grove?"

"That can I not do," answered Harold. "I am privily summoned hence to Normandy upon a mission of which I shall some time tell thee. And I pray thee, on thy love for me, go not to the feast in the sacred grove without me."

"What say'st thou?" cried Yseult. "Shall I not go to the feast of Ste. Ælfreda? My father would be sore displeased were I not there with the other maidens. 'T were greatest pity that I should despite his love thus."

"But do not, I beseech thee," Harold implored. "Go not to the feast of Ste. Ælfreda in the sacred grove! And thou would thus love me, go not—see, thou my life, on my two knees I ask it!"

"How pale thou art," said Yseult, "and trembling."

"Go not to the sacred grove upon the morrow night," he begged.

Yseult marvelled at his acts and at his speech. Then, for the first time, she thought him to be jealous—whereat she secretly rejoiced (being a woman).

"Ah," quoth she, "thou dost doubt my love," but when she saw a look of pain come on his face she added—as if she repented of the words she had spoken—"or dost thou fear the werewolf?"

Then Harold answered, fixing his eyes on hers, "Thou hast said it; it is the werewolf that I fear."

"Why dost thou look at me so strangely, Harold?" cried Yseult. "By the cruel light in thine eyes one might almost take thee to be the werewolf!"

"Come hither, sit beside me," said Harold tremblingly, "and I will tell thee why I fear to have thee go to the feast of Ste. Ælfreda tomorrow evening. Hear what I dreamed last night. I dreamed I was the werewolf—do not shudder, dear love, for 't was only a dream.

"A grizzled old man stood at my bedside and strove to pluck my soul from my bosom.

"'What would'st thou?' I cried.

"'Thy soul is mine,' he said, 'thou shalt live out my curse. Give me thy soul—hold back thy hands—give me thy soul, I say.'

"'Thy curse shall not be upon me,' I cried. 'What have I done that thy curse should rest upon me? Thou shalt not have my soul.'

"'For my offence shalt thou suffer, and in my curse thou shalt endure hell—it is so decreed.'

"So spake the old man, and he strove with me, and he prevailed against me, and he plucked my soul from my bosom, and he said, 'Go, search and kill'—and—and lo, I was a wolf upon the moor.

"The dry grass crackled beneath my tread. The darkness of the night was heavy and it oppressed me. Strange horrors tortured my soul, and it groaned and groaned gaoled in that wolfish body. The wind whispered to me; with its myriad voices it spake to me and said, 'Go, search and kill.' And above these voices sounded the hideous laughter of an old man. I fled the moor—whither I knew not, nor knew I what motive lashed me on.

"I came to a river and I plunged in. A burning thirst consumed me, and I lapped the waters of the river—they were waves of flame, and they flashed around me and hissed, and what they said was, 'Go, search and kill,' and I heard the old man's laughter again.

"A forest lay before me with its gloomy thickets and its sombre shadows—with its ravens, its vampires, its serprents, its reptiles, and all its hideous brood of night. I darted among its thorns and crouched amid the leaves, the nettles, and the brambles. The owls hooted at me and the thorns pierced my flesh. 'Go, search and kill,' said everything. The hares sprang from my pathway; the other beasts ran bellowing away; every form of life shrieked in my ears—the curse was on me—I was the werewolf.

"On, on I went with the fleetness of the wind, and my soul groaned in its wolfish prison, and the winds and the waters and the trees bade me, 'Go, search and kill, thou accursed brute; go, search and kill.'

"Nowhere was there pity for the wolf; what mercy, thus, should I, the werewolf, show? The curse was on me and it filled me with hunger and a thirst for blood. Skulking on my way within myself I cried, 'Let me have blood, oh, let me have human blood, that this wrath may be appeased, that this curse may be removed.'

"At last I came to the sacred grove. Sombre loomed the poplars, the oaks frowned upon me. Before me stood an old man—'twas he, grizzled and taunting, whose curse I bore. He feared me not. All other living things fled before me, but the old man feared me not. A maiden stood beside him. She did not see me, for she was blind.

"'Kill, kill,' cried the old man, and he pointed at the girl beside him.

"Hell raged within me—the curse impelled me—I sprang at her throat. I heard the old man's laughter once more, and then—then I awoke, trembling, cold, horrified."

Scarce was this dream told when Alfred strode the way.

"Now, by'r Lady," quoth he, "I bethink me never to have seen a sorrier twain."

Then Yseult told him of Harold's going away and how that Harold had besought her not to venture to the feast of Ste. Ælfreda in the sacred grove.

"These fears are childish," cried Alfred boastfully. "And thou sufferest me, sweet lady, I will bear thee company to the feast, and a score of my lusty yeoman with their good yew-bows and honest spears, they shall attend me. There be no werewolf, I trow, will chance about with us."

Whereat Yseult laughed merrily, and Harold said: "'T is well; thou shalt go to the sacred grove, and may my love and Heaven's grace forefend all evil."

Then Harold went to his abode, and he fetched old Siegfried's spear back unto Yseult, and he gave it into her two hands, saying, "Take this spear with thee to the feast to-morrow night. It is old Siegfried's spear, possessing mighty virtue and marvellous."

And Harold took Yseult to his heart and blessed her, and he kissed her upon her brow and upon her lips, saying, "Farewell, oh, my beloved. How wilt thou love me when thou know'st my sacrifice. Farewell, farewell, forever, oh, alder-liefest mine."

So Harold went his way, and Yseult was lost in wonderment.

On the morrow night came Yseult to the sacred grove wherein the feast was spread, and she bore old Siegfried's spear with her in her girdle. Alfred attended her, and a score of lusty yeomen were with him. In the grove there was great merriment, and with singing and dancing and games withal did the honest folk celebrate the feast of the fair Ste. Ælfreda.

But suddenly a mighty tumult arose, and there were cries of "The werewolf!" "The werewolf!" Terror seized upon all—stout hearts were frozen with fear. Out from the further forest rushed the werewolf, wood wroth, bellowing hoarsely, gnashing his fangs and tossing hither and thither the yellow foam from his snapping jaws. He sought Yseult straight, as if an evil power drew him to the spot where she stood. But Yseult was not afeared; like a marble statue she stood and saw the werewolf's coming. The yeomen, dropping their torches and casting aside their bows, had fled; Alfred alone abided there to do the monster battle.

At the approaching wolf he hurled his heavy lance, but as it struck the werewolf's bristling back the weapon was all to-shivered.

Then the werewolf, fixing his eyes upon Yseult, skulked for a moment in the shadow of the yews and thinking then of Harold's words, Yseult plucked old Siegfried's spear from her girdle, raised it on high, and with the strength of despair sent it hurtling through the air.

The werewolf saw the shining weapon, and a cry burst from his gaping throat—a cry of human agony. And Yseult saw in the werewolf's eyes the eyes of some one she had seen and known, but 't was for an instant only, and then the eyes were no longer human, but wolfish in their ferocity.

A supernatural force seemed to speed the spear in its flight. With fearful precision the weapon smote home and buried itself by half its length in the werewolf's shaggy breast just above the heart, and then, with a monstrous sigh—as if he yielded up his life without regret—the werewolf fell dead in the shadow of the yews.

Then, ah, then in very truth there was great joy, and loud were the acclaims, while, beautiful in her trembling pallor, Yseult was led unto her home, where the people set about to give great feast to do her homage, for the werewolf was dead, and she it was that had slain him.

But Yseult cried out: "Go, search for Harold—go, bring him to me. Nor eat, nor sleep till he be found."

"Good my lady," quoth Alfred, "how can that be, since he hath betaken himself to Normandy?"

"I care not where he be," she cried. "My heart stands still until I look into his eyes again."

"Surely he hath not gone to Normandy," outspake Hubert. "This very eventide I saw him enter his abode."

They hastened thither—a vast company. His chamber door was barred.

"Harold, Harold, come forth!" they cried, as they beat upon the door, but no answer came to their calls and knockings. Afeared, they battered down the door, and when it fell they saw that Harold lay upon his bed.

"He sleeps," said one. "See, he holds a portrait in his hand—and it is her portrait. How fair he is and how tranquilly he sleeps."

But no, Harold was not asleep. His face was calm and beautiful, as if he dreamed of his beloved, but his raiment was red with the blood that streamed from a wound in his breast—a gaping, ghastly spear wound just above his heart.

25

The Other Side
A Breton Legend

ERIC STENBOCK

À la joyouse Messe noire.

ot that I like it, but one does feel so much better after it—oh,
thank you, Mère Yvonne, yes just a little drop more." So the old
crones fell to drinking their hot brandy and water (although of course
they only took it medicinally, as a remedy for their rheumatics), all
seated round the big fire and Mère Pinquèle continued her story.

"Oh, yes, then when they get to the top of the hill, there is an
altar with six candles quite black and a sort of something in between,
that nobody sees quite clearly, and the old black ram with the man's
face and long horns begins to say Mass in a sort of gibberish nobody
understands, and two black strange things like monkeys glide about
with the book and the cruets—and there's music too, such music.
There are things the top half like black cats, and the bottom part like
men only their legs are all covered with close black hair, and they play
on the bag-pipes, and when they come to the elevation, then—" Amid
the old crones there was lying on the hearth-rug, before the fire, a boy,
whose large lovely eyes dilated and whose limbs quivered in the very
ecstacy of terror.

"Is that all true, Mère Pinquèle?" he said.

"Oh, quite true, and not only that, the best part is yet to come;
for they take a child and—." Here Mère Pinquèle showed her fang-like
teeth.

"Oh! Mère Pinquèle, are you a witch too?"

"Silence, Gabriel," said Mère Yvonne, "how can you say anything
so wicked? Why, bless me, the boy ought to have been in bed ages ago."

Just then all shuddered, and all made the sign of the cross except
Mère Pinquèle, for they heard that most dreadful of dreadful sounds—
the howl of a wolf, which begins with three sharp barks and then lifts

In *The Spirit Lamp* (Oxford), IV. 2 (June 1893): 52–68.

itself up in a long protracted wail of commingled cruelty and despair, and at last subsides into a whispered growl fraught with eternal malice.

There was a forest and a village and a brook, the village was on one side of the brook, none had dared to cross to the other side. Where the village was, all was green and glad and fertile and fruitful; on the other side the trees never put forth green leaves, and a dark shadow hung over it even at noon-day, and in the night-time one could hear the wolves howling—the were-wolves and the wolf-men and the men-wolves, and those very wicked men who for nine days in every year are turned into wolves; but on the green side no wolf was ever seen, and only one little running brook like a silver streak flowed between.

It was spring now and the old crones sat no longer by the fire but before their cottages sunning themselves, and everyone felt so happy that they ceased to tell stories of the "other side." But Gabriel wandered by the brook as he was wont to wander, drawn thither by some strange attraction mingled with intense horror.

His schoolfellows did not like Gabriel; all laughed and jeered at him, because he was less cruel and more gentle of nature than the rest, and even as a rare and beautiful bird escaped from a cage is hacked to death by the common sparrows, so was Gabriel among his fellows. Everyone wondered how Mère Yvonne, that buxom and worthy matron, could have produced a son like this, with strange dreamy eyes, who was as they said "pas comme les autres gamins." His only friends were the Abbé Félicien whose Mass he served each morning, and one little girl called Carmeille, who loved him, no one could make out why.

The sun had already set, Gabriel still wandered by the brook, filled with vague terror and irresistible fascination. The sun set and the moon rose, the full moon, very large and very clear, and the moonlight flooded the forest both this side and "the other side," and just on the "other side" of the brook, hanging over, Gabriel saw a large deep blue flower, whose strange intoxicating perfume reached him and fascinated him even where he stood.

"If I could only make one step across," he thought, "nothing could harm me if I only plucked that one flower, and nobody would know I had been over at all," for the villagers looked with hatred and suspicion on anyone who was said to have crossed to the "other side," so summing up courage he leapt lightly to the other side of the brook.

Then the moon breaking from a cloud shone with unusual brilliance, and he saw, stretching before him, long reaches of the same strange blue flowers each one lovelier than the last, till, not being able to make up his mind which one flower to take or whether to take several, he went on and on, and the moon shone very brightly, and a strange unseen bird, somewhat like a nightingale, but louder and lovelier, sang, and his heart was filled with longing for he knew not what, and the moon shone and the nightingale sang. But on a sudden a black cloud covered the moon entirely, and all was black, utter darkness, and through the darkness he heard wolves howling and shrieking in the hideous ardour of the chase, and there passed before him a horrible procession of wolves (black wolves with red fiery eyes), and with them men that had the heads of wolves and wolves that had the heads of men, and above them flew owls (black owls with red fiery eyes), and bats and long serpentine black things, and last of all seated on an enormous black ram with hideous human face the wolf-keeper on whose face was eternal shadow; but they continued their horrid chase and passed him by, and when they had passed the moon shone out more beautiful than ever, and the strange nightingale sang again, and the strange intense blue flowers were in long reaches in front to the right and to the left. But one thing was there which had not been before, among the deep blue flowers walked one with long gleaming golden hair, and she turned once round and her eyes were of the same colour as the strange blue flowers, and she walked on and Gabriel could not choose but follow. But when a cloud passed over the moon he saw no beautiful woman but a wolf, so in utter terror he turned and fled, plucking one of the strange blue flowers on the way, and leapt again over the brook and ran home.

When he got home Gabriel could not resist showing his treasure to his mother, though he knew she would not appreciate it; but when she saw the strange blue flower, Mère Yvonne turned pale and said, "Why child, where hast thou been? sure it is the witch flower"; and so saying she snatched it from him and cast it into the corner, and immediately all its beauty and strange fragrance faded from it and it looked charred as though it had been burnt. So Gabriel sat down silently and rather sulkily, and having eaten no supper went up to bed, but he did not sleep but waited and waited till all was quiet within the house. Then he crept downstairs in his long white night-shirt and bare feet on

the square cold stones and picked hurriedly up the charred and faded
flower and put it in his warm bosom next his heart, and immediately
the flower bloomed again lovelier than ever, and he fell into a deep
sleep, but through his sleep he seemed to hear a soft low voice singing
underneath his window in a strange language (in which the subtle
sounds melted into one another), but he could distinguish no word
except his own name.

When he went forth in the morning to serve Mass, he still kept
the flower with him next his heart. Now when the priest began Mass
and said "Intriobo ad altare Dei," then said Gabriel "Qui nequiquam
laetificavit juventutem meam." And the Abbé Félicien turned round on
hearing this strange response, and he saw the boy's face deadly pale,
his eyes fixed and his limbs rigid, and as the priest looked on him
Gabriel fell fainting to the floor, so the sacristan had to carry him home
and seek another acolyte for the Abbé Félicien.

Now when the Abbé Félicien came to see after him, Gabriel felt
strangely reluctant to say anything about the blue flower and for the
first time he deceived the priest.

In the afternoon as sunset drew nigh he felt better and Carmeille
came to see him and begged him to go out with her into the fresh air.
So they went out hand in hand, the dark haired, gazelle-eyed boy, and
the fair wavy haired girl, and something, he knew not what, led his
steps (half knowingly and yet not so, for he could not but walk thither)
to the brook, and they sat down together on the bank.

Gabriel thought at least he might tell his secret to Carmeille, so
he took out the flower from his bosom and said, "Look here, Carmeille, hast thou seen ever so lovely a flower as this?" but Carmeille
turned pale and faint and said, "Oh, Gabriel what is this flower? I but
touched it and I felt something strange come over me. No, no, I don't
like its perfume, no there's something not quite right about it, oh, dear
Gabriel, do let me throw it away," and before he had time to answer,
she cast it from her, and again all its beauty and fragrance went from it
and it looked charred as though it had been burnt. But suddenly where
the flower had been thrown on this side of the brook, there appeared a
wolf, which stood and looked at the children.

Carmeille said, "What shall we do," and clung to Gabriel, but the
wolf looked at them very steadfastly and Gabriel recognized in the
eyes of the wolf the strange deep intense blue eyes of the wolf-woman

he had seen on the "other side," so he said, "Stay here, dear Carmeille, see she is looking gently at us and will not hurt us."

"But it is a wolf," said Carmeille, and quivered all over with fear, but again Gabriel said languidly, "She will not hurt us." Then Carmeille seized Gabriel's hand in an agony of terror and dragged him along with her till they reached the village, where she gave the alarm and all the lads of the village gathered together. They had never seen a wolf on this side of the brook, so they excited themselves greatly and arranged a grand wolf hunt for the morrow, but Gabriel sat silently apart and said no word.

That night Gabriel could not sleep at all nor could he bring himself to say his prayers; but he sat in his little room by the window with his shirt open at the throat and the strange blue flower at his heart and again this night he heard a voice singing beneath his window in the same soft, subtle, liquid language as before—

> Ma zála liral va jé
> Cwamûlo zhajéla je
> Cárma urádi el javé
> Járma, symai, —carmé—
> Zhála javály thra je
> al vú al vlaûle va azré
> Safralje vairálje va já?
> Cárma serâja
> Lâja lâja
> Luzhà!

and as he looked he could see the silvern shadows slide on the limmering light of golden hair, and the strange eyes gleaming dark blue through the night and it seemed to him that he could not but follow; so he walked half clad and bare foot as he was with eyes fixed as in a dream silently down the stairs and out into the night.

And ever and again she turned to look on him with her strange blue eyes full of tenderness and passion and sadness beyond the sadness of things human—and as he foreknew his steps led him to the brink of the brook. Then she, taking his hand, familiarly said, "Won't you help me over Gabriel?"

Then it seemed to him as though he had known her all his life— so he went with her to the "other side" but he saw no one by him; and looking again beside him there were *two wolves*. In a frenzy of terror, he (who had never thought to kill any living thing before) seized a log of wood lying by and smote one of the wolves on the head.

Immediately he saw the wolf-woman again at his side with blood streaming from her forehead, staining her wonderful golden hair, and with eyes looking at him with infinite reproach, she said—"Who did this?"

Then she whispered a few words to the other wolf, which leapt over the brook and made its way towards the village, and turning again towards him she said, "Oh Gabriel, how could you strike me, who would have loved you so long and so well." Then it seemed to him again as though he had known her all his life but he felt dazed and said nothing—but she gathered a dark green strangely shaped leaf and holding it to her forehead, she said—"Gabriel, kiss the place all will be well again." So he kissed as she had bidden him and he felt the salt taste of blood in his mouth and then he knew no more.

Again he saw the wolf-keeper with his horrible troupe around him, but this time not engaged in the chase but sitting in strange conclave in a circle and the black owls sat in the trees and the black bats hung downwards from the branches. Gabriel stood alone in the middle with a hundred wicked eyes fixed on him. They seemed to deliberate about what should be done with him, speaking in that same strange tongue which he had heard in the songs beneath his window. Suddenly he felt a hand pressing in his and saw the mysterious wolf-woman by his side. Then began what seemed a kind of incantation where human or half human creatures seemed to howl, and beasts to speak with human speech but in the unknown tongue. Then the wolf-keeper whose face was ever veiled in shadow spake some words in a voice that seemed to come from afar off, but all he could distinguish was his own name Gabriel and her name Lilith. Then he felt arms enlacing him. —

Gabriel awoke—in his own room—so it was a dream after all— but what a dreadful dream. Yes, but was it his own room? Of course there was his coat hanging over the chair—yes but—the Crucifix— where was the Crucifix and the benetier and the consecrated palm branch and the antique image of Our Lady perpetuae salutis, with the little ever-burning lamp before it, before which he placed every day the flowers he had gathered, yet had not dared to place the blue flower.—

Every morning he lifted his still dream-laden eyes to it and said Ave Maria and made the sign of the cross, which bringeth peace to the soul—but how horrible, how maddening, it was not there, not at all. No surely he could not be awake, at least not *quite* awake, he would make the benedictive sign and he would be freed from this fearful illusion—yes but the sign, he would make the sign—oh, but what was the sign? Had he forgotten? or was his arm paralyzed? No he could not move. Then he had forgotten—and the prayer—he must remember that. A—vae—nunc—mortis—fructus. No surely it did not run thus—but something like it surely—yes, he was awake he could move at any rate—he would reassure himself—he would get up—he would see the grey old church with the exquisitely pointed gables bathed in the light of dawn, and presently the deep solemn bell would toll and he would run down and don his red cassock and lace-worked cotta and light the tall candles on the altar and wait reverently to vest the good and gracious Abbé Félicien, kissing each vestment as he lifted it with reverent hands.

But surely this was not the light of dawn; it was like sunset! He leapt from his small white bed, and a vague terror came over him, he trembled and had to hold on to the chair before he reached the window. No, the solemn spires of the grey church were not to be seen— he was in the depths of the forest; but in a part he had never seen before—but surely he had explored every part, it must be the "other side." To terror succeeded a languor and lassitude not without charm— passivity, acquiescence, indulgence—he felt, as it were, the strong caress of another will flowing over him like water and clothing him with invisible hands in an impalpable garment; so he dressed himself almost mechanically and walked downstairs, the same stairs it seemed to him down which it was his wont to run and spring. The broad square stones seemed singularly beautiful and irridescent with many strange colours—how was it he had never noticed this before—but he was gradually losing the power of wondering—he entered the room below—the wonted coffee and bread-rolls were on the table.

"Why Gabriel, how late you are to-day." The voice was very sweet but the intonation strange—and there sat Lilith, the mysterious wolf-woman, her glittering gold hair tied in a loose knot and an embroidery whereon she was tracing strange serpentine patterns, lay over the lap of her maize coloured garment—and she looked at Gabriel steadfastly with her wonderful dark blue eyes and said, "Why, Gabriel, you are late to-day," and Gabriel answered, "I was tired yesterday, give me some coffee."

A dream within a dream—yes, he had known her all his life, and they dwelt together; had they not always done so? And she would take him through the glades of the forest and gather for him flowers, such as he had never seen before, and tell him stories in her strange, low deep voice, which seemed ever to be accompanied by the faint vibration of strings, looking at him fixedly the while with her marvellous blue eyes.

Little by little the flame of vitality which burned within him seemed to grow fainter and fainter, and his lithe lissom limbs waxed languorous and luxurious—yet was he ever filled with a languid content and a will not his own perpetually overshadowed him.

One day in their wanderings he saw a strange dark blue flower like unto the eyes of Lilith, and a sudden half remembrance flashed through his mind.

"What is this blue flower?" he said, and Lilith shuddered and said nothing; but as they went a little further there was a brook—*the* brook he thought, and felt his fetters falling off him, and he prepared to spring over the brook; but Lilith seized him by the arm and held him back with all her strength, and trembling all over she said, "Promise me Gabriel that you will not cross over." But he said, "Tell me what is this blue flower, and why you will not tell me?" And she said, "Look Gabriel at the brook." And he looked and saw that though it was just like the brook of separation it was not the same, the waters did not flow.

As Gabriel looked steadfastly into the still waters it seemed to him as though he saw voices—some impression of the Vespers for the Dead. "Hei mihi quia incolatus sum," and again "De profundis clamavi ad te"—oh, that veil, that overshadowing veil! Why could he not hear properly and see, and why did he only remember as one looking through a threefold semi-transparent curtain. Yes they were praying for him—but who were they? He heard again the voice of Lilith in whispered anguish, "Come away!"

Then he said, this time in monotone, "What is this blue flower, and what is its use?"

And the low thrilling voice answered, "It is called 'lûli uzhûri,' two drops pressed upon the face of the sleeper and he will *sleep.*"

He was as a child in her hand and suffered himself to be led from thence, nevertheless he plucked listlessly one of the blue flowers, holding it downwards in his hand. What did she mean? Would the sleeper wake? Would the blue flower leave any stain? Could that stain be wiped off?

But as he lay asleep at early dawn he heard voices from afar off praying for him—the Abbé Félicien, Carmeille, his mother too, then some familiar words struck his ear: "Libera mea porta inferi." Mass was being said for the repose of his soul, he knew this. No, he could not stay, he would leap over the brook, he knew the way—he had forgotten that the brook did not flow. Ah, but Lilith would know—what should he do? The blue flower—there it lay close by his bedside—he understood now; so he crept very silently to where Lilith lay asleep, her long hair glistening gold, shining like a glory round about her. He pressed two drops on her forehead, she sighed once, and a shade of praeternatural anguish passed over her beautiful face. He fled—terror, remorse, and hope tearing his soul and making fleet his feet. He came to the brook—he did not see that the water did not flow—of course it was the brook for separation; one bound, he should be with things human again. He leapt over and—

A change had come over him—what was it? He could not tell— did he walk on all fours? Yes surely. He looked into the brook, whose still waters were fixed as a mirror, and there, horror, he beheld himself; or was it himself? His head and face, yes; but his body transformed to that of a wolf. Even as he looked he heard a sound of hideous mocking laughter behind him. He turned round—there, in a gleam of red lurid light, he saw one whose body was human, but whose head was that of a wolf, with eyes of infinite malice; and, while this hideous being laughed with a loud human laugh, he, essaying to speak, could only utter the prolonged howl of a wolf.

But we will transfer our thoughts from the alien things on the "other side" to the simple human village where Gabriel used to dwell. Mère Yvonne was not much surprised when Gabriel did not turn up to breakfast—he often did not, so absent-minded was he; this time she said, "I suppose he has gone with the others to the wolf hunt." Not that Gabriel was given to hunting, but, as she sagely said, "there was no knowing what he might do next." The boys said, "Of course that muff Gabriel is skulking and hiding himself, he's afraid to join the wolf hunt; why, he wouldn't even kill a cat," for their one notion of excellence was slaughter—so the greater the game the greater the glory. They were chiefly now confined to cats and sparrows, but they all hoped in after time to become generals of armies.

Yet these children had been taught all their life through with the gentle words of Christ—but alas, nearly all the seed falls by the way-side, where it could not bear flower or fruit; how little these know the suffering and bitter anguish or realize the full meaning of the words to those, of whom it is written "Some fell among thorns."

The wolf hunt was so far a success that they did actually see a wolf, but not a success, as they did not kill it before it leapt over the brook to the "other side," where, of course, they were afraid to pursue it. No emotion is more inrooted and intense in the minds of common people than hatred and fear of anything "strange."

Days passed by, but Gabriel was nowhere seen—and Mère Yvonne began to see clearly at last how deeply she loved her only son, who was so unlike her that she had thought herself an object of pity to other mothers—the goose and the swan's egg. People searched and pretended to search, they even went to the length of dragging the ponds, which the boys thought very amusing, as it enabled them to kill a great number of water rats, and Carmeille sat in a corner and cried all day long. Mère Pinquèle also sat in a corner and chuckled and said that she had always said Gabriel would come to no good. The Abbé Félicien looked pale and anxious, but said very little, save to God and those that dwelt with God.

At last, as Gabriel was not there, they supposed he must be nowhere—that is *dead*. (Their knowledge of other localities being so limited, that it did not even occur to them to suppose he might be living elsewhere than in the village.) So it was agreed that an empty catafalque should be put up in the church with tall candles round it, and Mère Yvonne said all the prayers that were in her prayer book, beginning at the beginning and ending at the end, regardless of their appropriateness—not even omitting the instructions of the rubrics.

And Carmeille sat in the corner of the little side chapel and cried, and cried. And the Abbé Félicien caused the boys to sing the Vespers for the Dead (this did not amuse them so much as dragging the pond), and on the following morning, in the silence of early dawn, said the Dirge and the Requiem—*and this Gabriel heard.*

Then the Abbé Félicien received a message to bring the Holy Viaticum to one sick. So they set forth in solemn procession with great torches, and their way lay along the brook of separation.

Essaying to speak he could only utter the prolonged howl of a wolf—the most fearful of all bestial sounds. He howled and howled again—perhaps Lilith would hear him! Perhaps she could rescue him? Then he remembered the blue flower—the beginning and end of all his woe. His cries aroused all the denizens of the forest—the wolves, the wolf-men, and the men-wolves. He fled before them in an agony of terror—behind him, seated on the black ram with human face, was the wolf-keeper, whose face was veiled in eternal shadow. Only once he turned to look behind—for among the shrieks and howls of bestial chase he heard one thrilling voice moan with pain. And there among them he beheld Lilith, her body too was that of a wolf, almost hidden in the masses of her glittering golden hair, on her forehead was a stain of blue, like in colour to her mysterious eyes, now veiled with tears she could not shed.

The way of the Most Holy Viaticum lay along the brook of separation. They heard the fearful howlings afar off, the torch bearers turned pale and trembled—but the Abbé Félicien, holding aloft the Ciborium, said "They cannot harm us."

Suddenly the whole horrid chase came in sight. Gabriel sprang over the brook, the Abbé Félicien held the most Blessed Sacrament before him, and his shape was restored to him and he fell down prostrate in adoration. But the Abbé Félicien still held aloft the Sacred Ciborium, and the people fell on their knees in the agony of fear, but the face of the priest seemed to shine with divine effulgence. Then the wolf-keeper held up in his hands the shape of something horrible and inconceivable—a monstrance to the Sacrament of Hell, and three times he raised it, in mockery of the blessed rite of Benediction. And on the third time streams of fire went forth from his fingers, and all the "other side" of the forest took fire, and great darkness was over all.

All who were there and saw and heard it have kept the impress thereof for the rest of their lives—nor till in their death hour was the remembrance thereof absent from their minds. Shrieks, horrible beyond conception, were heard till nightfall—then the rain rained.

The "other side" is harmless now—charred ashes only; but none dares to cross but Gabriel alone—for once a year for nine days a strange madness comes over him.

SECTION VI
Allegory

Introduction

The *Were-Wolf* by Clemence Housman is the classic werewolf story of the late nineteenth century. Like George Macdonald's stories from the same period (*At the Back of the North Wind; Lilith*), it is a blend of myth, fantasy, and allegory.

Rooted in, and adapted from, Norse mythology, the story is set in the Northern lands of ice and snow. Although the farmhouse and its inhabitants create a warm environment, the shadow of something sinister gives a chill to the air and creates a feeling that evil lurks in corners of the room and just outside the door. The story channels the reader's imagination into the realm of the numinous, where battles between Good and Evil are waged.

Its fantasy elements reveal characters who are not carefully delineated: they have the stereotypical features of fairy tales. The runners exceed human speed and endurance; the young child and the old woman are vulnerable; the dogs are prescient and sense the coming of evil into the lives of those they love; time seems to have indefinite boundaries; winter is eternal.

Christian allegory frames the tale. The hero is named Christian. He is the personification of Christian love. The beautiful young woman dressed in white furs is the werewolf, the personification of evil. The temptress has superhuman strength to destroy those she can get in her clutches. Christian must draw his strength from the Source of Love. Christian emerges as the hero: in the presence of hostility and distrust on the part of his beloved brother, he stands up to rejection. His quiet heroism springs from a humility that forces him to challenge the decision of his brother to love White Fell. He risks and receives ridicule when he tells his brother that White Fell is a werewolf. In the face of his brother's physical aggressiveness and spiritual opposition, Christian nevertheless pursues White Fell in a death struggle to save his brother from her.

The conflict between Christian and White Fell takes place under the dark sky of a Northern winter where the stars gradually illumine the sky and Christian's path. He clings to White Fell, after miles and hours of running, and, though maimed and suffering great pain, triumphs over her in death—his a sacrificial one, hers the death of a large white wolf at midnight. The blood-stained snow tells the story of sacrificial death, and the author, pointing the reader to the death of Christ, shows Him as the prototype of all such deaths.

Perhaps in the allegory the twin brothers are the personification of discordant elements in the human soul, reflecting the ongoing internal struggle between the forces of good and evil alluded to by almost all the writers on lycanthropy. It is difficult to tell in this story whether White Fell is a wolf metamorphosed into a temptress, or whether she is a human being transformed for evil purposes by demonic forces into a white wolf. In any case, White Fell personifies death—spiritual death—and its subtle attractiveness to the human spirit. To follow and love White Fell requires only acquiescence, not commitment; cowardice, not courage. Ultimately, those who follow White Fell are lost forever in the Shadowlands of the North. Theirs is a linear journey from which no traveller returns.

This section of the *Reader* ends with a quotation from George Macdonald, Housman's contemporary, which is the epitome of her werewolf story:

> Life is everything. Many doubtless mistake the joy of life for life itself, and, longing after the joy, languish with a thirst at once poor and inextinguishable; but even that, thirst points to the one spring. These love self, not life, and self is but the shadow of life. When it is taken for life itself, and set as the man's centre, it becomes a live death in the man, a devil he worships as his God: the worm of the death eternal he clasps to his bosom as his one joy. [1]

Notes

1. *George Macdonald*, C. S. Lewis (New York: Macmillan, 1947), 64–65.

26

The Were-Wolf

CLEMENCE HOUSMAN

𝕿he great farm hall was ablaze with the fire-light, and noisy with laughter and talk. None could be idle but the very young and the very old: little Rol, who was hugging a puppy, and old Trella, whose palsied hand fumbled over her knitting. The early evening had closed in, and the farm-servants, come from their outdoor work, had assembled in the ample hall, which gave space for a score or more of workers. Several of the men were engaged in carving, and to these were yielded the best place and light; others made or repaired fishing-tackle and harness, and a great seine net occupied three pairs of hands. Of the women most were sorting and mixing eider feather and chopping straw to add to it. Looms were there, though not in present use, but three wheels whirred, and the finest and swiftest thread of the three ran between the fingers of the house-mistress. Near her were some children, busy too, plaiting wicks for candles and lamps. Each group of workers had a lamp in its centre, and those farthest from the fire had live heat from two braziers filled with glowing wood embers, replenished now and again from the generous hearth. But the flicker of the great fire was manifest to remotest corners, and prevailed beyond the limits of the weaker lights.

Little Rol grew tired of his puppy, dropped it, and made an onslaught on Tyr, the old wolf-hound, who basked dozing, whimpering and twitching in his hunting dreams. Prone went Rol beside Tyr, his young arms round the shaggy neck, his curls against the black jowl. Tyr gave a perfunctory lick, and stretched with a sleepy sigh. Rol growled and rolled and shoved invitingly, but could only gain from the old dog placid toleration and a half-observant blink. "Take that then!" said Rol, indignant at this ignoring of his advances, and sent the puppy sprawling against the dignity that disdained him as playmate. The dog took no notice, and the child wandered off to find amusement elsewhere. . . .

The Were-Wolf (London: John Lane at the Bodley Head, Chicago: Way and Williams, 1896).

Rol sprawled forward to survey the room. . . . As he slipped in among the men, they looked up to see that their tools might be, as far as possible, out of reach of Rol's hands, and close to their own. Nevertheless, before long he managed to secure a fine chisel and take off its point on the leg of the table. The carver's strong objections to this disconcerted Rol, who for five minutes thereafter effaced himself under the table.

During this seclusion he contemplated the many pairs of legs that surrounded him, and almost shut out the light of the fire. . . . A few moments later Sweyn of the long legs felt a small hand caressing his foot, and looking down, met the upturned eyes of his little cousin Rol. Lying on his back, still softly patting and stroking the young man's foot, the child was quiet and happy for a good while. He watched the movement of the strong deft hands, and the shifting of the bright tools. Now and then, minute chips of wood, puffed off by Sweyn, fell down upon his face. At last he raised himself, very gently, lest a jog should wake impatience in the carver, and crossing his own legs round Sweyn's ankle, clasping with his arms too, laid his head against the knee. . . . Sweyn forgot he was near, hardly noticed when his leg was gently released, and never saw the stealthy abstraction of one of his tools.

Ten minutes thereafter was a lamentable wail from low on the floor, rising to the full pitch of Rol's healthy lungs; for his hand was gashed across, and the copious bleeding terrified him. Then was there soothing and comforting, washing and tending, and a modicum of scolding, till the loud outcry sank into occasional sobs, and the child, tear-stained and subdued, was returned to the chimney-corner settle, where Trella nodded.

In the reaction after pain and fright, Rol found that the quiet of that fire-lit corner was to his mind. Tyr, too, disdained him no longer, but, roused by his sobs, showed all the concern and sympathy that a dog can by licking and wistful watching. A little shame weighed also upon his spirits. He wished he had not cried quite so much. He remembered how once Sweyn had come home with his arm torn down from the shoulder, and a dead bear; and how he had never winced nor said a word, though his lips turned white with pain. Poor little Rol gave another sighing sob over his own faint-hearted shortcomings.

The light and motion of the great fire began to tell strange stories to the child, and the wind in the chimney roared a corroborative note now and then. The great black mouth of the chimney, impending high over the hearth, received as into a mysterious gulf murky coils of smoke and brightness of aspiring sparks; and beyond, in the high darkness, were muttering and wailing and strange doings, so that sometimes the smoke rushed back in panic, and curled out and up to the roof, and condensed itself to invisibility among the rafters. And then the wind would rage after its lost prey, and rush round the house, rattling and shrieking at window and door.

In a lull, after one such loud gust, Rol lifted his head in surprise and listened. A lull had also come on the babel of talk, and thus could be heard with strange distinctness a sound outside the door—the sound of a child's voice, a child's hands. "Open, open; let me in!" piped the little voice from low down, lower than the handle, and the latch rattled as though a tiptoe child reached up to it, and soft small knocks were struck. One near the door sprang up and opened it. "No one is here," he said. Tyr lifted his head and gave utterance to a howl, loud, prolonged, most dismal.

Sweyn, not able to believe that his ears had deceived him, got up and went to the door. It was a dark night; the clouds were heavy with snow, that had fallen fitfully when the wind lulled. Untrodden snow lay up to the porch; there was no sight nor sound of any human being. Sweyn strained his eyes far and near, only to see dark sky, pure snow, and a line of black fir trees on a hill brow, bowing down before the wind. "It must have been the wind," he said, and closed the door.

Many faces looked scared. The sound of a child's voice had been so distinct—and the words "Open, open; let me in!" The wind might creak the wood, or rattle the latch, but could not speak with a child's voice, nor knock with the soft plain blows that a plump fist gives. And the strange unusual howl of the wolf-hound was an omen to be feared. Strange things were said by one and another, till the rebuke of the house-mistress quelled them into far-off whispers. For a time after there was uneasiness, constraint, and silence; then the chill fear thawed by degrees, and the babble of talk flowed on again.

Yet half-an-hour later a very slight noise outside the door sufficed to arrest every hand, every tongue. Every head was raised, every eye fixed in one direction. "It is Christian; he is late," said Sweyn.

No, no; this is a feeble shuffle, not a young man's tread. With the sound of uncertain feet came the hard tap-tap of a stick against the door, and the high-pitched voice of eld, "Open, open; let me in!" Again Tyr flung up his head in a long doleful howl.

Before the echo of the tapping stick and the high voice had fairly died away, Sweyn had sprung across to the door and flung it wide. "No one again," he said in a steady voice, though his eyes looked startled as he stared out. He saw the lonely expanse of snow, the clouds swagging low, and between the two the line of dark fir-trees bowing in the wind. He closed the door without a word of comment, and re-crossed the room.

A score of blanched faces were turned to him as though he must be solver of the enigma. He could not be unconscious of this mute eye-questioning, and it disturbed his resolute air of composure. He hesitated, glanced towards his mother, the house-mistress, then back at the frightened folk, and gravely, before them all, made the sign of the cross. There was a flutter of hands as the sign was repeated by all, and the dead silence was stirred as by a hugh sigh, for the held breath of many was freed as though the sign gave magic relief.

Even the house-mistress was perturbed. She left her wheel and crossed the room to her son, and spoke with him for a moment in a low tone that none could overhear. But a moment later her voice was high-pitched and loud, so that all might benefit by her rebuke of the "heathen chatter" of one of the girls. Perhaps she essayed to silence thus her own misgivings and forebodings.

No other voice dared speak now with its natural fulness. Low tones made intermittent murmurs, and now and then silence drifted over the whole room. The handling of tools was as noiseless as might be, and suspended on the instant if the door rattled in a gust of wind. After a time Sweyn left his work, joined the group nearest the door, and loitered there on the pretence of giving advice and help to the unskillful.

A man's tread was heard outside in the porch. "Christian!" said Sweyn and his mother simultaneously, he confidently, she authoritatively, to set the checked wheels going again. But Tyr flung up his head with an appalling howl.

"Open, open; let me in!"

It was a man's voice, and the door shook and rattled as a man's strength beat against it. Sweyn could feel the planks quivering, as on the instant his hand was upon the door, flinging it open, to face the blank porch, and beyond only snow and sky, and firs aslant in the wind.

He stood for a long minute with the open door in his hand. The bitter wind swept in with its icy chill, but a deadlier chill of fear came swifter, and seemed to freeze the beating of hearts. Sweyn stepped back to snatch up a great bearskin cloak.

"Sweyn, where are you going?"

"No farther than the porch, mother," and he stepped out and closed the door.

He wrapped himself in the heavy fur, and leaning against the most sheltered wall of the porch, steeled his nerves to face the devil and all his works. No sound of voices came from within; the most distinct sound was the crackle and roar of the fire.

It was bitterly cold. His feet grew numb, but he forbore stamping them into warmth lest the sound should strike panic within; nor would he leave the porch, nor print a foot-mark on the untrodden white that declared so absolutely how no human voices and hands could have approached the door since snow fell two hours or more ago. "When the wind drops there will be more snow," thought Sweyn.

For the best part of an hour he kept his watch, and saw no living thing—heard no unwonted sound. "I will freeze here no longer," he muttered, and re-entered.

One woman gave a half-suppressed scream as his hand was laid on the latch, and then a gasp of relief as he came in. No one questioned him, only his mother said, in a tone of forced unconcern, "Could you not see Christian coming?" as though she were made anxious only by the absence of her younger son. Hardly had Sweyn stamped near to the fire than clear knocking was heard at the door. Tyr leapt from the hearth, his eyes red as the fire, his fangs showing white in the black jowl, his neck ridged and bristling; and overleaping Rol, ramped at the door, barking furiously.

Outside the door a clear mellow voice was calling. Tyr's bark made the words undistinguishable.

No one offered to stir towards the door before Sweyn.

He stalked down the room, resolutely lifted the latch, and swung back the door.

A white-robed woman glided in.

No wraith! Living—beautiful—young.

Tyr leapt upon her.

Lithely she baulked the sharp fangs with folds of her long fur robe, and snatching from her girdle a small two-edged axe, whirled it up for a blow of defence.

Sweyn caught the dog by the collar, and dragged him off yelling and struggling.

The stranger stood in the doorway motionless, one foot set forward, one arm flung up, till the house-mistress hurried down the room; and Sweyn, relinquishing to others the furious Tyr, turned again to close the door, and offer excuse for so fierce a greeting. Then she lowered her arm, slung the axe in its place at her waist, loosened the furs about her face, and shook over her shoulders the long white robe—all as it were with the sway of one movement.

She was a maiden, tall and very fair. The fashion of her dress was strange, half masculine, yet not unwomanly. A fine fur tunic, reaching but little below the knee, was all the skirt she wore; below were the cross-bound shoes and leggings that a hunter wears. A white fur cap was set low upon the brows, and from its edge strips of fur fell lappet-wise about her shoulders; two of these at her entrance had been drawn forward and crossed about her throat, but now, loosened and thrust back, left unhidden long plaits of fair hair that lay forward on shoulder and breast, down to the ivory-studded girdle where the axe gleamed.

Sweyn and his mother led the stranger to the hearth without question or sign of curiosity, till she voluntarily told her tale of a long journey to distant kindred, a promised guide unmet, and signals and landmarks mistaken.

"Alone!" exclaimed Sweyn in astonishment. "Have you journeyed thus far, a hundred leagues, alone?"

She answered "Yes" with a little smile.

"Over the hills and the wastes! Why, the folk there are savage and wild as beasts."

She dropped her hand upon her axe with a laugh of some scorn.

"I fear neither man nor beast; some few fear me." And then she told strange tales of fierce attack and defence, and of the bold free huntress life she had led.

Her words came a little slowly and deliberately, as though she spoke in a scarce familiar tongue; now and then she hesitated, and stopped in a phrase, as though for lack of some word.

She became the centre of a group of listeners. The interest she excited dissipated, in some degree, the dread inspired by the mysterious voices. There was nothing ominous about this young, bright, fair reality, though her aspect was strange.

Little Rol crept near, staring at the stranger with all his might. Unnoticed, he softly stroked and patted a corner of her soft white robe that reached to the floor in ample folds. He laid his cheek against it caressingly, and then edged up close to her knees.

"What is your name?" he asked.

The stranger's smile and ready answer, as she looked down, saved Rol from the rebuke merited by his unmannerly questions.

"My real name," she said, "would be uncouth to your ears and tongue. The folk of this country have given me another name, and from this" (she laid her hand on the fur robe) "they call me 'White Fell.'"

Little Rol repeated it to himself, stroking and patting as before. "White Fell, White Fell."

The fair face, and soft, beautiful dress pleased Rol. He knelt up, with his eyes on her face and an air of uncertain determination, like a robin's on a doorstep, and plumped his elbows into her lap with a little gasp at his own audacity.

"Rol!" exclaimed his aunt; but, "Oh, let him!" said White Fell, smiling and stroking his head; and Rol stayed.

He advanced farther, and panting at his own adventurousness in the face of his aunt's authority, climbed up on to her knees. Her welcoming arms hindered any protest. He nestled happily, fingering the axe head, the ivory studs in her girdle, the ivory clasp at her throat, the plaits of fair hair; rubbing his head against the softness of her fur-clad shoulder, with a child's full confidence in the kindness of beauty.

White Fell had not uncovered her head, only knotted the pendant fur loosely behind her neck. Rol reached up his hand towards it, whispering her name to himself, "White Fell, White Fell," then slid his arms round her neck, and kissed her—once—twice. She laughed delightedly, and kissed him again.

"The child plagues you?" said Sweyn.

"No, indeed," she answered, with an earnestness so intense as to seem disproportionate to the occasion.

Rol settled himself again on her lap, and began to unwind the bandage bound round his hand. He paused a little when he saw where the blood had soaked through; then went on till his hand was bare and the cut displayed, gaping and long, though only skin deep. He held it up towards White Fell, desirous of her pity and sympathy.

At sight of it, and the blood-stained linen, she drew in her breath suddenly, clasped Rol to her—hard, hard—till he began to struggle. Her face was hidden behind the boy, so that none could see its expression. It had lighted up with a most awful glee.

Afar, beyond the fir-grove, beyond the low hill behind, the absent Christian was hastening his return. From daybreak he had been afoot, carrying notice of a bear hunt to all the best hunters of the farms and hamlets that lay within a radius of twelve miles. Nevertheless, having been detained till a late hour, he now broke into a run, going with a long smooth stride of apparent ease that fast made the miles diminish.

He entered the midnight blackness of the fir-grove with scarcely slackened pace, though the path was invisible; and passing through into the open again, sighted the farm lying a furlong off down the slope. Then he sprang out freely, and almost on the instant gave one great sideways leap, and stood still. There in the snow was the track of a great wolf.

His hand went to his knife, his only weapon. He stopped, knelt down, to bring his eyes to the level of the beast, and peered about; his teeth set, his heart beat a little harder than the pace of his running insisted on. A solitary wolf, nearly always savage and of large size, is a formidable beast that will not hesitate to attack a single man. This wolf-track was the largest Christian had ever seen, and, so far as he could judge, recently made. It led from under the fir-trees down the slope. Well for him, he thought, was the delay that had so vexed him before: well for him that he had not passed through the dark fir-grove when that danger of jaws lurked there. Going warily, he followed the track.

It led down the slope, across a broad ice-bound stream, along the level beyond, making towards the farm. A less precise knowledge had doubted, and guessed that here might have come straying big Tyr or his like; but Christian was sure, knowing better than to mistake between footmark of dog and wolf.

Straight on—straight on towards the farm.

Surprised and anxious grew Christian, that a prowling wolf should dare so near. He drew his knife and pressed on, more hastily, more keen-eyed. Oh that Tyr were with him!

Straight on, straight on, even to the very door, where the snow failed. His heart seemed to give a great leap and then stop. There the track ended.

Nothing lurked in the porch, and there was no sign of return. The firs stood straight against the sky, the clouds lay low; for the wind had fallen and a few snowflakes came drifting down. In a horror of surprise, Christian stood dazed a moment: then he lifted the latch and went in. His glance took in all the old familiar forms and faces, and with them that of the stranger, fur-clad and beautiful. The awful truth flashed upon him: he knew what she was.

Only a few were startled by the rattle of the latch as he entered. The room was filled with bustle and movement, for it was the supper hour, when all tools were laid aside, and trestles and tables shifted. Christian had no knowledge of what he said and did; he moved and spoke mechanically, half thinking that soon he must wake from this horrible dream. Sweyn and his mother supposed him to be cold and dead-tired, and spared all unnecessary questions. And he found himself seated beside the hearth, opposite that dreadful Thing that looked like a beautiful girl; watching her every movement, curdling with horror to see her fondle the child Rol.

Sweyn stood near them both, intent upon White Fell also; but how differently! She seemed unconscious of the gaze of both—neither aware of the chill dread in the eyes of Christian, nor of Sweyn's warm admiration.

These two brothers, who were twins, contrasted greatly, despite their striking likeness. They were alike in regular profile, fair brown hair, and deep blue eyes; but Sweyn's features were perfect as a young god's, while Christian's showed faulty details. Thus, the line of his mouth was set too straight, the eyes shelved too deeply back, and the contour of the face flowed in less generous curves than Sweyn's. Their height was the same, but Christian was too slender for perfect proportion, while Sweyn's well-knit frame, broad shoulders, and muscular arms, made him pre-eminent for manly beauty as well as for strength. As a hunter Sweyn was without rival; as a fisher without rival. All the countryside acknowledged him to be the best wrestler, rider, dancer, singer. Only in speed could he be surpassed, and in that only by his younger brother. All others Sweyn could distance fairly; but Christian could outrun him easily. Ay, he could keep pace with Sweyn's most breathless burst, and laugh and talk the while. Christian took little pride in his fleetness of foot, counting a man's legs to be the least worthy of his members. He had no envy of his brother's athletic superiority, though to several feats he had made a moderate second. He loved as only a twin can love—proud of all that Sweyn did, content with all that Sweyn was; humbly content also that his own great love should not be so exceedingly returned, since he knew himself to be so far less love-worthy.

Christian dared not, in the midst of women and children, launch the horror that he knew into words. He waited to consult his brother; but Sweyn did not, or would not, notice the signal he made, and kept his face always turned towards White Fell. Christian drew away from the hearth, unable to remain passive with that dread upon him.

"Where is Tyr?" he said suddenly. Then, catching sight of the dog in a distant corner, "Why is he chained there?"

"He flew at the stranger," one answered.

Christian's eyes glowed. "Yes?" he said, interrogatively.

"He was within an ace of having his brain knocked out."

"Tyr?"

"Yes; she was nimbly up with that little axe she has at her waist. It was well for old Tyr that his master throttled him off."

Christian went without a word to the corner where Tyr was chained. The dog rose up to meet him, as piteous and indignant as a dumb beast can be. He stroked the black head. "Good Tyr! brave dog!"

They knew, they only; and the man and the dumb dog had comfort of each other.

Christian's eyes turned again towards White Fell: Tyr's also, and he strained against the length of the chain. Christian's hand lay on the dog's neck, and he felt it ridge and bristle with the quivering of impotent fury. Then he began to quiver in like manner, with a fury born of reason, not instinct; as impotent morally as was Tyr physically. Oh! the woman's form that he dare not touch! Anything but that, and he with Tyr would be free to kill or be killed.

Then he returned to ask fresh questions.

"How long has the stranger been here?"

"She came about half-an-hour before you."

"Who opened the door to her?"

"Sweyn: no one else dared."

The tone of the answer was mysterious.

"Why?" queried Christian. "Has anything strange happened? Tell me."

For answer he was told in a low undertone of the summons at the door thrice repeated without human agency; and of Tyr's ominous howls; and of Sweyn's fruitless watch outside.

Christian turned towards his brother in a torment of impatience for a word apart. The board was spread, and Sweyn was leading White Fell to the guest's place. This was more awful: she would break bread with them under the roof-tree!

He started forward, and touching Sweyn's arm, whispered an urgent entreaty. Sweyn stared, and shook his head in angry impatience.

Thereupon Christian would take no morsel of food.

His opportunity came at last. White Fell questioned of the land-marks of the country, and of one Cairn Hill, which was an appointed meeting-place at which she was due that night. The house-mistress and Sweyn both exclaimed.

"It is three long miles away," said Sweyn; "with no place for shelter but a wretched hut. Stay with us this night, and I will show you the way to-morrow."

White Fell seemed to hesitate. "Three miles," she said; "then I should be able to see or hear a signal."

"I will look out," said Sweyn; "then, if there be no signal, you must not leave us."

He went to the door. Christian rose silently, and followed him out.

"Sweyn, do you know what she is?"

Sweyn, surprised at the vehement grasp, and low hoarse voice, made answer:

"She? Who? White Fell?"

"Yes."

"She is the most beautiful girl I have ever seen."

"She is a Were-Wolf."

Sweyn burst out laughing. "Are you mad?" he asked.

"No; here, see for yourself."

Christian drew him out of the porch, pointing to the snow where the footmarks had been. Had been, for now they were not. Snow was falling fast, and every dint was blotted out.

"Well?" asked Sweyn.

"Had you come when I signed to you, you would have seen for yourself."

"Seen what?"

"The footprints of a wolf leading up to the door; none leading away."

It was impossible not to be startled by the tone alone, though it was hardly above a whisper. Sweyn eyed his brother anxiously, but in the darkness could make nothing of his face. Then he laid his hands kindly and re-assuringly on Christian's shoulders and felt how he was quivering with excitement and horror.

"One sees strange things," he said, "when the cold has got into the brain behind the eyes; you came in cold and worn out."

"No," interrupted Christian. "I saw the track first on the brow of the slope, and followed it down right here to the door. This is no delusion."

Sweyn in his heart felt positive that it was. Christian was given to day-dreams and strange fancies, though never had he been possessed with so mad a notion before.

"Don't you believe me?" said Christian desperately. "You must. I swear it is sane truth. Are you blind? Why, even Tyr knows."

"You will be clearer headed to-morrow after a night's rest. Then come too, if you will, with White Fell, to the Hill Cairn; and if you have doubts still, watch and follow, and see what footprints she leaves."

Galled by Sweyn's evident contempt Christian turned abruptly to the door. Sweyn caught him back.

"What now, Christian? What are you going to do?"

"You do not believe me; my mother shall."

Sweyn's grasp tightened. "You shall not tell her," he said authoritatively.

Customarily Christian was so docile to his brother's mastery that

it was now a surprising thing when he wrenched himself free vig-
orously, and said as determinedly as Sweyn, "She shall know!" but
Sweyn was nearer the door and would not let him pass.

"There has been scare enough for one night already. If this notion
of yours will keep, broach it to-morrow." Christian would not yield.

"Women are so easily scared," pursued Sweyn, "and are ready to
believe any folly without shadow of proof. Be a man, Christian, and
fight this notion of a Were-Wolf by yourself."

"If you would believe me," began Christian.

"I believe you to be a fool," said Sweyn, losing patience. "Another, who was not your brother, might believe you to be a knave, and
guess that you had transformed White Fell into a Were-Wolf because
she smiled more readily on me than on you."

The jest was not without foundation, for the grace of White Fell's
bright looks had been bestowed on him, on Christian never a whit.
Sweyn's coxcombery was always frank, and most forgiveable, and not
without fair colour.

"If you want an ally," continued Sweyn, "confide in old Trella.
Out of her stores of wisdom, if her memory holds good, she can
instruct you in the orthodox manner of tackling a Were-Wolf. If I
remember aright, you should watch the suspected person till midnight,
when the beast's form must be resumed, and retained ever after if a
human eye sees the change; or, better still, sprinkle hands and feet
with holy water, which is certain death. Oh! never fear, but old Trella
will be equal to the occasion."

Sweyn's contempt was no longer good-humoured; some touch of
irritation or resentment rose at this monstrous doubt of White Fell. But
Christian was too deeply distressed to take offence.

"You speak of them as old wives' tales; but if you had seen the
proof I have seen, you would be ready at least to wish them true, if not
also to put them to the test."

"Well," said Sweyn, with a laugh that had a little sneer in it, "put
them to the test! I will not object to that, if you will only keep your
notions to yourself. Now, Christian, give me your word for silence,
and we will freeze here no longer."

Christian remained silent.

Sweyn put his hands on his shoulders again and vainly tried to see
his face in the darkness.

"We have never quarrelled yet, Christian?"

"*I* have never quarrelled," returned the other, aware for the first time that his dictatorial brother had sometimes offered occasion for quarrel, had he been ready to take it.

"Well," said Sweyn emphatically, "if you speak against White Fell to any other, as to-night you have spoken to me—*we shall.*"

He delivered the words like an ultimatum, turned sharp round, and re-entered the house. Christian, more fearful and wretched than before, followed.

"Snow is falling fast: not a single light is to be seen."

White Fell's eyes passed over Christian without apparent notice, and turned bright and shining upon Sweyn.

"Nor any signal to be heard?" she queried. "Did you not hear the sound of a sea-horn?"

"I saw nothing, and heard nothing; and signal or no signal, the heavy snow would keep you here perforce."

She smiled her thanks beautifully. And Christian's heart sank like lead with a deadly foreboding, as he noted what a light was kindled in Sweyn's eyes by her smile.

That night, when all others slept, Christian, the weariest of all, watched outside the guest-chamber till midnight was past. No sound, not the faintest, could be heard. Could the old tale be true of the midnight change? What was on the other side of the door, a woman or a beast? He would have given his right hand to know. Instinctively he laid his hand on the latch, and drew it softly, though believing that bolts fastened the inner side. The door yielded to his hand; he stood on the threshold; a keen gust of air cut at him; the window stood open; the room was empty.

So Christian could sleep with a somewhat lightened heart.

In the morning there was surprise and conjecture when White Fell's absence was discovered. Christian held his peace. Not even to his brother did he say how he knew that she had fled before midnight; and Sweyn, though evidently greatly chagrined, seemed to disdain reference to the subject of Christian's fears. . . .

All that day, and for many a day after, Christian would never go out of sight of his home. Sweyn alone noticed how he manoeuvred for this, and was clearly annoyed by it. White Fell's name was never mentioned between them, though not seldom was it heard in general talk. Hardly a day passed but little Rol asked when White Fell would come again: pretty White Fell, who kissed like a snowflake. And if Sweyn answered, Christian would be quite sure that the light in his eyes, kindled by White Fell's smile, had not yet died out.

Little Rol! Naughty, merry, fair-haired little Rol. A day came when his feet raced over the threshold never to return; when his chatter and laugh were heard no more; when tears of anguish were wept by eyes that never would see his bright head again: never again, living or dead.

He was seen at dusk for the last time, escaping from the house with his puppy, in freakish rebellion against old Trella. Later, when his absence had begun to cause anxiety, his puppy crept back to the farm, cowed, whimpering and yelping, a pitiful, dumb lump of terror, without intelligence or courage to guide the frightened search.

Rol was never found, nor any trace of him. Where he had perished was never known; how he had perished was known only by an awful guess—a wild beast had devoured him.

Christian heard the conjecture "a wolf"; and a horrible certainty flashed upon him that he knew what wolf it was. He tried to declare what he knew, but Sweyn saw him start at the words with white face and struggling lips; and, guessing his purpose, pulled him back, and kept him silent, hardly, by his imperious grip and wrathful eyes, and one low whisper.

That Christian should retain his most irrational suspicion against beautiful White Fell was, to Sweyn, evidence of a weak obstinacy of mind that would but thrive upon expostulation and argument. But this evident intention to direct the passions of grief and anguish to a hatred and fear of the fair stranger, such as his own, was intolerable, and Sweyn set his will against it. Again Christian yielded to his brother's stronger words and will, and against his own judgment consented to silence.

Repentance came before the new moon, the first of the year, was old. White Fell came again, smiling as she entered, as though assured of a glad and kindly welcome; and, in truth, there was only one who saw again her fair face and strange white garb without pleasure. Sweyn's face glowed with delight, while Christian's grew pale and rigid as death. He had given his word to keep silence; but he had not thought that she would dare to come again. Silence was impossible,

face to face with that Thing, impossible. Irrepressibly he cried out:
"Where is Rol?"

Not a quiver disturbed White Fell's face. She heard, yet remained
bright and tranquil. Sweyn's eyes flashed round at his brother dangerously. Among the women some tears fell at the poor child's name;
but none caught alarm from its sudden utterance, for the thought of
Rol rose naturally. Where was little Rol, who had nestled in the stranger's arms, kissing her; and watched for her since; and prattled of her
daily?

Christian went out silently. . . . The swiftest runner of the coun-
try-side had started on his hardest race: little less than three leagues
and back, which he reckoned to accomplish in two hours, though the
night was moonless and the way rugged. He rushed against the still
cold air till it felt like a wind upon his face. . . . He took no conscious
heed of landmarks, not even when all sign of a path was gone under
depths of snow. His will was set to reach his goal with unexampled
speed; and thither by instinct his physical forces bore him, without
one definite thought to guide.

And the idle brain lay passive, inert, receiving into its vacancy
restless siftings of past sights and sounds: Rol, weeping, laughing,
playing, coiled in the arms of that dreadful Thing: Tyr—O Tyr!—
white fangs in the black jowl: the women who wept on the foolish
puppy, precious for the child's last touch: footprints from pine wood to
door: the smiling face among furs, of such womanly beauty—smiling—smiling: and Sweyn's face.

"Sweyn, Sweyn, O Sweyn, my brother!"

Sweyn's angry laugh possessed his ear within the sound of the
wind of his speed; Sweyn's scorn assailed more quick and keen than the
biting cold at his throat. And yet he was unimpressed by any thought
of how Sweyn's anger and scorn would rise, if this errand were known.

Sweyn was a sceptic. His utter disbelief in Christian's testimony
regarding the footprints was based upon positive scepticism. His reason refused to bend in accepting the possibility of the supernatural
materialised. That a living beast could ever be other than palpably
bestial—pawed, toothed, shagged, and eared as such, was to him
incredible; far more that a human presence could be transformed from
its god-like aspect, upright, free-handed, with brows, and speech, and
laughter. The wild and fearful legends that he had known from child-

hood and then believed, he regarded now as built upon facts distorted, overlaid by imagination, and quickened by superstition. Even the strange summons at the threshold, that he himself had vainly answered, was, after the first shock of surprise, rationally explained by him as malicious foolery on the part of some clever trickster, who withheld the key to the enigma.

To the younger brother all life was a spiritual mystery, veiled from his clear knowledge by the density of flesh. Since he knew his own body to be linked to the complex and antagonistic forces that constitute one soul, it seemed to him not impossibly strange that one spiritual force should possess divers forms for widely various manifestation. Nor, to him, was it great effort to believe that as pure water washes away all natural foulness, so water, holy by consecration, must needs cleanse God's world from that supernatural evil Thing. Therefore, faster than ever man's foot had covered those leagues, he sped under the dark, still night, over the waste, trackless snowridges to the far-away church, where salvation lay in the holy-water stoup at the door. His faith was as firm as any that wrought miracles in days past, simple as a child's wish, strong as a man's will.

He was hardly missed during these hours, every second of which was by him fulfilled to its utmost extent by extremist effort that sinews and nerves could attain. Within the homestead the while, the easy moments went bright with words and looks of unwonted animation, for the kindly, hospitable instincts of the inmates were roused into cordial expression of welcome and interest by the grace and beauty of the returned stranger.

But Sweyn was eager and earnest, with more than a host's courteous warmth. The impression that at her first coming had charmed him, that had lived since through memory, deepened now in her actual presence. Sweyn, the matchless among men, acknowledged in this fair White Fell a spirit high and bold as his own, and a frame so firm and capable that only bulk was lacking for equal strength. Yet the white skin was moulded most smoothly, without such muscular swelling as made his might evident. Such love as his frank self-love could concede was called forth by an ardent admiration for this supreme stranger. More admiration than love was in his passion, and therefore he was free from a lover's hesitancy and delicate reserve and doubts. Frankly and boldly he courted her favour by looks and tones, and an address that came of natural ease, needless of skill by practice.

Nor was she a woman to be wooed otherwise. Tender whispers and sighs would never gain her ear; but her eyes would brighten and shine if she heard of a brave feat, and her prompt hand in sympathy fall swiftly on the axe-haft and clasp it hard. That movement ever fired Sweyn's admiration anew; he watched for it, strove to elicit it, and glowed when it came. Wonderful and beautiful was that wrist, slender and steel-strong; also the smooth shapely hand, that curved so fast and firm, ready to deal instant death.

Desiring to feel the pressure of these hands, this bold lover schemed with palpable directness, proposing that she should hear how their hunting songs were sung, with a chorus that signalled hands to be clasped. So his splendid voice gave the verses, and, as the chorus was taken up, he claimed her hands, and even through the easy grip, felt, as he desired, the strength that was latent, and the vigour that quickened the very fingertips, as the song fired her, and her voice was caught out of her by the rhythmic swell, and rang clear on the top of the closing surge.

Afterwards she sang alone. For contrast, or in the pride of swaying moods by her voice, she chose a mournful song that drifted along in a minor chant, sad as a wind that dirges. . . .

Old Trella came tottering from her corner, shaken to additional palsy by an aroused memory. She strained her dim eyes towards the singer, and then bent her head, that the one ear yet sensible to sound might avail of every note. At the close, groping forward, she murmured with the high-pitched quaver of old age:

"So she sang, my Thora; my last and brightest. What is she like, she whose voice is like my dead Thora's? Are her eyes blue?"

"Blue as the sky."

"So were my Thora's! Is her hair fair, and in plaits to the waist?"

"Even so," answered White Fell herself, and met the advancing hands with her own, and guided them to corroborate her words by touch.

"Like my dead Thora's," repeated the old woman; and then her trembling hands rested on the fur-clad shoulders, and she bent forward and kissed the smooth fair face that White Fell upturned, nothing loth, to receive and return the caress.

So Christian saw them as he entered.

He stood a moment. After the starless darkness and the icy night air, and the fierce silent two hours' race, his senses reeled on sudden entrance into warmth, and light, and the cheery hum of voices. A sudden unforeseen anguish assailed him, as now first he entertained the possibility of being overmatched by her wiles and her daring, if at the approach of pure death she should start up at bay transformed to a terrible beast, and achieve a savage glut at the last. He looked with horror and pity on the harmless, helpless folk, so unwitting of outrage to their comfort and security. The dreadful Thing in their midst, that was veiled from their knowledge by womanly beauty, was a centre of pleasant interest. There, before him, signally impressive, was poor old Trella, weakest and feeblest of all, in fond nearness. And a moment might bring about the revelation of a monstrous horror—a ghastly, deadly danger, set loose and at bay, in a circle of girls and women and careless defenceless men: so hideous and terrible a thing as might crack the brain, or curdle the heart stone dead.

And he alone of the throng prepared!

For one breathing space he faltered, no longer than that, while over him swept the agony of compunction that yet could not make him surrender his purpose.

He alone? Nay, but Tyr also; and he crossed to the dumb sole sharer of his knowledge.

So timeless is thought that a few seconds only lay between his lifting of the latch and his loosening of Tyr's collar; but in those few seconds succeeding his first glance, as lightning-swift had been the impulses of others, their motion as quick and sure. Sweyn's vigilant eye had darted upon him, and instantly his every fibre was alert with hostile instinct; and, half divining, half incredulous, of Christian's object in stooping to Tyr, he came hastily, wary, wrathful, resolute to oppose the malice of his wild-eyed brother.

But beyond Sweyn rose White Fell, blanching white as her furs, and with eyes grown fierce and wild. She leapt down the room to the door, whirling her long robe closely to her. "Hark!" she panted. "The signal horn! Hark, I must go!" as she snatched at the latch to be out and away.

For one precious moment Christian had hesitated on the half-loosened collar; for, except the womanly form were exchanged for the bestial, Tyr's jaws would gnash to rags his honour of manhood. Then he heard her voice, and turned—too late.

As she tugged at the door, he sprang across grasping his flask, but Sweyn dashed between, and caught him back irresistibly, so that a most frantic effort only availed to wrench one arm free. With that, on the impulse of sheer despair, he cast at her with all his force. The door swung behind her, and the flask flew into fragments against it. Then, as Sweyn's grasp slackened, and he met the questioning astonishment of surrounding faces, with a hoarse inarticulate cry: "God help us all!" he said. "She is a Were-Wolf."

Sweyn turned upon him, "Liar, coward!" and his hands gripped his brother's throat with deadly force, as though the spoken word could be killed so; and as Christian struggled, lifted him clear off his feet and flung him crashing backward. So furious was he, that, as his brother lay motionless, he stirred him roughly with his foot, till their mother came between, crying shame; and yet then he stood by, his teeth set, his brows knit, his hands clenched, ready to enforce silence again violently, as Christian rose staggering and bewildered.

But utter silence and submission were more than he expected, and turned his anger into contempt for one so easily cowed and held in subjection by mere force. "He is mad!" he said, turning on his heel as he spoke, so that he lost his mother's look of pained reproach at this sudden free utterance of what was a lurking dread within her.

Christian was too spent for the effort of speech. His hard-drawn breath laboured in great sobs; his limbs were powerless and unstrung in utter relax after hard service. Failure in his endeavour induced a stupor of misery and despair. In addition was the wretched humiliation of open violence and strife with his brother, and the distress of hearing misjudging contempt expressed without reserve; for he was aware that Sweyn had turned to allay the scared excitement half by imperious mastery, half by explanation and argument, that showed painful disregard of brotherly consideration. All this unkindness of his twin he charged upon the fell Thing who had wrought this their first dissension, and, ah! most terrible thought, interposed between them so effectually, that Sweyn was wilfully blind and deaf on her account, resentful of interference, arbitrary beyond reason.

Dread and perplexity unfathomable darkened upon him; unshared, the burden was overwhelming: a foreboding of unspeakable calamity, based upon his ghastly discovery, bore down upon him, crushing out hope of power to withstand impending fate.

Sweyn the while was observant of his brother. . . . Observation

set him wondering on Christian's exhausted condition. The heavy labouring breath and the slack inert fall of the limbs told surely of
unusual and prolonged exertion. And then why had close upon two
hours' absence been followed by open hostility against White Fell?

Suddenly, the fragments of the flask giving a clue, he guessed all,
and faced about to stare at his brother in amaze. He forgot that the
motive scheme was against White Fell, demanding derision and resentment from him; that was swept out of remembrance by astonishment
and admiration for the feat of speed and endurance. In eagerness to
question he inclined to attempt a generous part and frankly offer to
heal the breach; but Christian's depression and sad following gaze
provoked him to self-justification by recalling the offence of that out-
rageous utterance against White Fell; and the impulse passed. . . .

That night Sweyn and his mother talked long and late together,
shaping into certainty the suspicion that Christian's mind had lost its
balance, and discussing the evident cause. For Sweyn, declaring his
own love for White Fell, suggested that his unfortunate brother, with a
like passion, they being twins in loves as in birth, had through jealousy
and despair turned from love to hate, until reason failed at the strain,
and a craze developed, which the malice and treachery of madness
made a serious and dangerous force.

So Sweyn theorised, convincing himself as he spoke; convincing
afterwards others who advanced doubts against White Fell; fettering
his judgment by his advocacy, and by his staunch defence of her
hurried flight silencing his own inner consciousness of the unaccount-
ability of her action.

But a little time and Sweyn lost his vantage in the shock of a fresh
horror at the homestead. Trella was no more, and her end a mystery.
The poor old woman crawled out in a bright gleam to visit a bed-
ridden gossip living beyond the firgrove. Under the trees she was last
seen, halting for her companion, sent back for a forgotten present.
Quick alarm sprang, calling every man to the search. Her stick was
found among the brushwood only a few paces from the path, but no
track or stain, for a gusty wind was sifting the snow from the branches,
and hid all sign of how she came by her death.

So panic-stricken were the farm folk that none dared go singly on
the search. Known danger could be braced, but not this stealthy Death
that walked by day invisible, that cut off alike the child in his play and
the aged woman so near to her quiet grave.

"Rol she kissed; Trella she kissed!" So rang Christian's frantic cry again and again, till Sweyn dragged him away and strove to keep him apart, albeit in his agony of grief and remorse he accused himself wildly as answerable for the tragedy, and gave clear proof that the charge of madness was well founded, if strange looks and desperate, incoherent words were evidence enough.

But thenceforward all Sweyn's reasoning and mastery could not uphold White Fell above suspicion. He was not called upon to defend her from accusation when Christian had been brought to silence again; but he well knew the significance of this fact, that her name, formerly uttered freely and often, he never heard now: it was huddled away into whispers that he could not catch.

The passing of time did not sweep away the superstitious fears that Sweyn despised. He was angry and anxious; eager that White Fell should return, and, merely by her bright gracious presence, reinstate herself in favour; but doubtful if all his authority and example could keep from her notice an altered aspect of welcome; and he foresaw clearly that Christian would prove unmanageable, and might be capable of some dangerous outbreak. . . .

Christian's surveillance galled him incessantly, and embarrassment and danger he foresaw as the outcome. Therefore, that suspicion might be lulled, he judged it wise to make overtures for peace. Most easily done. A little kindliness, a few evidences of consideration, a slight return of the old brotherly imperiousness, and Christian replied by a gratefulness and relief that might have touched him had he understood all, but instead, increased his secret contempt.

So successful was this finesse, that when, late on a day, a message summoning Christian to a distance was transmitted by Sweyn, no doubt of its genuineness occurred. When, his errand proved useless, he set out to return, mistake or misapprehension was all that he surmised. Not till he sighted the homestead, lying low between the night-grey snow ridges, did vivid recollection of the time when he had tracked that horror to the door rouse an intense dread, and with it a hardly-defined suspicion.

His grasp tightened on the bear-spear that he carried as a staff; every sense was alert, every muscle strung; excitement urged him on, caution checked him, and the two governed his long stride, swiftly, noiselessly, to the climax he felt was at hand.

As he drew near to the outer gates, a light shadow stirred and went, as though the grey of the snow had taken detached motion. A darker shadow stayed and faced Christian, striking his life-blood chill with utmost despair.

Sweyn stood before him, and surely, the shadow that went was White Fell.

They had been together—close. Had she not been in his arms, near enough for lips to meet?

There was no moon, but the stars gave light enough to show that Sweyn's face was flushed and elated. The flush remained, though the expression changed quickly at sight of his brother. How, if Christian had seen all, should one of his frenzied outbursts be met and managed: by resolution? by indifference? He halted between the two, and as a result, he swaggered.

"White Fell?" questioned Christian, hoarse and breathless.

"Yes?"

Sweyn's answer was a query, with an intonation that implied he was clearing the ground for action.

From Christian came: "Have you kissed her?" like a bolt direct, staggering Sweyn by its sheer prompt temerity.

He flushed yet darker, and yet half-smiled over this earnest of success he had won. Had there been really between himself and Christian the rivalry that he imagined, his face had enough of the insolence of triumph to exasperate jealous rage.

"You dare ask this?"

"Sweyn, O Sweyn, I must know! You have!"

The ring of despair and anguish in his tone angered Sweyn, misconstruing it. Jealousy urging to such presumption was intolerable.

"Mad fool!" he said, constraining himself no longer. "Win for yourself a woman to kiss. Leave mine without question. Such an one as I should desire to kiss is such an one as shall never allow a kiss to you."

Then Christian fully understood his supposition.

"I—I!" he cried. "White Fell—that deadly Thing! Sweyn, are you blind, mad? I would save you from her: a Were-Wolf!"

Sweyn maddened again at the accusation—a dastardly way of revenge, as he conceived; and instantly, for the second time, the brothers were at strife violently.

But Christian was now too desperate to be scrupulous; for a dim glimpse had shot a possibility into his mind, and to be free to follow it the striking of his brother was a necessity. Thank God! he was armed, and so Sweyn's equal.

Facing his assailant with the bearspear, he struck up his arms, and with the butt end hit hard so that he fell. The matchless runner leapt away on the instant, to follow a forlorn hope.

Sweyn, on regaining his feet, was as amazed as angry at this unaccountable flight. He knew in his heart that his brother was no coward, and that it was unlike him to shrink from an encounter because defeat was certain, and cruel humiliation from a vindictive victor probable. Of the uselessness of pursuit he was well aware: he must abide his chagrin, content to know that his time for advantage would come. Since White Fell had parted to the right, Christian to the left, the event of a sequent encounter did not occur to him.

And now Christian, acting on the dim glimpse he had had, just as Sweyn turned upon him, of something that moved against the sky along the ridge behind the homestead, was staking his only hope on a chance, and his own superlative speed. If what he saw was really White Fell, he guessed she was bending her steps towards the open wastes; and there was just a possibility that, by a straight dash, and a desperate perilous leap over a sheer bluff, he might yet meet her or head her. And then: he had no further thought.

It was past, the quick, fierce race, and the chance of death at the leap; and he halted in a hollow to fetch his breath and to look: did she come? had she gone?

She came.

She came with a smooth, gliding, noiseless speed, that was neither walking nor running; her arms were folded in her furs that were drawn tight about her body; the white lappets from her head were wrapped and knotted closely beneath her face; her eyes were set on a far distance. So she went till the even sway of her going was startled to a pause by Christian.

"Fell!"

She drew a quick, sharp breath at the sound of her name thus mutilated, and faced Sweyn's brother. Her eyes glittered; her upper lip was lifted, and shewed the teeth. The half of her name, impressed with an ominous sense as uttered by him, warned her of the aspect of a deadly foe. Yet she cast loose her robes till they trailed ample, and spoke as a mild woman.

"What would you?"

Then Christian answered with his solemn dreadful accusation:

"You kissed Rol—and Rol is dead! You kissed Trella: she is dead! You have kissed Sweyn, my brother; but he shall not die!"

He added: "You may live till midnight."

The edge of the teeth and the glitter of the eyes stayed a moment, and her right hand also slid down to the axe haft. Then, without a word, she swerved from him, and sprang out and away swiftly over the snow.

And Christian sprang out and away, and followed her swiftly over the snow, keeping behind, but half-a-stride's length from her side.

So they went running together, silent, towards the vast wastes of snow, where no living thing but they two moved under the stars of night.

Never before had Christian so rejoiced in his powers. The gift of speed, and the training of use and endurance were priceless to him now. Though midnight was hours away, he was confident that, go where that Fell Thing would, hasten as she would, she could not outstrip him nor escape from him. Then, when came the time for transformation, when the woman's form made no longer a shield against a man's hand, he could slay or be slain to save Sweyn. He had struck his dear brother in dire extremity, but he could not, though reason urged, strike a woman.

For one mile, for two miles they ran: White Fell ever foremost, Christian ever at equal distance from her side, so near that, now and again, her out-flying furs touched him. She spoke no word; nor he. She never turned her head to look at him, nor swerved to evade him; but, with set face looking forward, sped straight on, over rough, over smooth, aware of his nearness by the regular beat of his feet, and the sound of his breath behind.

In a while she quickened her pace. From the first, Christian had judged of her speed as admirable, yet with exulting security in his own excelling and enduring whatever her efforts. But, when the pace increased, he found himself put to the test as never had he been before in any race. Her feet, indeed, flew faster than his; it was only by the length of stride that he kept his place at her side. But his heart was high and resolute, and he did not fear failure yet.

So the desperate race flew on. . . . White Fell held on without

Christian keeping pace with White Fell. From Clemence Housman, *The Were-Wolf*. Illus. Laurence Housman (London, 1896). Courtesy of The Newberry Library, Chicago.

slack. She, it was evident, with confidence in her speed proving matchless, as resolute to outrun her pursuer as he to endure till midnight and fulfil his purpose. And Christian held on, still self-assured. He could not fail; he would not fail. To avenge Rol and Trella was motive enough for him to do what man could do; but for Sweyn more. She had kissed Sweyn, but he should not die too: with Sweyn to save he could not fail.

Never before was such a race as this; no, not when in old Greece man and maid raced together with two fates at stake; for the hard running was sustained unabated, while star after star rose and went wheeling up towards midnight, for one hour, for two hours.

Then Christian saw and heard what shot him through with fear. Where a fringe of trees hung round a slope he saw something dark moving, and heard a yelp, followed by a full horrid cry, and the dark spread out upon the snow, a pack of wolves in pursuit.

Of the beasts alone he had little cause for fear; at the pace he held he could distance them, four-footed though they were. But of White Fell's wiles he had infinite apprehension, for how might she not avail herself of the savage jaws of these wolves, akin as they were to half her nature. She vouchsafed to them nor look nor sign; but Christian, on a impulse to assure himself that she should not escape him, caught and held the back-flung edge of her furs, running still.

She turned like a flash with a beastly snarl, teeth and eyes gleaming again. Her axe shone, on the upstroke, on the downstroke, as she hacked at his hand. She had lopped it off at the wrist, but that he parried with the bear-spear. Even then, she shore through the shaft and shattered the bones of the hand at the same blow, so that he loosed perforce.

Then again they raced on as before, Christian not losing a pace, though his left hand swung useless, bleeding and broken.

The snarl, indubitable, though modified from a woman's organs, the vicious fury revealed in teeth and eyes, the sharp arrogant pain of her maiming blow, caught away Christian's heed of the beasts behind, by striking into him close vivid realisation of the infinitely greater danger that ran before him in that deadly Thing.

When he bethought him to look behind, lo! the pack had but reached their tracks, and instantly slunk aside, cowed; the yell of pursuit changing to yelps and whines. So abhorrent was that fell creature to beast as to man.

She had drawn her furs more closely to her, disposing them so that, instead of flying loose to her heels, no drapery hung lower than her knees, and this without a check to her wonderful speed, nor embarrassment by the cumbering of the folds. She held her head as before; her lips were firmly set, only the tense nostrils gave her breath; not a sign of distress witnessed to the long sustaining of that terrible speed.

But on Christian by now the strain was telling palpably. His head weighed heavy, and his breath came labouring in great sobs; the bear-spear would have been a burden now. His heart was beating like a hammer, but such a dulness oppressed his brain, that it was only by degrees he could realise his helpless state; wounded and weaponless, chasing that terrible Thing, that was a fierce, desperate, axe-armed woman, except she should assume the beast with fangs yet more formidable.

And still the far slow stars went lingering nearly an hour from midnight.

So far was his brain astray that an impression took him that she was fleeing from the midnight stars, whose gain was by such slow degrees that a time equalling days and days had gone in the race round the northern circle of the world, and days and days as long might last before the end—except she slackened, or except he failed.

But he would not fail yet.

How long had he been praying so? He had started with a self-confidence and reliance that had felt no need for that aid; and now it seemed the only means by which to restrain his heart from swelling beyond the compass of his body, by which to cherish his brain from dwindling and shrivelling quite away. Some sharp-toothed creature kept tearing and dragging on his maimed left hand; he never could see it, he could not shake it off; but he prayed it off at times.

The clear stars before him took to shuddering, and he knew why: they shuddered at sight of what was behind him. He had never divined before that strange things hid themselves from men under pretence of being snow-clad mounds or swaying trees; but now they came slipping out from their harmless covers to follow him, and mock at his impotence to make a kindred Thing resolve to truer form. He knew the air behind him was thronged; he heard the hum of innumerable murmurings together; but his eyes could never catch them, they were too swift and nimble. Yet he knew they were there, because, on a backward glance, he saw the snow mounds surge as they grovelled flatlings out of sight; he saw the trees reel as they screwed themselves rigid past recognition among the boughs.

And after such glance the stars for awhile returned to steadfastness, and an infinite stretch of silence froze upon the chill grey world, only deranged by the swift even beat of the flying feet, and his own—slower from the longer stride, and the sound of his breath. And for some clear moments he knew that his only concern was, to sustain his speed regardless of pain and distress, to deny with every nerve he had her power to outstrip him or to widen the space between them, till the stars crept up to midnight. Then out again would come that crowd invisible, humming and hustling behind, dense and dark enough, he knew, to blot out the stars at his back, yet ever skipping and jerking from his sight.

A hideous check came to the race. White Fell swirled about and leapt to the right, and Christian, unprepared for so prompt a lurch, found close at his feet a deep pit yawning, and his own impetus past control. But he snatched at her as he bore past, clasping her right arm with his one whole hand, and the two swung together upon the brink.

And her straining away in self preservation was vigorous enough to counter-balance his headlong impulse, and brought them reeling together to safety.

Then, before he was verily sure that they were not to perish so, crashing down, he saw her gnashing in wild pale fury as she wrenched to be free; and since her right hand was in his grasp, used her axe left-handed, striking back at him.

The blow was effectual enough even so; his right arm dropped powerless, gashed, and with the lesser bone broken, that jarred with horrid pain when he let it swing as he leaped out again, and ran to recover the few feet she had gained from his pause at the shock.

The near escape and this new quick pain made again every faculty alive and intense. He knew that what he followed was most surely Death animate: wounded and helpless, he was utterly at her mercy if so she should realise and take action. Hopeless to avenge, hopeless to save, his very despair for Sweyn swept him on to follow, and follow, and precede the kiss-doomed to death. Could he yet fail to hunt that Thing past midnight, out of the womanly form alluring and treacherous, into lasting restraint of the bestial, which was the last shred of hope left from the confident purpose of the outset?

"Sweyn, Sweyn, O Sweyn!" He thought he was praying, though his heart wrung out nothing but this: "Sweyn, Sweyn, O Sweyn!"

The last hour from midnight had lost half its quarters, and the stars went lifting up the great minutes; and again his greatening heart, and his shrinking brain, and the sickening agony that swung at either side, conspired to appal the will that had only seeming empire over his feet.

Now White Fell's body was so closely enveloped that not a lap nor an edge flew free. She stretched forward strangely aslant, leaning from the upright poise of a runner. She cleared the ground at times by long bounds, gaining an increase of speed that Christian agonised to equal.

Because the stars pointed that the end was nearing, the black brood came behind again, and followed, noising. . . . What shape had they? Should he ever know? If it were not that he was bound to compel the fell Thing that ran before him into her truer form, he might face about and follow them. No—no—not so; if he might do anything but what he did—race, race, and racing bear this agony, he would just stand still and die, to be quit of the pain of breathing. . . .

Why did the stars stop to shudder? Midnight else had surely come!

The leaning, leaping Thing looked back at him with a wild, fierce look, and laughed in savage scorn and triumph. He saw in a flash why, for within a time measurable by seconds she would have escaped him utterly. As the land lay, a slope of ice sunk on the one hand; on the other hand a steep rose, shouldering forwards; between the two was space for a foot to be planted, but none for a body to stand; yet a juniper bough, thrusting out, gave a handhold secure enough for one with a resolute grasp to swing past the perilous place, and pass on safe.

Though the first seconds of the last moment were going, she dared to flash back a wicked look, and laugh at the pursuer who was impotent to grasp.

The crisis struck convulsive life into his last supreme effort; his will surged up indomitable, his speed proved matchless yet. He leapt with a rush, passed her before her laugh had time to go out, and turned short, barring the way, and braced to withstand her.

She came hurling desperate, with a feint to the right hand, and then launched herself upon him with a spring like a wild beast when it leaps to kill. And he, with one strong arm and a hand that could not hold, with one strong hand and an arm that could not guide and sustain, he caught and held her even so. And they fell together. And because he felt his whole arm slipping, and his whole hand loosing, to slack the dreadful agony of the wrenched bone above, he caught and held with his teeth the tunic at her knee, as she struggled up and wrung off his hands to overleap him victorious.

Like lightning she snatched her axe, and struck him on the neck, deep—once, twice—his life-blood gushed out, staining her feet.

The stars touched midnight.

The death scream he heard was not his, for his set teeth had hardly yet relaxed when it rang out; and the dreadful cry began with a woman's shriek, and changed and ended as the yell of a beast. And before the final blank overtook his dying eyes, he saw that She gave place to It; he saw more, that Life gave place to Death—causelessly, incomprehensibly.

For he did not presume that no holy water could be more holy, more potent to destroy an evil thing than the life-blood of a pure heart poured out for another in free willing devotion.

His own true hidden reality that he had desired to know grew palpable, recognisable. It seemed to him just this: a great glad abounding hope that he had saved his brother; too expansive to be contained by the limited form of a sole man, it yearned for a new embodiment infinite as the stars.

What did it matter to that true reality that the man's brain shrank, shrank, till it was nothing; that the man's body could not retain the huge pain of his heart, and heaved it out through the red exit riven at the neck; that the black noise came again hurtling from behind, reinforced by that dissolved shape, and blotted out for ever the man's sight, hearing, sense.

In the early grey of day Sweyn chanced upon the footprints of a man— of a runner, as he saw by the shifted snow; and the direction they had taken aroused curiosity, since a little farther their line must be crossed by the edge of a sheer height. He turned to trace them. And so doing, the length of the stride struck his attention—a stride long as his own if he ran. He knew he was following Christian.

In his anger he had hardened himself to be indifferent to the night-long absence of his brother; but now, seeing where the footsteps went, he was seized with compunction and dread. He had failed to give thought and care to his poor frantic twin, who might—was it possible?—have rushed to a frantic death.

His heart stood still when he came to the place where the leap had been taken. A piled edge of snow had fallen too, and nothing but snow lay below when he peered. Along the upper edge he ran for a furlong, till he came to a dip where he could slip and climb down, and then back again on the lower level to the pile of fallen snow. There he saw that the vigorous running had started afresh.

He stood pondering; vexed that any man should have taken that leap where he had not ventured to follow; vexed that he had been beguiled to such painful emotions; guessing vainly at Christian's object in this mad freak. He began sauntering along, half unconsciously following his brother's track; and so in a while he came to the place where the footprints were doubled.

Small prints were these others, small as a woman's, though the pace from one to another was longer than that which the skirts of women allow.

Did not White Fell tread so?

A dreadful guess appalled him, so dreadful that he recoiled from belief. Yet his face grew ashy white, and he gasped to fetch back motion to his checked heart. Unbelievable? Closer attention showed how the smaller footfall had altered for greater speed, striking into the snow with a deeper onset and a lighter pressure on the heels. Unbelievable? Could any woman but White Fell run so? Could any man but Christian run so? The guess became a certainty. He was following where alone in the dark night White Fell had fled from Christian pursuing.

Such villainy set heart and brain on fire with rage and indignation: such villainy in his own brother, till lately love-worthy, praiseworthy, though a fool for meekness. He would kill Christian; had he lives many as the footprints he had trodden, vengeance should demand them all. In a tempest of murderous hate he followed on in haste, for the track was plain enough, starting with such a burst of speed as could not be maintained, but brought him back soon to a plod for the spent, sobbing breath to be regulated. He cursed Christian aloud and called White Fell's name on high in a frenzied expense of passion. His grief itself was a rage, being such an intolerable anguish of pity and shame at the thought of his love, White Fell, who had parted from his kiss free and radiant, to be hounded straightway by his brother mad with jealousy, fleeing for more than life while her lover was housed at his ease. If he had but known, he raved, in impotent rebellion at the cruelty of events, if he had but known that his strength and love might have availed in her defence; now the only service to her that he could render was to kill Christian.

As a woman he knew she was matchless in speed, matchless in strength; but Christian was matchless in speed among men, nor easily to be matched in strength. Brave and swift and strong though she were, what chance had she against a man of his strength and inches, frantic, too, and intent on horrid revenge against his brother, his successful rival?

Mile after mile he followed with a bursting heart; more piteous, more tragic, seemed the case at this evidence of White Fell's splendid supremacy, holding her own so long against Christian's famous speed. So long, so long that his love and admiration grew more and more boundless, and his grief and indignation therewith also. Whenever the track lay clear he ran, with such reckless prodigality of strength, that it soon was spent, and he dragged on heavily, till, sometimes on the ice of a mere, sometimes on a wind-swept place, all signs were lost; but, so undeviating had been their line that a course straight on, and then short questing to either hand, recovered them again.

Hour after hour had gone by through more than half that winter day, before ever he came to the place where the trampled snow showed that a scurry of feet had come—and gone! Wolves' feet—and gone most amazingly! Only a little beyond he came to the lopped point of Christian's bear-spear; farther on he would see where the remnant of the useless shaft had been dropped. The snow here was dashed with blood, and the footsteps of the two had fallen closer together. Some hoarse sound of exultation came from him that might have been a laugh had breath sufficed. "O White Fell, my poor, brave love! Well struck!" he groaned, torn by his pity and great admiration, as he guessed surely how she had turned and dealt a blow. . . .

On—on—on—through the aching time, toiling and straining in the track of those two superb runners, aware of the marvel of their endurance, but unaware of the marvel of their speed, that, in the three hours before midnight had overpassed all that vast distance that he could only traverse from twilight to twilight. For clear daylight was passing when he came to the edge of an old marl-pit, and saw how the two who had gone before had stamped and trampled together in desperate peril on the verge. And here fresh blood stains spoke to him of a valiant defence against his infamous brother; and he followed where the blood had dripped till the cold had staunched its flow, taking a savage gratification from this evidence that Christian had been gashed deeply, maddening afresh with desire to do likewise more excellently, and so slake his murderous hate. And he began to know that through all his despair he had entertained a germ of hope, that grew apace, rained upon by his brother's blood.

He strove on as best he might, wrung now by an access of hope, now of despair, in agony to reach the end, however terrible, sick with the aching of the toiled miles that deferred it.

And the light went lingering out of the sky, giving place to uncertain stars.

He came to the finish.

Two bodies lay in a narrow place. Christian's was one, but the other beyond not White Fell's. There where the footsteps ended lay a great white wolf.

At the sight Sweyn's strength was blasted; body and soul he was struck down grovelling.

The stars had grown sure and intense before he stirred from where he had dropped prone. Very feebly he crawled to his dead brother, and laid his hands upon him, and crouched so, afraid to look or stir farther.

Cold, stiff, hours dead. Yet the dead body was his only shelter and stay in that most dreadful hour. His soul, stripped bare of all sceptic comfort, cowered, shivering, naked, abject; and the living clung to the dead out of piteous need for grace from the soul that had passed away.

He rose to his knees, lifting the body. Christian had fallen face forward in the snow, with his arms flung up and wide, and so had the frost made him rigid: strange, ghastly, unyielding to Sweyn's lifting, so that he laid him down again and crouched above, with his arms fast round him, and a low heart-wrung groan.

When at last he found force to raise his brother's body and gather it in his arms, tight clasped to his breast, he tried to face the Thing that lay beyond. The sight set his limbs in a palsy with horror and dread.

His senses had failed and fainted in utter cowardice, but for the strength that came from holding dead Christian in his arms, enabling him to compel his eyes to endure the sight, and take into the brain the complete aspect of the Thing. No wound, only blood stains on the feet. The great grim jaws had a savage grin, though dead-stiff. And his kiss: he could bear it no longer, and turned away, nor ever looked again.

And the dead man in his arms, knowing the full horror, had followed and faced it for his sake; had suffered agony and death for his sake; in the neck was the deep death gash, one arm and both hands were dark with frozen blood, for his sake! Dead he knew him, as in life he had not known him, to give the right meed of love and worship. Because the outward man lacked perfection and strength equal to his, he had taken the love and worship of that great pure heart as his due; he, so unworthy in the inner reality, so mean, so despicable, callous, and contemptuous towards the brother who had laid down his life to save him. He longed for utter annihilation, that so he might lose the agony of knowing himself so unworthy such perfect love. The frozen calm of death on the face appalled him. He dared not touch it with lips that had cursed so lately, with lips fouled by kiss of the horror that had been death.

He struggled to his feet, still clasping Christian. The dead man stood upright within his arm, frozen rigid. The eyes were not quite closed; the head had stiffened, bowed slightly to one side; the arms stayed straight and wide. It was the figure of one crucified, the blood-stained hands also conforming.

So living and dead went back along the track that one had passed in the deepest passion of love, and one in the deepest passion of hate. All that night Sweyn toiled through the snow, bearing the weight of dead Christian, treading back along the steps he before had trodden, when he was wronging with vilest thoughts, and cursing with murderous hatred, the brother who all the while lay dead for his sake.

Cold, silence, darkness encompassed the strong man bowed with the dolorous burden; and yet he knew surely that that night he entered hell, and trod hell-fire along the homeward road, and endured through it only because Christian was with him. And he knew surely that to him Christian had been as Christ, and had suffered and died to save him from his sins.

Bibliography

Selected Primary Sources

Baxter, Richard. *The Certainty of the World of Spirits.* London, 1691.

Beauvoys De Chauvincourt, Le Sieur de. *Discours de la Lycanthropie.* Paris, 1599.

Bodin, Jean. *De la Demonomanie des Sorciers.* Paris, 1580.

Boguet, Henri. *Discours des Sorciers.* Lyons, 1590. Translated by E. Allen Ashwin as *An Examen of Witches.* London: John Rodker, 1929.

Boulton, Richard. *A Complete History of Magic.* London, 1715.

Bovet, Richard. *Pandaemonium.* London, 1684.

Burton, Robert. *The Anatomy of Melancholy.* (1621). Edited by A. R. Shilleto. 3 vols. London, 1926–27.

Camerarius, Philippus. *Operae Horarum Subcisiuarum,* 1591.

Cotta, John. *The Triall of Witchcraft.* London, 1616.

Crouch, Nathaniel. *The Kingdom of Darkness.* London, 1688.

Culpeper, Nicholas. *The Complete Herbal.* London, 1653.

Daneau, Lambert. *A Dialogue of Witches.* Translated by R. W. London, 1575.

Deacon and Walker. *Dialogicall Discourses of Spirits and Divils.* London, 1601.

Della Porta, Giambattista. *Natural Magick.* Edited by Derek J. Price. New York, 1957.

Drage, William. *Daimonomageia.* London, 1665.

Fairfax, Edward. *Daemonologia* (1621). Harrogate: Ackrill, 1882.

Ferrand, Jacques. *Erotomania.* Trans. Edmund Chilmead. Oxford, 1640.

Fincel, Job. *Wunderzeichen.* Jhena, 1556.

Fromann, Johann Christian. *De Fascinatione.* Norimbergae, 1675.

Garzoni, Tommaso. *The Hospitall of Incurable Fooles.* London, 1600.

Geiler, Johann von Kaiserberg. *Die Emeis.* Strassburg, 1516.

Gerard, John. *The Herball.* London, 1597. Enlarged and amended, Johnson, Thomas. London, 1633, 1636.

Gifford, George. *A Discourse of the Subtill Practises of Devilles.* 1587.

———. *A Dialogue Concerning Witches and Witchcraftes.* 1593.

Godelmann, Johann Georg. *De Magis, Veneficis, et Lamiis Tractatus.* Frankfort, 1601.

Goulart, Simon. *Admirable and Memorable Histories . . .* Translated by Edward Grimeston. London, 1607.

Guazzo, Frencesco-Maria. *Compendium Maleficarum.* Milan, 1608.

Harsnett, Samuell. *A Discovery of the Fraudulent Practises of J. Darrell.* 1599.

———. *A Declaration of Egregious Popish Impostors.* 1603.

Hewin, Jan van. *Heurnii Opera Omnia.* Lugduni, 1658.

Holland, Henry. *A Treatise Against Witchcraft.* London, 1590.

James I. *Daemonologie.* Edinburgh, 1597.

Krause, Michael Henricus. *Theranthropismus Fictus.* Wittenbergae, 1673.

Lancre, Pierre De. *L'incredulité et Mescréance.* Paris, 1622.

———. *Tableau de l' Inconstance des Mauvais Anges et Demons.* Paris, 1613.

Lauben, Theophilus. *Dialogi und Gespräche von der Lycanthropia.* Frankfurt, 1686.

Lemnius, Levinus. *The Secret Miracles of Nature.* London, 1658.

———. *The Touchstone of Complexions.* Translated by Thomas Newton. London, 1576.

Licetus, Fortunius. *Ulisses apud Circen.* Utini, 1636.

Loyer, Pierre le. *Discours des Spectres.* Paris, 1608.

Majolus, Simon. *Dies Caniculares.* Helenopolis, 1612.

Mei, Michael. *De Lycanthropia.* Wittenburgae, 1654.

Middleton, Thomas. *The Changeling.* Edited by A. H. Bullen. London, 1935.

———. *The Witch.* Edited by A. H. Bullen. London, 1935.

Müller, Jacobus Fridericus. *De Transmutatione Hominum in Lupos.* Lipsiae, 1673.

Niphanius, Concord. *De Lycanthropia.* Wittenburgae, 1654.

Nynauld, Jean de. *De La Lycanthropie.* Paris, 1615.

Paulus Aegineta. *The Seven Books of Paulus Aegineta.* Translated by Francis Adams. 3 vols. London, 1844–47.

Perkins, William. *A Discourse of the Damned Art of Witchcraft.* London, 1608.

Peucer, Casper. *De Praecipibus Divinationum Generibus.* 1560.

Prieur, Claude. *Dialogue de la Lycanthropie.* Louvain, 1596.

Remy, Nicolas. *Daemonolatria.* Lyons, 1595. Translated by E. A. Ashwin. London, 1930.

The Romance of William of Palerne. Edited by W. W. Skeat. Early English Text Society. London, 1867.

Scot, Reginald. *The Discoverie of Witchcraft.* London, 1584.

Sennert, Daniel. *Opera Omnia.* Paris, 1641.

Seligmann, Gottlieb Frid. *De Dubiis Hominibus.* Lipsiae, 1679.

Shadwell, Thomas. *The Lancashire Witches.* Edited by Montague Summers. London, 1927.

Verstegan, Richard. *A Restitution of Decayed Intelligence.* Antwerp, 1605.

Wantscherus, Christopherus. *De Lupo et Lycanthropia.* Witteburgae, 1666.

Webster, John. *The Duchess of Malfi. The Complete Works of John Webster.* Edited by F. L. Lucas. 4 vols. London, 1927.

Webster, John. *The Displaying of Supposed Witchcraft.* London, 1677.

Weyer (Wier), Johann. *De Praestigiis Daemonum.* Basle, 1563.

Wolfeshusius, Joannes Fridericus. *De Lycanthropis.* Lipsiae, 1591.

Ziegrae, Conrad. *Disputatio contra Opliantriam, Lycanthropiam, et Metempsychosim.* Witteburgae, 1650.

Selected Modern Studies

Anglo, Sydney, ed. *The Damned Art.* London: Routledge and Kegan Paul, 1977.

_____. "Melancholia and Witchcraft: The Debate Between Wier, Bodin and Scot" in A. Gerlo, ed., *Folie et deraison à la Renaissance.* (Brussels, 1976), pp. 209–22.

_____. "Reginald Scot's *Discoverie of Witchcraft:* Scepticism and Sadduceeism." In *The Damned Art,* 106–39.

B., H. G. "Lycanthropy." *The Occult Review* 25 (1917): 214–17.

Babb, Lawrence. *The Elizabethan Malady.* East Lansing: Michigan State University Press, 1951.

Baring-Gould, Sabine. *The Book of Were-Wolves.* London, 1865.

Baxter, Christopher. "Jean Bodin's *De La Démonomanie Des Sorciers:* The Logic of Persecution." In *The Damned Art,* 76–105.

_____. "Johann Weyer's *De Praestigiis Daemonum:* Unsystematic Psychopathology." In *The Damned Art,* 53–75.

Black, George F. *A List of Works Relating to Lycanthropy.* New York, 1920.

Bourquelot, Félix. *Recherches sur la lycanthropie.* In the *Société des Antiquaires de France* 19 (Paris, 1849): 193–262.

Clark, Stuart. King James's *Daemonologie:* Witchcraft and Kingship." In *The Damned Art,* 156–81.

Cobben, J. J. *De Opvattingen van Johannes Wier Over Bezetenheid, Hekserij En Magie.* Assen: Van Gorcum, 1960.

Davidson, H. R. Ellis. "Shape-Changing in the Old Norse Sagas." In *Animals in Folklore.* Edited by J. R. Porter and W. M. S. Russell, 126–42, 258–59. London: D. S. Brewer, Ltd., and Totowa: Rowman & Littlefield, 1978.

Eisler, Robert. *Man into Wolf, an Anthropological Interpretation of Sadism, Masochism and Lycanthropy.* New York, 1951.

Fletcher, Robert. "The Witches' Pharmacopeia." *Bulletin of the Johns Hopkins Hospital* 7 (August 1896): 147–53.

Grieve, Mrs. M. *A Modern Herbal.* New York: Dover, 1971.

Hamel, Frank. *Human Animals.* London, 1915.

Hardwick, Charles. *Traditions, Superstitions and Folklore.* Manchester, 1872.

Kittredge, George Lyman. *Witchcraft in Old and New England.* Cambridge: Harvard, 1928.

Macfarlane, Alan. "A Tudor Anthropologist: George Gifford's *Discourse* and *Dialogue.*" In *The Damned Art,* 140–55.

Monter, E. William. *Witchcraft in France and Switzerland.* Ithaca: Cornell University Press, 1976.

O'Donnell, Elliott. *Werewolves.* London, 1912.

Robbins, Rossell Hope. *The Encyclopedia of Witchcraft and Demonology.* New York: Crown, 1959.

Russell, W. M. S. and Claire Russell. "The Social Biology of Werewolves." In *Animals in Folklore.* Edited by J. R. Porter and W. M. S. Russell, 156–77, 260–64. London: D. S. Brewer, Ltd., and Totowa: Rowman & Littlefield, 1978.

Smith, Kirby Flower. "An Historical Study of the Werewolf in Literature." *PMLA* 9:1–42.

Summers, Montague. *The Werewolf.* London, 1933.

Thomas, Keith. *Religion and the Decline of Magic.* New York: Scribner's, 1971.

Vickers, Brian, ed. *Occult and Scientific Mentalities in the Renaissance.* Cambridge: Cambridge University Press, 1984.

Walker, D. P. *Unclean Spirits.* Philadelphia: University of Pennsylvania Press, 1981.

Index